MILLER'S

COLLECTING MODERN
DESIGN

# The Consultants

**Alex Payne** (Consultant Editor)

is an expert in Modern Design and has worked at major London auction houses. He is currently consultant to Phillips Auctioneers Modern Design department for whom he organizes sales in London and New York.

**Nigel Benson** (Glass)

originally trained as a landscape architect. He started to collect glass in the mid 1970s and began dealing in British, Scandinavian, and Continental glass in 1986. He now runs a shop, Twentieth Century Glass, in Kensington Church Street, London.

**Will Farmer** (Jewellery and Metalware)

trained as a silversmith and jeweller at the Birmingham School of Jewellery. He has been an auctioneer for three years, currently with Fieldings Auctioneers. He writes for various antiques magazines and is now filming a television series on collecting 20th century icons.

**Sarah Hodgson** (Graphics)

studied History of Art at Warwick University and joined the Film and Entertainment department at Christie's South Kensington in 1994. Her special interest is in film memorabilia and her first sale devoted to film posters was in 1995.

**Ben Williams** (Ceramics)

worked first at Bonhams, London, and then at Phillips International Auctioneers, where he is currently head of the Contemporary Ceramics department. He has arranged sales in London and New York, including the estate sales of Dame Lucie Rie and Janet Leach.

# COLLECTING MODERN
# DESIGN

## SALLY HOBAN

### CONSULTANT EDITOR: ALEXANDER PAYNE

# Miller's Collecting Modern Design

## Sally Hoban

## Consultant Editor: Alex Payne

First published in Great Britain in 2001 by Miller's,
an imprint of Octopus Publishing Group Ltd,
2–4 Heron Quays, London, E14 4JP
Miller's is a registered trademark of Octopus Publishing Group Ltd
© 2001 Octopus Publishing Group Ltd

Commissioning Editor **Anna Sanderson**
Executive Art Editor **Rhonda Fisher**
Project Editor **Emily Asquith**
Design **Jester Designs**
Picture Researcher **Maria Gibbs**
Editor **Selina Mumford**
Editorial Assistant **Rose Hudson**
Proofreader **Jane Donovan**
Indexer **Sue Farr**
Production **Angela Couchman, Nancy Roberts**

ISBN 1 84000 405 3
A CIP catalogue record for this book is available from the British Library
Set in Industria and Frutiger
Printed and bound by Mladinska knjiga tiskarna d.d., Slovenia

**Front of jacket**
top left: "Patchwork" vase by Ansolo Fuga, c.1955
top right: "Ball" or "Globe" chair by Eero Aarnio, 1963–5
bottom left: "Lapis" screen-printed cotton for Heal's by Lucienne Day, 1953
bottom right: Flared bowl by Lucie Rie, c.1955

**Back of jacket**, left to right:
"UP 3 Lounge" chair by Gaetano Pesce, 1969
Jimi Hendrix poster, late 1960s
Stainless steel "Cylinda" line coffee pot by Arne Jacobsen, 1961

**Spine**
Vase by Flavio Poli, c.1957

**Title Page**
"Butterfly" stool by Sori Yanagi, 1954

# Contents

# STARTING TO COLLECT

Since the mid 1990s the direction of the decorative arts market in Europe and the USA has shifted and expanded to include 20th century design classics. Today, modern design is probably the fastest growing collectable area. In Britain the leading auction houses are Phillips, de Pury & Luxembourg; Bonhams & Brooks; Sotheby's; and Christie's, and they now hold regular sales of modern design across the world, with regional auction houses also tapping into the new market. Collectors are finally recognizing the quality of pre- and post-war furniture and will be prepared to pay for a design classic.

Thanks to more efficient production techniques and exciting new materials, the 20th century was the first to mass-produce design objects of good quality. In the 18th and 19th centuries, production was dominated by workshop industry, so less designs were made and fewer items reached the market. Top quality design was elitist and only available to the middle and upper classes. All this had changed by c.1930 when good design was finally available to all.

After World War I, the focus was on top quality design for mass production. Furniture designers were interested in how a chair would fit in a space and how a person would sit in it, as well as how it would look. As a result of this, modern design pieces will often be of better quality and more comfortable than many of today's flat-packed tables and chairs and will also give your home considerably more originality.

Some pieces, such as Bauhaus School products, were to prove instrumental in shaping the look of the century, as forward-thinking designers created functional streamlined furniture and applied art that still influence design today.

Modern design is appealing to a new generation of collectors fuelled by publicity through "lifestyle" magazines such as *Elle Decoration* and *Wallpaper*. Interior design has succumbed to the whims of fashion design, with 1960s and 1970s the trend at the time of writing. The media too has embraced design classics, for example sales of the Eames chair and ottoman have soared since they featured on the set of the television series *Frasier*.

People are also redefining the way they live in the 21st century, and new types of homes are leading to new spaces to furnish. The sleek, cool lines of Modernist furniture fit much better than a Chippendale chair in large, minimal loft spaces.

Collecting modern design is also flourishing because there are still plenty of items from the high and low ends of the market available to buy. Even if you are unable to afford an original designer piece, you can find good quality contemporary copies. Modern design pieces, if

A glass tea service, designed
c.1930 by Wilhelm Wagenfeld
for Jenaer Glaswerk Schott & Gen.
£600–£1,000/$900–$1,500

you know what you're looking for, can still be found in provincial auctions, house clearance sales and, if you are very lucky, at junk shops.

## HOW TO BEGIN AND WHERE TO BUY

Firstly, read as much as you can about modern design and learn about the key designers and their most celebrated pieces. Books, magazines, auction house catalogues, and the internet will yield a wealth of information about the more famous designers, but as this is such a new collecting field, the amount written about lesser-known designers and manufacturers is relatively small. You can still find contemporary catalogues and magazines such as 1960s issues of *Homes & Gardens* or vintage editions of the *Design Yearbook* at antique fairs, auctions, and in specialist art libraries and these will tell you how items were received at the time. These publications are becoming increasingly collectable in their own right.

Major British auction houses now hold regular modern design sales in the USA, in Britain, and in other countries within Europe. They also have themed sales if you are looking to buy just chairs or lighting, for example. Most offer on-line catalogues and on-line bidding facilities.

An "Elda" armchair, designed by Joe Colombo for Comfort in 1965.
£1,500–£2,000,/$2,250–$3,000

A "Libri" chest bureau, designed by Piero Fornasetti c.1952.
£20,000–£26,650/$30,000–$40,000

The rise of specialist shops, fairs, and dealers since the mid 1990s also makes it easy to buy modern design. In Britain, although most dealers tend to be in London, there are plenty of specialists elsewhere in the country and some of these are listed in the directory of suppliers at the back of this book. Their shops are quickly becoming the hippest places to buy goods to furnish your home.

In Britain the fairs circuit, traditionally datelined at about 1940, has opened up to modern design classics, with big events such as the Olympia Fine Art Fair now allowing modern pieces from across Europe, as well as contemporary objects by designers such as Danny Lane. The shift has even spread to the antique textiles market, with regular specialist sales featuring Mary Quant, Pierre Cardin, and space-age Courrèges pieces. Museums too are beginning to include 20th century design classics.

Sites on modern design on the internet are booming, and include those dedicated to individual designers (the one for Charles and Ray Eames is particularly comprehensive) and for 20th century design as a whole. Many dealers have their own sites, which can be especially useful should you wish to purchase items from abroad.

The newest way to purchase modern design is through internet auctions. At the time of writing these are especially good for American pieces by Herman Miller and Charles and Ray Eames, and Scandinavian glass and furniture. The most popular sites are insured so you can buy in confidence, and internet eBay has a feedback facility where buyers can leave positive or negative responses to a seller after a transaction. The only drawback with buying on the internet is that you cannot see or feel the piece before you purchase it and so have to rely on the seller's honesty in condition reports. Paying for the item can be a problem too, as unless a vendor will take a credit card you will have to send payment in an international draft in the relevant currency, attracting bank charges. You will also have to pay extra for postage and with larger items, shipping, and depending on the value of the object you may be liable for customs import tax.

A ceramic charger, designed by Salvatore Meli in 1973.
**£300–£500/$450–$750**

A cyclindrical storage system, designed by Anna Castelli Ferrieri for Kartell in 1969.
**£80–£120/$120–$180**

Other sites such as antiques.co.uk offer a range of selected dealer items for sale on the internet and these will have been vetted for quality, condition, and authenticity before being offered for sale. (*See p.234 for further information*).

## WHAT TO COLLECT

You can specialize in collecting one area such as ceramics, glass, or textiles, or you can theme an entire room or house. The beauty of modern design is that the key styles filtered through into every aspect of design and individual piece will complement and reflect each other.

Designers were directly influenced by the work of their contemporaries in different countries, so you can also build up a collection of geographical origin, specializing in, say, Scandinavian or American design. You can also collect by material, such as plywood or tubular steel furniture. An alternative is to theme a collection around an historical event such as the 1951 *Festival of Britain* (*see pp.70–1*). All these will be discussed in detail in this book.

For investment purposes, if you buy pieces by design pioneers that are already recognized as classics then there is little chance that your purchases will depreciate in value, making them a sound investment for the future. But now is also the time to buy reasonably priced pieces by designers that are not yet recognized. Look for quality of design and items that show the influence of major designers such as Alvar Aalto or Hans Wegner.

Damaged pieces will never attract a premium. It is particularly difficult to spot restorations in ceramics and glass. Chips on the rim of a glass vase, for example, can be ground out, which although not immediately noticeable will detract from an object's value and will be easily spotted by an auction house specialist, should you wish to part with the item.

Furniture design companies in particular are recognizing the popularity of modern design, and beginning to reissue classic designs, so beware of later-designed examples. These do, however, provide an ideal purchase if you cannot afford an original, and stamped designs by a recognized manufacturer such as the Italian furniture company Cassina will always have a value in the future as original examples become harder to find.

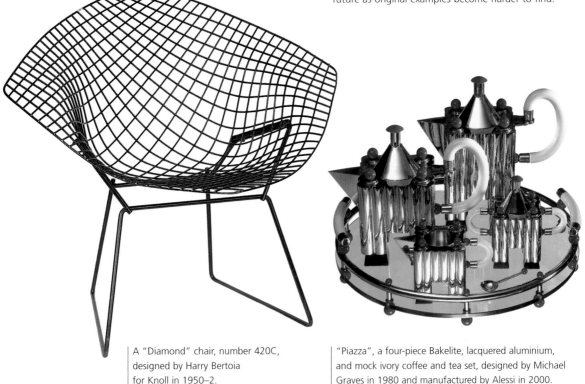

A "Diamond" chair, number 420C, designed by Harry Bertoia for Knoll in 1950–2.
£100–£150/$150–$225

"Piazza", a four-piece Bakelite, lacquered aluminium, and mock ivory coffee and tea set, designed by Michael Graves in 1980 and manufactured by Alessi in 2000.
£13,350–£20,000/$20,000–$30,000

# Timeline

1918 The unpainted "Red-Blue" chair is designed by Gerrit Rietveld.

1926 The Bauhaus group moves to Dessau after the authorities close its Weimar school in 1925. New staff include Gunta Stölzl, Marcel Breuer, and Herbert Bayer.

1928 Le Corbusier, Pierre Jeanneret, and Charlotte Perriand design the "B306" chaise longue.

1934—5 Gerald Summers' groundbreaking one-piece plywood armchair is designed.

1941 Charles and Ray Eames begin plywood experiments, inspired by the 1940s avant-garde movement.

1947 George Nelson becomes design director of Herman Miller.

1951 *Festival of Britain*, an exhibition celebrating British design, is held in London.

1959—60 Verner Panton's "Panton" chair, the first single-form injection-moulded plastic chair, is designed.

1972 The *Italy: New Domestic Landscape* exhibition, now cited as one of the most important surveys on Italian design, is held at the Museum of Modern Art in New York.

1978 *bau.haus 1* exhibition by Studio Alchimia is held in Milan, the first exhibition showcasing Studio Alchimia's design.

1981 The "Rover" chair is designed by Ron Arad.

1993 Marc Newson's elongated "Orgone" chair is produced.

MODERNISM

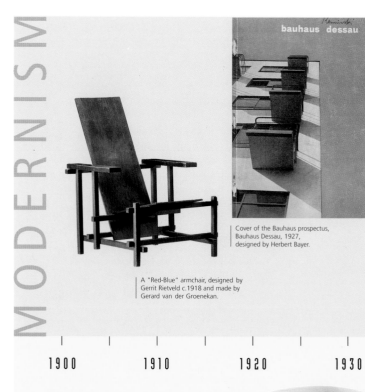

Cover of the Bauhaus prospectus, Bauhaus Dessau, 1927, designed by Herbert Bayer.

A "Red-Blue" armchair, designed by Gerrit Rietveld c.1918 and made by Gerard van der Groenekan.

1900    1910    1920    1930

A "B306" chaise longue ("LC1"), designed by Le Corbusier, Pierre Jeanneret, and Charlotte Perriand in 1928–9 for Thonet & Embru (this is a later example).

A brass and nickel-plated ashtray, designed by Marianne Brandt in 1924, at the Bauhaus metal workshop in Weimar.

Bauhaus

De Stijl

A plywood armchair, designed by Gerald Summers in 1933–4.

1900    1910    1920    1930

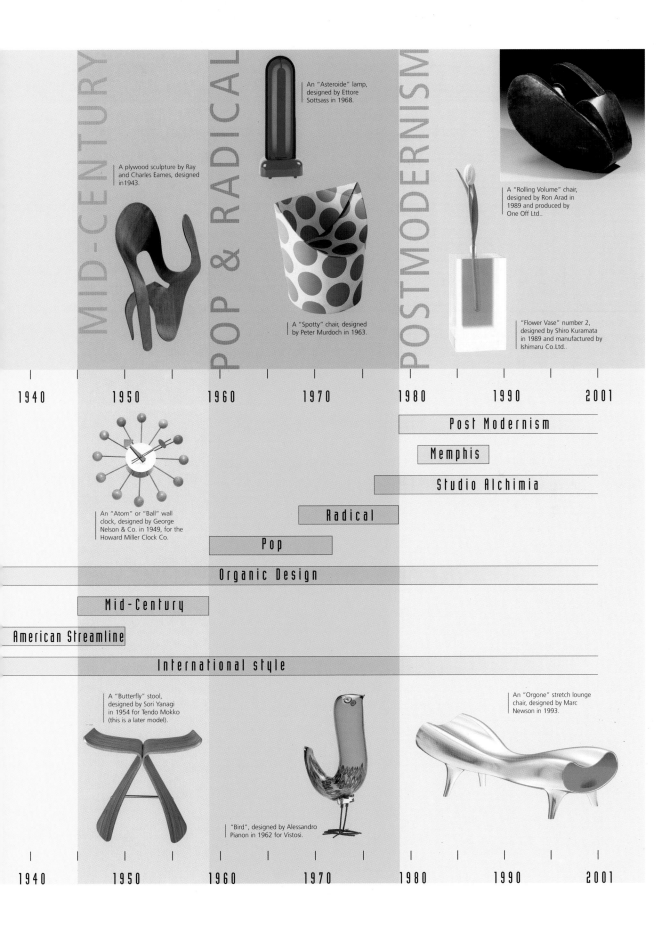

MID-CENTURY

POP & RADICAL

POSTMODERNISM

A plywood sculpture by Ray and Charles Eames, designed in 1943.

An "Asteroide" lamp, designed by Ettore Sottsass in 1968.

A "Spotty" chair, designed by Peter Murdoch in 1963.

A "Rolling Volume" chair, designed by Ron Arad in 1989 and produced by One Off Ltd..

"Flower Vase" number 2, designed by Shiro Kuramata in 1989 and manufactured by Ishimaru Co.Ltd..

| 1940 | 1950 | 1960 | 1970 | 1980 | 1990 | 2001 |

Post Modernism

Memphis

Studio Alchimia

An "Atom" or "Ball" wall clock, designed by George Nelson & Co. in 1949, for the Howard Miller Clock Co.

Radical

Pop

Organic Design

Mid-Century

American Streamline

International style

A "Butterfly" stool, designed by Sori Yanagi in 1954 for Tendo Mokko (this is a later model).

An "Orgone" stretch lounge chair, designed by Marc Newson in 1993.

"Bird", designed by Alessandro Pianon in 1962 for Vistosi.

| 1940 | 1950 | 1960 | 1970 | 1980 | 1990 | 2001 |

MODERNISM

# MODERNISM

The early 20th century saw the beginnings of a break in traditional design and manufacturing processes. Modernism was never a cohesive movement, but rather groups of artists and designers working to a set of common goals in a similar style. Designers across Germany, France, and the Netherlands were the chief exponents of early Modernism, although it later spread to Britain and the USA. New, innovative styles of furniture, ceramics, glass, and textiles appeared from c.1915 onwards.

Technological and industrial advances in the first quarter of the 20th century meant that new materials and methods of construction were available for the first time. Increased wealth led to greater consumerism, which meant that designers had a larger number of richer patrons to buy their work and allow the style to become established.

World War I caused massive destruction across much of Europe but left artists and designers with a feeling of social responsibility. Many believed that design could play a part in creating a new world of truth, beauty, and simplicity. These aims were central to the new schools of art and design workshops that sprang up from 1907 to 1930, such as the Deutscher Werkbund (see p.22) and the Bauhaus (see pp.22–5) in Germany.

Modernist designers believed the arts should work together through a fusion of art, design, and architecture to create a harmonious whole, such as in the buildings and interiors of Le Corbusier and Ludwig Mies van der Rohe. The origins of Modernism can be traced back to the late 19th century with William Morris (1834–96) and the Arts and Crafts movement in Britain. Morris

and his followers believed that industrialization had led to mass-produced, poorly designed goods. Morris had an underlying social purpose too, for he had a theory that a craftsman engaged in useful work would bring about a happier society. His ideas led to the formation of crafts guilds and workshops in Britain and the USA, but inevitably hand production cost more than mass production so the products of Morris & Co. and groups such as the Guild of Handicrafts were really only available to the rich.

Some of the design that was produced in the mid to late 19th century was way ahead of its time. The English designer Dr Christopher Dresser actively promoted industrial production in his designs from c.1870 onwards in his pursuit of "truth, beauty and power" with botanical and Japanese influences.

Modernism in the early 20th century took up Morris' and Dresser's vision and began to make it a reality. New techniques meant that good design could be mass-produced and yet retain its integrity. Like Morris, the early Modernists rejected the use of mass ornamentation; so their pieces are stark, pure, and harmonious. The brass piano lamp shown here was designed by the Dutch architect J. J. Pieter Oud in 1927 and is a perfect example of Modernist styling with its sleek chrome form.

The early strands of Modernism became the International Style in France, the USA, and, to a lesser extent, in Britain. International Style stayed true to many of the underlying ideas of Modernism but developed the mode further. In the USA this led to streamlined design (based on the sleek styling of aeroplanes and other innovations such as skyscrapers and sheer speed of transportation) while in Europe, particularly Scandinavia, a more earthy style developed with a reliance on natural, organic forms.

Early Modernist pieces can be identified by: use of industrial materials such as plywood, aluminium, tubular steel and glass; radical new forms; lack of ornament; visible internal structure; functionality, and practicality.

Detail from "Giso" number 404, a chrome-plated brass piano lamp, designed by J. J. Pieter Oud for W. H. Gispen & Co. in 1927.
£6,650–£10,000/$10,000–$15,000

# FURNITURE

To say that Modernist furniture was revolutionary is by no means an exaggeration. By the end of the late 19th and early 20th centuries, little had changed in furniture manufacture for at least a hundred years. Pieces were still either handcrafted, such as those from the English Arts and Crafts movement, or else were mass-produced and of poor quality. In the 1860s, Michael Thonet's (1796–1871) bentwood armchairs and dining chairs represented a major break from the past and can be seen as the first chairs that were designed for mass production. The bentwoods were successful, selling hundreds of thousands across Europe, and the fluid lines of the rocking version reflect early 20th century plywood chairs by Marcel Breuer (1902–81). But it was left to the young designers of the early 1900s to late 1920s to completely revolutionize the way furniture was produced and the materials it was made from. Designers in Germany, France, and Scandinavia were particularly innovative, with Britain and the USA adopting the new style and techniques slightly later.

For the first time designers gave serious consideration to a piece of furniture's purpose as well as its form, so design began to take on a social function. Furniture made from new materials such as plywood, tubular steel, and even glass could be designed for mass production. Aluminium, too, was harnessed for use in furniture and this was completely new.

An aluminium chaise longue, designed by Marcel Breuer in 1932 for Embru AG, and retailed at Wohnbedarf shops in Switzerland.
**£25,000–£35,000/$37,500–$52,500**

Breuer's aluminium chaise longue was created in 1932 and was a feat of modern engineering coupled with the sleek lines of the Modern movement. Likewise Erich Dieckmann's tubular steel and cane chair with its streamlined modern form, designed in 1931.

The use of aluminium in furniture was perhaps the most radical of changes to occur in design during the Modern movement and was to have a huge impact on designers in the 20th century. Breuer was completely aware of the possibilities of this new material and the need for such pieces in everyday life. In 1928 he said, "This metal furniture is intended to be nothing but a necessary apparatus for contemporary life."

Modernist furniture gives great scope for the collector because it is so original. You can specialize in collecting pieces made from a new material, such as moulded plywood, and trace the evolution of that material in furniture design through your collection. Alternatively you can concentrate on the work of a particular designer, or collect items from an important school such as the Bauhaus.

Rare nickel-plated tubular steel, stained
wood, and cane chair, model number 8162,
designed by Erich Dieckmann in 1931
and manufactured by Cebaro.
**£3,350–£4,500/$5,000–$7,000**

It is still possible to find reasonably priced pieces of modern
design for sale because it is a relatively new collecting area.
The value of an item may be affected if it is worn, scratched
or distressed, but if it is very rare this might not be an issue. It
is possible to get modern design furniture restored but this
can be very expensive, so be aware of extra costs when
buying the item. Many of the tubular steel chairs from this
period were made with canvas, leather or hide seats and
examples with the original seats still intact will be worth much
more than those where it has been lost or damaged.

The rarity of a table or sofa, for example, will also greatly
affect its value, particularly if it is by a key designer, such as
the cane and chromed "B35" armchair by Breuer shown here.
Prototypes made by major designers are worth much more
than mass-produced pieces and fetch high prices, with
examples from initial, small manufacturing runs following
closely behind. It is always best to buy a piece of furniture
made by a recognized designer if it is within your budget.
Although some copies are of high quality, they will never be
as good as the real thing in investment terms. Some designs
are being reissued today under licence from the original
manufacturer, and these will hold their value and can be a
good alternative if you want to own a particular piece but are
unable to invest in a more expensive original example.

Rare cane and chromed tubular
steel model "B35" armchair,
designed by Marcel Breuer in 1929 and
manufactured by Thonet c.1930.
**£3,000–£5,000/$4,500–$7,500**

# Gerrit Rietveld

errit Rietveld (1888–1964) was the most important designer to be influenced by De Stijl and as such his work is highly collectable. His pioneering designs are recognized as the first pieces of modern design furniture. Rietveld was born in Utrecht and trained in his father's cabinet-making workshop and at evening classes before opening his own furniture-making business in 1911.

His most famous design is the "Red-Blue" chair, which is synonymous with the De Stijl style and is one of the most important chairs of the 20th century. Its design is highly original as nothing like it had ever been manufactured before. It was to prove highly influential to generations of designers and architects. Rietveld wrote about the chair, "It never occurred to me that it would prove all that meaningful for myself and possibly for others; that it would even have an impact on architecture."

The chair is a perfect example of how form and colour can combine to produce a startlingly original piece of furniture that owes more to sculpture than existing furniture designs. A 1919 edition of the *De Stijl* journal described the chair as "a new answer to the question of what place sculpture will have in the new interior". It was also exhibited at the Bauhaus and influenced furniture design in Germany.

The "Red-Blue" chair is striking because it lacks surface ornamentation. Rietveld was one of the first avant-garde designers in Europe to turn away from the use of highly decorative ornament that was popularized by Art Nouveau. He also rejected the common practice of covering up the internal structure of a chair with upholstery. Instead, the joints of the "Red-Blue" chair are exposed and form an integral part of the overall design.

Consisting of standardized components of painted solid beechwood and plywood, Rietveld wrote that he designed the chair "to the end of showing that a thing of beauty eg a spatial object, could be made of nothing but straight machined materials."

The prototype of this chair was originally designed in 1917–18 with a natural wood finish. Rietveld painted it in its famous red, blue, black, and yellow colours in c.1922 after he had become immersed in De Stijl and admired Piet Mondrian's painted geometric canvases with their heavy use of line. Mondrian was De Stijl's most influential follower and his flat canvases reduced the natural world into arrangements of abstract lines and colour.

Between 1918 and 1923 Rietveld produced unpainted, naturally stained, and black and white versions of the chair. Its standardized, simple construction made it ideally suited to mass production but only a small number were made, which heightens its value today.

The rarest, and most expensive versions, of the "Red-Blue" chair were constructed in Rietveld's workshop by his assistant. The firm Cvt Hellenaar manufactured cheaper models. In 1971 the Italian firm Cassina started to reissue the chair and examples of these are fairly easy to find today and are relatively inexpensive compared to original versions. They are visually very similar to the original examples but, as with any furniture that has been reproduced from an original design, the Cassina chairs lack signs of aging, such as split and cracked paint and general wear and tear on the body.

Rietveld continued to explore geometric use of line in his unpainted wood "Zig-Zag" chair, which dates from c.1932–4. The chair is constructed from four individual planes of wood that are joined together to make a striking whole. Both the shape and construction of this chair are highly original, and its influence can be seen in many later furniture designs throughout the 20th century. It too was reissued by Cassina.

A hardwood prototype model of the "Zig-Zag" chair was produced for Mrs Schröder, an important patron of Rietveld in Utrecht. Several versions of the chair then went into production, including a softwood example made by the furniture company Metz & Co. from 1934 onwards.

## De Stijl — 1917 to c.1928

The members of De Stijl (The Style), a design collective in Europe active in the 1920s, are often credited as the pioneers of 20th century Modernism. The Dutch painter and designer Theo van Doesburg was the founding father of the group. The De Stijl designers believed in the abandonment of natural forms and superfluous decoration in design, and called for them to be replaced with a purer style based upon stripping down the traditional forms of furniture and architecture to their geometric elements and utilizing bold, unbroken primary colours in their decoration.

The group included avant-garde painters, designers, intellectuals, and architects who were brought together through the *De Stijl* journal, first published in the Netherlands in 1917. The journal showcased the work of architects, designers, and painters and tried to break down the barriers between high and low art. There was a strong social element to their work, as they wanted to create a new international style to counteract the devastation in Europe after World War I. By the mid 1920s, De Stijl encompassed all aspects of design including graphics, architecture, painting, and interiors, and held several acclaimed exhibitions in France.

"Red-Blue" armchair, designed c.1918 and made by Gerard van der Groenekan.
**£120,000–£150,000/ $180,000–$225,000**

Wooden Buffet Sideboard, designed c.1919 and manufactured by Gerard van de Groenekan in 1983.
**£3,000–£4,000/$4,500–$6,000**

"Zig-Zag" chair, designed c.1932–4 and manufactured by Cassina c.1970s.
**£300–£500/$450–$750**

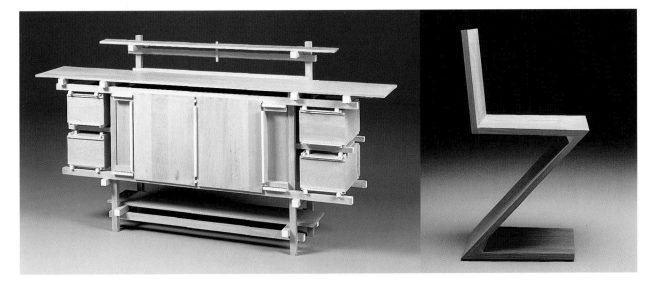

Mrs Schröder also gave Rietveld his first and most famous commission for a complete building project, which he started in 1924 and finished the following year. The Schröder House is truly innovative in that the interior spaces can be changed according to the occupier's needs through a series of ingenious open and closing partitions on tracks. Each of the partitioned spaces has built-in furniture and the emphasis is on functionality. The Wooden Buffet Sideboard shown on the previous page is the best surviving example of a Rietveld interior and a perfect illustration of the De Stijl belief that the individual elements of a building should work together to form a unified whole, a principle that the influential Modernist designer Le Corbusier took up slightly later when he described houses as "machines for living in".

Rietveld continued to design furniture and buildings throughout his life, although after 1945 he is perhaps best remembered for his architecture, including further projects for Mrs Schröder. One of his last architectural commissions was for the Van Gogh Museum in Amsterdam between 1963 and 1974.

Following the success of the "Red-Blue" chair and the Schröder House, Rietveld helped form the CIAM (International Congress of Modern Architecture) in 1928 and his chairs continued to find worldwide acclaim. They also influenced Mid-Century designers such as Charles Eames in the USA and Verner Panton in Scandinavia, who were also interested in creating single form, moulded plywood furniture.

Some of Rietveld's later designs reflected trends in society, for example the "Crate" range designed c.1935 for the furniture company Metz and Co. These pieces were made out of spruce wood packing crate components and were designed to be low-cost furniture suitable for home assembly in the economic recession of the 1930s.

Rietveld also embraced the new materials of Modernism in tandem with the next generation of designers, working with aluminium and bent metal in the 1930s. He was probably influenced by Marcel Breuer's experiments with these materials at the Bauhaus, creating pieces in the Mid-Century style in the 1950s.

The price of Rietveld furniture very much depends on its rarity. This can be in terms of the number of other surviving examples or how a piece relates to other existing items of the same design. For instance, a chair of which several examples are known to exist can be worth several thousand pounds but extremely rare one-off editions can fetch five figure sums. This is the case with the unique "Zig-Zag" armchair that is illustrated here (see opposite). It was made by Rietveld himself in 1934 out of four solid, stained cantilevered elm wood parts and bears a paper label printed "Woppen-Rietveld Mient 593 Den Haag, Holland", which helps give it a desirable provenance and authenticity. The chair was made for Rietveld's own use and is of interest to collectors because it differs in proportions from all the other known existing models. The reason for this is unclear, although the critic Peter Vöge suggests that it could be because Rietveld used a cushion for this chair.

The "Piano" chair dates from 1923 and was again designed and made by Rietveld himself. Its styling is almost primitive but retains his love of geometric form. The frame consists of nine mahogany tubes secured with nails, and the chair is stained and dyed with violet on the terminals. The seat and backrest are made from brown leather, and the chair is similar in design to a child's chair executed by Rietveld at around the same time. This item of furniture is also highly collectable today.

The "Beugel Stoel", which means "frame chair" in Dutch, dates from 1928 and is startlingly modern in its construction, looking forward to Mid-Century styling with its fluid, yet simple plywood shape and tubular metal legs and frame. It is a wonderful example of Rietveld's early experiments utilizing new man-made materials in furniture design. This chair was manufactured by Gerard van de Groenekan for Metz & Co. in Amsterdam in 1928 and has a stamped mark underneath the white painted laminated wood seat and back which gives it authenticity. Versions of this chair also exist with black painted laminated wood.

This example is a later model of the "Beugel Stoel" chair and very few early chairs are documented. They were made from fibreboard, Rietveld's original preferred material, but because this wasn't particularly strong and was prone to cracking Rietveld made later models from laminated wood. Fibreboard versions are even more desirable to collectors today because of their extreme rarity.

The "Nijland Buffet" was given to the daughter of D. Nijland, who was a close friend of Rietveld, as a wedding present in 1924. It was designed and made by Rietveld himself and is constructed from stained pine. Its design reflects Rietveld's other work from this period, particularly its elegant, geometric proportions.

"Piano" chair,
designed and built by
Gerrit Rietveld in 1923.
**£14,000–£18,000/$21,000–$27,000**

"Nijland Buffet",
designed and built by
Gerrit Rietveld in 1924.
**£30,650–£34,650/
$46,000–$52,000**

Important and unique "Zig-Zag"
chair with armrests, designed and
built by Gerrit Rietveld in 1934.
**£30,000–£32,000/$45,000–$48,000**

"Beugel Stoel", designed in 1928
and manufactured by Gerard van de
Groenekan for Metz & Co.
**£6,000–£7,350/$9,000–$11,000**

# The Bauhaus

The Bauhaus was arguably the most important design school of the 20th century, thanks to its innovative teaching methods and the extraordinary talent of the pupils and teachers who worked and studied there. Modernism really became established at the school, and so any serious modern design collection should have some Bauhaus or Bauhaus-inspired pieces, although they are rare because many designs did not make it past small batch production stage. Bauhaus graphics, posters, sample books, and catalogues are highly sought after by collectors, for example the poster by Herbert Bayer and the Bauhaus prospectus (*see opposite*).

It is difficult to define the Bauhaus style, given that many of its designers were multi-disciplinary and multi-talented. Students learnt architecture, weaving, ceramics and glass, typography, metalwork, and fine art. Some produced work that included bright colours and abstract patterns, while others took a more minimal approach working with new materials, such as tubular steel, to create a much more functionalist style. Industrial design in Germany began to change round about the turn of the 20th century, and several influential people helped this to happen. The architect Hermann Muthesius (1861–1927) called for the production of affordable, mass-produced design with decoration that would not detract from an object's essential function. Muthesius visited England in the 1890s where he would no doubt have learnt of William Morris' design theories and the popularity of the English Arts and Crafts movement.

In 1907, Muthesius founded the Deutsche Werkbund, which was one of the first attempts to bring about a change in the traditional manufacture of industrial objects in Germany. The Werkbund, consisting of a dozen artists and a dozen industrialists, aimed to bring good design to industrially manufactured goods and to assist in the employment of designers in industry.

One of the most important members of the Werkbund was the designer and architect Peter Behrens (1868–1940). He revolutionized the way the German electricity company AEG (Allgemeine Elektrizitäts Gesellschaft) produced everyday products through his designs for fans, electric kettles, and telephones. These items are already collectable today. Behrens was also an important figure in the early careers of some of the key Bauhaus designers, because many of them worked in his architectural office, including Walter Gropius, Le Corbusier, and Ludwig Mies van der Rohe.

The name Bauhaus derives from *bauen* (*to build*) and *haus* (*house*). The first stage of the Bauhaus began in 1919 when Gropius (1883–1969) took over the state funded School of Art and Craft in Weimar. He wanted to train designers who were able to work with industry and (like William Morris in the late 19th century) aimed to unite art and traditional crafts. Johannes Itten, the painters Paul Klee (1897–1940) and Wassily Kandinsky (1866–1944), László Moholy-Nagy (1895–1946), and Wilhelm Wagenfeld (1900–90) are some of the key designers and teachers of the early Bauhaus. Methods of teaching were innovative and are still used today. Students enrolled for a preliminary course for one year in which they learnt the basics in several disciplines in both art and design before entering one of the specialist workshops in their second year.

In 1923 Gropius was giving lectures entitled "Art and Technology – a new unity" and the theme of the later Bauhaus was born. The school now aimed to train designers capable of making goods that could be mass-produced using machines and by the mid 1920s, catalogues were published to try to sell Bauhaus products outside the school.

The first public Bauhaus exhibition took place in 1923, but despite this and increasing production and output the Weimar authorities closed the school in 1925. The Bauhaus moved to Dessau and in 1926 took on the new name Hochschule fur Gestaltung (Institute for Design). Several of the workshops were closed down or amalgamated, and a department of architecture was set up in 1927. New staff included Gunta Stölzl (weaving), Marcel Breuer (carpentry and cabinet-making), and Herbert Bayer (printing), all of whom had trained at the Weimar Bauhaus. The weaving workshops produced geometric fabrics and wall hangings for commercial sale typified by the wall hanging illustrated opposite, which was designed by Anni Albers in 1926.

Gropius resigned in 1928 and Hannes Meyer became director. Architecture became the principal department, as Meyer was professor of architecture before he became director. He was looking towards the masses as his students were encouraged to explore design for mass housing and those in the other departments were urged to produce goods for sale to industry. Some of these, particularly the weaving workshop under Gunta Stölzl, commercial wallpaper production, and the metal workshop were very successful, but the rise of the National Socialists in Germany meant that the school only had a few years left.

In August 1930 Mies van der Rohe replaced Meyer as director. In the late 1920s a proportion of the students at the Bauhaus took up left wing ideas and this began to cause problems with the authorities. To the Nazis,

Staatliches Bauhaus in Weimar
1919–23, printed book, 1923.
£1,350–£2,000/$2,000–$3,000

"MT8" table lamp,
designed by Karl J. Jucker
and Wilhelm Wagenfeld in
1923–4 at the Bauhaus metal
workshop in Weimar
(later manufactured example).
£150–£200/$225–$300

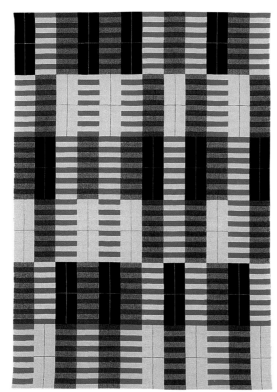

A wall hanging,
designed by Anni Albers
in 1926.
£4,000–£6,000/$6,000–$9,000

Cover of the Bauhaus prospectus,
Bauhaus Dessau, 1927,
designed by Herbert Bayer.
£300–£500/$450–$750

Modernism meant Communism and decadence, and many of the older teachers began to leave the school; one of the last to go was Paul Klee in 1931. It was finally closed down in 1933.

Many of the key Bauhaus designers and teachers, such as Mies van der Rohe, Albers, and Moholy-Nagy, emigrated to America and continued teaching and spreading their ideas. The "New Bauhaus" was set up in 1937 in Chicago by Moholy-Nagay.

The main characteristics of Bauhaus style can be outlined as follows: use of modern, new materials such as plywood; geometric and abstract patterns in bright primary colours; pieces were designed for mass production; items were functional and clearly constructed.

Functionalism and truth to materials was perhaps the most important theory taught at the Bauhaus. Albers said, "Today, something is beautiful if its form serves its function, if it is well made of well-chosen material." Marianne Brandt produced one of the most striking designs to come out of the Bauhaus. It is an abstract brass and nickel-plated ashtray that was produced for the Bauhaus metal workshop in 1924. This superbly designed piece, combining spherical and semicircular shapes, turns an everyday household object into a work of art and encapsulates the key Bauhaus ideals of functionalism and beauty. This ashtray was handmade, but the design was perfectly suited for mass production. It is still produced today by the Italian manufacturer Alessi, under licence from the Bauhaus archive in Berlin. It is easy to tell these reproductions from an original because new examples are made in stainless steel and do not bear the signature "Bauhaus" on the foot of the ashtray.

Otto Lindig enrolled at the school in 1919 and joined the ceramics workshop and began to produce stark, yet beautiful designs that were suited to mass production. In 1926 he became the master of the ceramics workshop at the Weimar Bauhaus where he continued to make his characteristic semi-opaque glazed ceramics. Lindig's ceramics work so well because the total lack of surface decoration allows the form of each piece to speak for itself. The terracotta tea and coffee service (see opposite) is still strikingly modern today.

Ludwig Mies van der Rohe (1886–1969) was a principal figure at the Bauhaus, designing everything from tables and chairs to buildings. He worked in Peter Behren's office in Berlin between 1908 and 1911 and in his own architectural studio in the same city from 1912. He was involved with the Deutsche Werkbund from the early 1920s and was director of the Dessau Bauhaus from 1930 until 1933. Mies van der Rohe's most famous design to have been produced at the Bauhaus is arguably the "Barcelona" chair (see p.37), but pretty much all the furniture that he produced at the Bauhaus is collectable today, for example the elegant and minimal occasional table (see opposite).

The work of Gerrit Rietveld was a great influence on the early work of designers at the Bauhaus, most probably because he exhibited at the school in 1921. Marcel Breuer's "Lattenstuhl", or "Slatted" chair, is highly reminiscent of Rietveld's work. The joints of the "Lattenstuhl" are left exposed as an integral part of the design and it has a similar pared down, minimal feel to Rietveld's furniture of the same time.

Lamps and other lighting from the Bauhaus are now highly sought after, for example the "MT8" table lamp, which was designed by Karl J. Jucker and Wilhelm Wagenfeld between 1923 and 1924 in the Bauhaus metal workshop. It is a perfect illustration of the key aspects of the Bauhaus style – economy of design, truth to materials, functionalism, and lack of excess surface decoration.

The graphic designer and typographer Herbert Bayer (1900–85) studied at the Bauhaus between 1921 and 1923, and in 1925 began to teach at the school. His graphics were bold and used lower-case sans serif lettering, which heightened their modern appearance (this can be seen in the prospectus on page 23).

## KEY BAUHAUS DESIGNERS:

| | |
|---|---|
| Anni Albers (1899–1994) | textiles |
| Josef Albers (1888–1976) | glass |
| Marianne Brandt (1893–1983) | metalware |
| Marcel Breuer (1902–81) | architecture, furniture |
| Walter Gropius (1883–1969) | architecture, furniture |
| Otto Lindig (1895–1966) | ceramics |
| Mies van der Rohe (1886–1969) | architecture, furniture |
| Gunta Stölzl (1897–1983) | textiles |
| Wilhelm Wagenfeld (1900–90) | glass, lighting, metalware |

### Walter Gropius 1883–1969

GROPIUS

Walter Gropius trained as an architect and took his first job in the offices of Peter Behrens in Berlin in 1907. He joined the Deutsche Werkbund in 1910. The Werkbund was a group of designers and industrialists led by Hermann Muthesius who had joined together in 1906 to unite art and industry, very much in the tradition of the English Arts and Crafts movement. Gropius fought in World War I and formed the Weimar Bauhaus in 1919 until his resignation in 1928. He designed buildings, interiors, furniture, and metalware. In 1934 he moved to London and became director of Isokon (see p.28) and three years later he emigrated to the USA to teach at Harvard.

"The Bauhaus workshops are essentially laboratories in which prototypes suitable for mass production and typical of their time are developed with care and constantly improved. In these laboratories the Bauhaus intends to train an entirely new form of collaborator for industry and the crafts who has an equal command of technology and design."

Extract taken from: W. Gropius, *Dessau Bauhaus* (principles of Bauhaus production sheet), Bauhaus, 1926.

A brass and nickel-plated ashtray, designed by Marianne Brandt in 1924, at the Bauhaus metal workshop in Weimar.
£8,000–£10,650/$12,000–$16,000

A lemonwood occasional table, designed by Ludwig Mies van der Rohe c.1932 for the Breugleman's House, Antwerp, and manufactured by Thonet.
£4,000–£6,000/$6,000–$9,000

"Lattenstuhl", or "Slatted" chair, designed by Marcel Breuer in 1922–4, at the Bauhaus workshop in Weimar.
£25,000–£35,000/$37,500–$52,500

A terracotta tea and coffee service, designed by Otto Lindig c.1932.
£1,650–£2,350/$2,500–$3,500

# New materials in furniture

Early examples of European and American furniture made from the new 20th century man-made materials, particularly plywood, tubular steel, glass and chrome, are extremely collectable today.

As a general rule, a designer's original prototypes, limited production pieces, and early examples of well-known designs are the most desirable of all. Condition is important, but if an item is exceptionally rare then this can become a secondary consideration.

The price of a piece of early modern design furniture generally depends on who designed it, its rarity, its importance within the context of modern design as a whole, what similar examples fetched at auction, the number of collectors determined to own it, and if it has a provenance – for example, original sales documentation or a photograph of the designer with the piece.

Some of the classic early 20th century furniture that used new materials, for example Marcel Breuer's "Wassily" or "B3" chair, has been produced under licence from the original design by selected companies. These represent a good way to own a piece if original examples are out of your price range. But beware of investing in an unlicenced version of a classic design as these are often of inferior quality and will have little or no re-sale value. The "Wassily" chair must have appeared to be completely revolutionary when it was designed by Breuer in 1925–6. It utilized bent tubular steel for the frame and versions exist with either leather, canvas or Eisengarn sections for the arms and back supports. Original "Wassily" chairs are very rare and desirable today because so few were made, and of those most will already be in museums and private collections. It is available today, reissued by Knoll, most commonly with black leather seat and back sections.

The early work of Breuer, Alvar Aalto, Ludwig Mies van der Rohe, and other early Modernist designers is highly collectable today. Their pioneering designs meant that for the first time the aesthetic appearance of a piece of furniture was expressed through the material itself, predominantly plywood or machine-tooled steel or aluminium. Also revolutionary was the fact that they used no surface ornament, believing that the beauty came directly from the form of the piece, allowing the material to speak for itself. As the Viennese architect Adolf Loos said in his famous essay *Ornament and Crime* in 1908, "A plain piece of furniture is more beautiful than inlaid and carved museum pieces." In fact Loos took this idea one step further when he said, "we have outgrown ornament... it is no longer the expression of our culture." He was setting the scene for the modern movement in design which arguably began with Gerrit Rietveld's "Red-Blue" chair of 1918–23 (*see pp.*18–19).

By the 1920s, therefore, design no longer relied on surface decoration and it was the new materials available to designers that helped make this idea a success. Michael Thonet's famous bentwood chairs began this pared-down revolution in the 19th century, but it was left to later designers to bring it to fruition as they moved from using natural to man-made materials in furniture for the first time.

Natural wood was the traditional material for furniture construction for centuries. But it has drawbacks - for example it is very wasteful as only about a quarter of the wood from a tree actually appears in a piece of furniture.

By the early 20th century, man-made woods such as plywood were easily at hand for the first time. The American piano industry initially popularized the use of plywood in the mid 19th century and by the late 1890s machines were available to make it in greater quantities. This increased availability meant that it was also more affordable to make furniture in plywood and manufacturers quickly realized that it would be ideal for mass production.

Plywood manufacture required the assembly of three or more cross layers of wood joined together by a suitable adhesive. At first this would have been an animal- or plant-based glue but by the 1920s scientific advances had led to a new range of synthetic resin adhesives, which also made furniture manufacture much easier. There are two types of plywood – the first made from hardwoods such as ash, beech, birch, chestnut, elm, oak, and walnut, and the second made from softwoods, which are evergreen trees including pine, fir, and spruce.

When plywood is made, the veneers from a tree trunk are peeled away from the main body of the trunk using a long blade fitted to a machine and the resulting thin strips of veneer are cut to the required length. Hardwood plywoods were most commonly used in Modernist furniture manufacturing, and the lightness and malleability of this new material lent itself well to the simple geometric and curved shapes of much of the furniture produced in the 1920s and 1930s. Some of the radical new designs would have been impossible to produce in solid wood because it simply could not have been moulded into the required shape.

Aalto's model number 31 armchair (*see opposite*) was designed for the Paimio Tuberculosis Sanatorium *c.*1932 and its design was revolutionary because it was the first chair to use specially laminated wood in a cantilevered structure. Early examples of this piece are highly collectable. The chair also demonstrates Aalto's masterful use of plywood with its beautifully modelled seat. From 1935 it was reissued by Artek (*see p.*32) and is still in production today. Also collectable today are a series of occasional tables known as model

Designed by Alvar Aalto for the Paimio Tuberculosis Sanatorium. Above: model number 915 occasional table, c.1931–2 **£800–£1,200/$1,200–$1,800**; Right: model number 31 armchair, c.1932, (*see below* for mark). **£2,800–£3,200/$4,200–$4,800**

Details of mark on Alvar Aalto's early model number 31 armchair (*see above right*).

MR20 armchairs, designed by Ludwig Mies van der Rohe in 1927 and manufactured by Belliner Metallgewerbe Josef Müller, Berlin. **£6,000–£8,000/$9,000–$12,000**

number 915 (*see p.27*) that Aalto produced for the same commission and were used in the sanatorium.

Alongside the development of man-made materials, machine-produced materials were also becoming popular. The designer and architect Le Corbusier summed up the machine aesthetic as early as 1924 when he said, "the machine produces surfaces which are faultless". Soon after this, furniture designers began to experiment with other new materials such as tubular steel, reinforced glass, lacquerwork (especially seen in the work of Eileen Gray, *see pp.*38–9), and painted machine-tooled wood.

Aluminium in particular was a popular material with designers. A relatively new metal, it was first isolated in the 19th century and developed for commercial application. In the Paris Exposition of 1855 aluminium bars were exhibited next to the crown jewels. Aluminium was used extensively in the munitions industry during World War I, particularly in the manufacture of aeroplanes, which utilized its potential as a strong yet light material. These qualities were quickly exploited by the new generation of furniture designers who used it to create their new sculptural pieces with great success. Designers found that, like plywood, aluminium was extremely light, and could be strengthened by alloying; it also had a high resistance to corrosion. Aluminium was ideally suited for geometric Modernist furniture shapes such as the square, cube, and circle. Individual components for furniture manufacture could be standardized and each chair assembled from a set of parts which would make production much cheaper and well-designed furniture available to all. In 1926 Walter Gropius, the founder of the Bauhaus, said, "The creation of standard types for all practical commodities of everyday use is a social necessity."

Mies van der Rohe's MR20 armchair (*see p.27*) was designed in 1927. It combines a fluidly styled nickel-plated bent tubular steel frame with a more traditional woven cane seat and back, which gives it strength. Original examples were made from 1927 to 1930 and the chair was later reissued by Thonet and Knoll International. A similar model to this chair, the MR10, was designed without arms.

Breuer's organically styled "Long Chair" (*see opposite*) is one of his most important designs and was created for Isokon in 1935–6. This chair and his laminated wood armchairs from the mid 1930s represent his progression from designing furniture in metal in the 1920s. He did, however, continue to design in metal in the 1930s, for example his slatted aluminium number 313 chaise longue, which was designed in 1932–4. This chaise also exhibits Breuer's love of organic styling utilizing new materials suitable for mass production. Isokon was an important patron for Breuer, bringing his work to a wider audience in Britain. Isokon was founded by Jack Pritchard in the early 1930s and the company also produced Breuer's set of laminated birch stacking tables in 1936 (*see opposite*). Breuer's work, although expensive, was popular in Britain and after his success with Isokon he also designed a range of furniture for the retailer Heal's *c.*1936.

Model No. B3 designed by Marcel Breuer *c.*1925–27, and manufactured by Standard-Möbel and Gebrüder Thonet *c.*1929–31.
**£10,000–£15,000/$15,000–$22,500**

## Marcel Breuer [1902–81]

Marcel Breuer was born in Hungary and joined the Weimar Bauhaus in 1920, studying there until 1924. In 1925 he became master of the furniture workshop and continued in this role when the Bauhaus moved to Dessau. In the same year he created perhaps his most famous and iconic chair the "Wassily" or "B3" chair, which was designed specifically to furnish the painter Wassily Kandinsky's quarters at the Bauhaus.

Breuer left the Dessau Bauhaus in 1928 to practice as an architect in Berlin and his chairs were mass-produced by the firm Thonet after 1931. In 1935 Breuer moved to England. He worked for a short time at Isokon, a company co-founded by Jack Pritchard in an attempt to introduce plywood-made Modernist furniture into British homes. Pritchard wanted Isokon furniture to "make contemporary living pleasanter, comfortable and more efficient." Breuer's most famous design for Isokon was a chaise longue, a plywood model of his earlier aluminium version.

Breuer moved to the USA in 1937 and became an associate professor at Harvard in the same year. His earlier Bauhaus and Bauhaus-inspired designs were mass-produced from the mid 1960s.

"Long Chair",
designed by Marcel Breuer
in 1935–6 for Isokon.
£4,000–£6,000/$6,000–$9,000

Plastic nesting tables,
designed by Marcel Breuer
in 1936 for Isokon.
£700–£900/$1,000–1,350

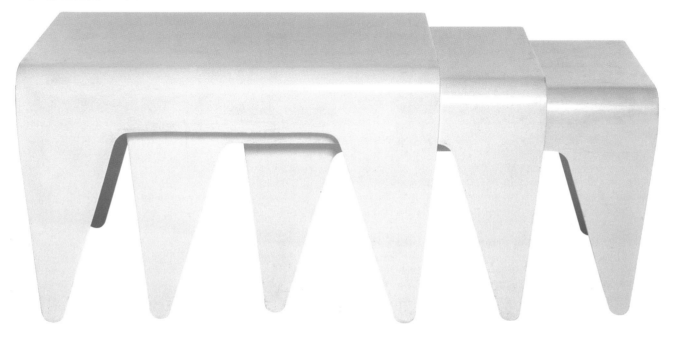

# New materials in furniture

In the 1920s designers in the USA began to use new materials in their work and they were influenced by the sleek lines and minimal styling coming out of Europe, especially the work produced at the Bauhaus. For example, this "Airline" chair (see opposite) designed by Karl Emmanuel Martin (Kem) Weber (1889–1963) clearly demonstrates the influence of Aalto's experiments with plywood in furniture and particularly reflects the design of Aalto's number 31 armchairs (see p.27) Weber was a furniture and industrial designer, as well as an architect and teacher. He was originally from Berlin and emigrated to the USA after World War I, becoming a US citizen in 1924. He opened his own industrial design studio in Hollywood in the late 1920s. The "Airline" chair was created in the mid 1930s and was Weber's attempt to design "a comfortable, hygienic, and beautiful chair inexpensively." The chair came flat-packed for home assembly. It has a maple frame and examples with their original corduroy upholstery are particularly appealing to collectors today. Weber also designed tubular chrome furniture for the Lloyd Company in the late 1930s.

The influence of European Modernism in America can also be seen in this stylish Pittsburgh plate glass chair (see opposite), which reflects Eileen Gray's and Le Corbusier's International Style designs, with its beautifully curved, yet functional reinforced glass frame and plain upholstered seat.

The new materials were ideal for the streamlined industrial designs of the 1930s that were designed to give a feel for speed and efficiency in the machine age, particularly in the USA. The king of streamlined design was undoubtedly the great 20th century American designer and theorist Raymond Loewy. His Modernist industrial design has become very popular among collectors today.

Loewy styled the famous American Greyhound Buses in the 1930s and redesigned the iconic Lucky Strike cigarette packet in 1942. His fantastic, streamlined creations stamped their mark on design right across the USA in the 1930s and 1940s. He opened his own design studio in New York in 1929 and produced fashion illustrations for magazines including *Vogue* and *Vanity Fair*. During his long and respected career he also designed streamlined refrigerators and even locomotives.

Loewy designed the pencil sharpener (see opposite) in the 1930s and its moulded, sleek metal body and attenuated form shows perfectly how streamlined design crossed over into everyday product design.

Another important new material was plastic, especially Bakelite and celluloid plastics. These materials were used in a range of household products, notably radios (which were cheaper to make with a plastic rather than a wooden case) and items that would traditionally have been made from wood such as cigarette boxes and serving trays. Bakelite household items are collectable today. You can buy reconditioned Bakelite telephones from antique fairs and specialist suppliers, as well as picture frames, lamp bases, and even kitchen equipment. Cigarette boxes are often good examples of Bakelite style, but the popularity of smoking related ephemera is falling so this might affect future values.

Plastics were seen by many people as futuristic "miracle" materials that allowed designers to mould and style the exciting new shapes. They were also easy to keep clean, and were strong and relatively simple to manufacture as they could be moulded in a single shape.

Bakelite (made from phenol-formaldehyde resin) was the first synthetic plastic. It was the creation of the Belgian Leo Baekeland (1863–1944) who had emigrated to the USA in 1889. He invented the new product in New York in 1907 and it was quick to catch on with both designers and manufacturers. It was used in furniture design, with the first Bakelite chair produced in 1926, and even in jewellery.

Bakelite has become a popular collecting field in its own right, with prices still reasonable today. It is most commonly found in a dark brown or black colour but the nature of the material allowed it to be dyed different colours. Coloured Bakelite was very popular in jewellery design. Radios and Bakelite televisions are becoming desirable among collectors today but nowadays the latter can really only be used as a decorative item.

Isamu Noguchi (1904–88) was born in Los Angeles but trained as a cabinet-maker in Japan and retained a love of traditional Japanese culture and styling throughout his career. His work is extremely collectable today, and one of his most popular designs showing the influence of new materials was the "Radio Nurse", which was a nursery monitor designed for the Zenith Radio Corporation in 1937 (see opposite).

The new plastics gave Noguchi the freedom to sculpt this radio's wonderfully evocative form, reflecting the shape of a samurai warrior. This symbolic design was chosen to make the piece look like a protective, guiding force in a child's room. Its Modernist design also reflects his sculpture training in Paris in the mid to late 1920s when he worked for two years as an assistant to the Modernist sculptor Constantin Brancusi.

A prototype metal
pencil sharpener, designed by
Raymond Loewy in 1933.
£80,000–£100,000/$120,000–$150,000

"Radio Nurse", designed by
Isamu Noguchi c.1937 for
Zenith Radio Corporation.
£1,350–£2,000/$2,000–$3,000

"Airline" chair, designed
by Kem Weber in 1938.
£6,650–£10,000/
$10,000–$15,000

Glass chair, designer unknown,
manufactured by Pittsburgh Plate
Glass Co. c.1939.
£800–£1,200/$1,200–$1,800

# Alvar Aalto

Alvar Aalto
(1898–1976).

Alvar Aalto (1898–1976) was arguably Finland's greatest architect and furniture designer. He produced interior designs, lighting, textiles, bentwood furniture, and glass that complemented his many architectural commissions and he also designed for and exhibited at international competitions and exhibitions throughout the 1930s. His experiments with plywood furniture were to prove highly influential to Mid-Century designers such as Charles and Ray Eames.

Aalto was a prolific designer working from the beginnings of Modernism through Scandinavian Modernism and into the 1970s, therefore it is impossible to place his work within a single style. However, throughout his life he remained true to the key Modernist principle that a piece of furniture's form should relate to its function.

From 1916 to 1921 Aalto studied architecture at the Helsinki Polytechnic and in Jyväskyla he opened his first architectural office in 1923, and was then based in Helsinki between 1933 and 1976. He began to design furniture from c.1929. Early pieces were manufactured by the Otto Korhonen factory and later pieces by Artek, a

commercial company set up in 1935 especially to produce his designs. In 1933 Aalto moved his thriving architectural practice to Helsinki where he continued to work until his death in 1976. In 1939 he designed the Finnish Pavilion for the New York World's Fair, so gaining recognition in the USA from this date onwards. His work was also available in Britain where it was marketed by the firm Finmar Ltd.

Aalto is particularly famous for his organically styled bentwood seating. His bent plywood chairs are feats of engineering, as each piece has fluid and beautifully curved plywood arms effortlessly supporting the seat. However, his chairs were produced in a manner that was fairly labour intensive so although in principle they aimed to bring good design to the mass market limited numbers were made, often for architectural commissions. This makes original examples rare and highly desirable among collectors. Also popular are the functional, yet beautifully styled tea trolleys he designed for Finmar Ltd. and Artek in the mid 1930s.

One of Aalto's most famous architectural commissions was for the Paimio Tuberculosis Sanatorium between

A birch tea trolley model number 90, designed in 1936–7 and manufactured by Oy Huonekalu-ja Rakennustyötehdas AB for Artek.
£1,500–£2,000/$2,250–$3,000

Laminated beech and plywood lounge chair model number 41, designed c.1932 and manufactured by Oy Huonekalu-ja Rakennustyötehdas AB specifically for use in the Paimio Tuberculosis Sanatorium, with red painted ward number II stencilled underneath.
£14,000–£18,000/
$21,000–$27,800

1929 and 1933. This project yielded the designs for two of his most celebrated chairs, the number 31 (*see p*.27) and number 41 armchairs. He worked with Otto Korhonen, a skilled joiner, to develop laminated wood and plywood furniture from 1929. Aalto would have seen Marcel Breuer's tubular steel furniture (*see pp*.16–17) and he combined the innovative shape and new technology of Breuer's pieces with the use of a Finnish raw material – wood.

The number 31 chair was first produced in *c*.1932 and is revolutionary because it was the first chair to employ laminated wood in a cantilevered section in two dimensions, prior to the Eames three dimensional pieces in the middle of the 20th century. The number 41 chair was produced at the same time by the company Huonekalu-ja Rakennustyötehdas and was constructed from birch and plywood. Approximately one hundred of these chairs were made for use in the Paimio Sanatorium. The example illustrated opposite has a single moulded, ebonized scrolling plywood seat on a laminated and solid birch frame, and still has its hospital ward number stencilled underneath the seat, which makes it especially

Pair of "402" armchairs with upholstered seats, designed in 1933 for Artek.
£1,200–£1,800/$1,800–$2,700

collectable as it is an original example. The design of this armchair made it suitable for mass production, but it was not manufactured in huge numbers. Later examples were made by Artek and have birch arms and four horizontal perforations in the back of the seat. Another collectable design is the elegant "402" armchair which was designed in 1933 for Artek, Aalto's own company. The "402" is very similar in style to another of Aalto's more famous designs, the number 31 armchair, except the former models have upholstered seats.

Although Aalto is particularly known for his chair designs he also produced other pieces of furniture which have the same refined elegance and functionalism. In 1934 he designed a birch desk with a corresponding side chair (*see below*) for the office of G. M. Boumphrey. Boumphrey, who was a writer for the *Architectural Review*, was a founding member of Finmar Ltd., a company that was set up specifically to sell and promote Aalto's furnishings in Britain. This desk and chair is especially appealing to collectors because it has such a strong provenance, having been passed down through

Boumphrey's family before coming on the market. Aalto also designed a range of birch tea trolleys (*see p.32*), and these have also become collectable. Versions exist with and without a wicker basket.

Aalto's furniture was designed to be functional, light, and practical, so many pieces could be stacked. One of his most enduring designs is model number 60 (*see opposite*), a laminated birch stacking stool which was made in 1932–3 and was the first of his designs to use the "L-Leg", the success of which led him to set up Artek. The stool was produced by Artek from 1935 and is still in production today. The model number 60 design has been extensively copied by other manufacturers but these pieces are often of inferior quality to originals and as such will not attract a high price among collectors.

Artek was set up in 1935 by Alvar Aalto, his wife Aino, who also designed furniture, and the art critic Nils-Gustav Hahl to promote the work of the Aaltos and other Finnish products that were sympathetic to them. The firm opened a shop in Helsinki in 1936. At first the company tended to gain commissions from public

A birch desk, designed *c*.1934 for
the office of G.M. Boumphrey.
**£4,000–£6,000/$6,000–$9,000**

interiors, including that for the Savoy Hotel and other hotels and restaurants in Finland, but by 1939 Artek was furnishing domestic interiors.

Artek held regular art exhibitions in the shop from 1936 onwards, showing paintings by contemporary modern artists such as Paul Gauguin, Henri Matisse, and Pablo Picasso, and glass pieces by Gunnel Nyman. These were so successful that a gallery for art exhibitions, Gallerie Artek, was founded in 1950. This provided a platform from which to launch the careers of young designers in Finland in this decade, and helped bring modern design to the attentions of a wider public. The company also exhibited and sold Aalto's furniture throughout the world, most notable successes being the 1933 Milan Triennale and the Paris Exposition of 1937.

Set of three stacking stools, model number 60, designed in 1932 for Artek.
**£200–£300/$300–$450**

### Alvar Aalto glass

**GLASSWARE**

Aalto is well known for his glassware and the most famous example of this is the vase he designed in c.1936 for the Savoy Restaurant in Turjku, Finland, which is made from clear glass with no surface decoration. The example illustrated here was produced for the glass factory Karhula in 1936.

These vases, commonly known as Savoy vases, are a perfect example of Aalto's love of organic styling, as the biomorphic vases resemble amoebas or single-celled natural organisms. They were also made in a traditional and truthful way by being blown into a wooden mould and then cut to shape. Original examples from the 1930s are highly desirable among glass and modern design collectors and can sell for up to £4,000–£6,000/$6,000–$9,000. Later examples were manufactured by the Iittala glassworks and are worth around £200–£250/$300–$400. These come up for sale frequently in auctions and at specialist antique fairs.

A Savoy glass vase, designed for Karhula in 1936 and later manufactured by Iittala. This is a later, post-war example.
**£100–£150/$150–$225**

# International style

The first stage of Modernism really came to an end with the closure of the Bauhaus by the Nazis in 1933. The style had spread throughout Europe in the late 1920s, and by the early 1930s Modernist architecture and design was becoming much more international in scope. The trend for designing functional, unadorned furniture was to continue throughout the decade and the second stage of Modernism became known as International Style.

Many of the designers who adopted International Style, c.1929–39, continued to follow Modernist principles of functionalism and geometric styling. They carried on experimenting with new materials, such as plywood, glass, and tubular steel, and new construction technology. Ludwig Mies van der Rohe's (1886–1969) "Barcelona" or model number "MR90" chair was designed in 1929 and become one of the most famous chair designs of the 20th century, as well as a perfect example of the International Style. It was designed specifically for use in the German pavilion at the International Exhibition in Barcelona in 1929, and was later manufactured by Knoll. Despite its machine tooled appearance, the "Barcelona" chair was almost completely handmade. It was constructed from a curved steel frame and had leather straps and leather upholstered cushions. Original examples are rare and highly collectable, although it has been reissued and is available to buy new today.

Many designs at this time were mass-produced, so there are plenty of pieces available. In the USA a vast amount of items were made in this style, particularly showing the effects of streamlining. Industrial and product design took up the new style, leading to a host of mass-produced items which are still relatively easy to find today.

The 1930s saw the mass-production of Modernist furniture in Britain with firms such as PEL and Isokon interpreting some of Modernism's key theories. Some designers, including Gerald Summers, preferred a more traditional approach and worked within a workshop system. In France, Le Corbusier, Charlotte Perriand, and Eileen Gray continued many of the traditions begun at the Bauhaus with their sleek tubular steel, leather, and glass furniture. These designers produced many designs for commissioned projects. Desny was a short-lived, though influential French interior design firm and is particularly famed for the manufacture of Modernist metalware. The silver-plated centrepiece (*see opposite*) is a wonderful example of the International Style, with its precise, geometric form crafted from sleek metal and its total lack of surface decoration.

The International Style was adopted by the commercial mass market in the USA fairly quickly, whereas in Europe it tended to be restricted to architecture and applied art.

Streamlining, which derived from aerodynamics with its connotations of speed, sleekness, and efficiency, became extremely popular. In furniture design, early pieces from Knoll and the Herman Miller Co. brought well-designed furniture within the reach of the American public.

## KEY INTERNATIONAL STYLE DESIGNERS/FIRMS:

| | |
|---|---|
| Le Corbusier (1887–1965) | architecture, furniture |
| Desny (1927–33) | interiors, metalware |
| Norman Bel Geddes (1893–1958) | architecture, industrial design |
| Eileen Gray (1878–1976) | furniture, interior design |
| Isokon (1932–9) | architecture, furniture |
| Raymond Loewy (1893–1986) | industrial design |
| Ludwig Mies van der Rohe (1886–1969) | architecture, furniture |
| PEL – Practical Equipment Ltd. (founded 1931) | furniture |
| Charlotte Perriand (1903–99) | furniture, interior design |
| Gerald Summers (1899–1967) | furniture |
| Walter Dorwin Teague (1883–1960) | graphics, industrial design |

## International Style America

The new style came to the USA through an exhibition entitled *The International Style: Architecture since 1922*, which was held at the Museum of Modern Art in New York in 1932.

Key figures from the Bauhaus, such as Walter Gropius and Mies van der Rohe, emigrated to the USA in the mid 1930s and brought their ideas and the Bauhaus style with them.

International Style began with architecture and then spread to the decorative arts. Gropius and Mies van der Rohe taught in American universities and their commitment to break away from architectural tradition and design simple, functional and unadorned buildings led to monuments of the International Style such as the Seagram Building, a skyscraper in Manhattan, New York designed by Mies van der Rohe and the American architect Philip Johnson.

In the USA commercial items such as cars, buildings, cash registers, graphic design and packaging, and refrigerators became icons of Modernism due to their styling and materials, particularly through the work of industrial designers Norman Bel Geddes (1893–1958), Raymond Loewy (1893–1986), (*see p. 30–1*), and Walter Dorwin Teague (1883–1960).

A silver-plated metal centrepiece, by Desny in the late 1920s to early 1930s.
**£46,650–£60,000/$70,000–$90,000**

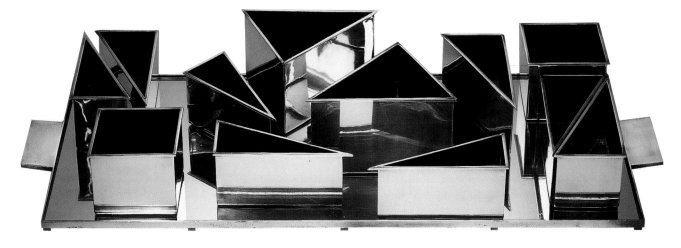

Red leather and chromed-steel stool, designed by Eileen Gray c.1930.
**£15,000–£20,000/$22,500–$30,000**

Leather and chromed steel model "MR90" "Barcelona" chair, designed by Ludwig Mies van der Rohe in 1929. This example is manufactured by Bamberg Metallwerkstätten, Berlin, c.1931.
**£50,000–£70,000/$75,000–$105,000**

# International style France

The main style that came out of France in the late 1920s and early 1930s was Art Deco and many pieces made in the country at this time incorporate elements of both Deco and International Style. They shared some common features such as extensive use of chromed-steel and glass, and streamlined furniture shapes, as well as geometric patterns in rugs and other textile designs as seen in the carpet designed by Paul Follot in 1938 (*see opposite*). As a general rule Deco objects tended to utilize more expensive materials and were much more decorative, while International Style pieces were closer to Modernism with sleek, clear lines, little or no decoration, and consideration of function as well as form. International Style designers also tended to reject the expensive materials but some designers, such as Eileen Gray, mixed Modernist styling with a subtle use of costly materials in their work.

Eileen Gray (1879–1976) is one of the most reclusive figures in 20th century modern design. Although she didn't assign herself to a particular group, many of her pieces from the late 1920s and early 1930s epitomize the International Style. She lived and worked in the same apartment, 21 rue Bonaparte, Paris for 70 years from 1907 until her death. She is most famous for her doors, screens, divans, sofas, chairs, mirrors, and several architecture commissions. She also designed carpets from 1917 and by 1932 her textile designs had become extremely abstract.

Gray was born in County Wexford, Ireland and was brought up in the comfortable surroundings of her family's country house. When she was 20 she attended the Slade School of Art in London and moved to Paris in 1902 to study at the Académie Julian.

The Secessionists were a group of radical young artists and architects working in Vienna from 1897 onwards. They were impressed by the crisp, minimal style of the Scottish designer Charles Rennie Mackintosh and elements of the English Arts and Crafts movement. The Secessionists broke away from what they saw as the conservative design in Vienna at the time and built a magnificent purpose-built building in Vienna to act as a temple to their new artistic expression.

The English Arts and Crafts movement and the Vienna Secession influenced Gray's early work, but on a brief return to London in 1905 she became interested in Japanese lacquerwork.

Gray met Sougawara, master of Japanese lacquerwork, and worked with him for over 40 years. In 1922 she established her own shop, the Galerie Jean Désert. This closed in 1930 but she continued to design. Some of her pieces were reproduced in the 1970s and the "E-1027" table and "Bibendum" chair are still in production today.

The "Bibendum" chair must have seemed way ahead of its time when it was produced in 1932–4. The seat and back of this chair consists of three curved leather tubes, stacked on top of each other and set on a chromed-tubular base. "Transat", another of Gray's chairs, was designed in 1925–6. It too reflects a strong sense of Modernism with its geometrically styled lacquered wood frame, its sparse use of line, chromed-metal fittings, and sling seat. This design is clearly indebted to Gerrit Rietveld and De Stijl, (Gray saw an exhibition of Dutch design in Paris in 1923). But it is the "S" chair, designed in 1932–4, that was to prove to be Gray's most original design, with its sinuous curved metal structure, geometric cut-outs, and padded seat.

Gray's most famous architectural commission was the "E-1027" house designed with Jean Badovici in 1926–9. Badovici was a friend of Le Corbusier and it is easy to see his influence in the style of the house and the furnishings that Gray designed for the interior. The classic "E-1027" tubular glass and chrome adjustable table came out of this project, and it has been widely copied throughout the 20th century to the present day.

The other key designer working in the International Style in France was Jean Prouvé. Prouvé (1901–84) collaborated with several of the International Style's greatest designers such as Le Corbusier and Charlotte Perriand. He trained in metalwork and opened his own workshop in Paris in 1923. A year after this he developed a new method of using tubular metal for chair construction that he called *tube aplati*, which made his chairs stronger by reinforcing areas that bore the greatest amount of strain when the chair was in use. Like Perriand and Le Corbusier, Prouvé was interested in a chair's function as well as its form, so many of his designs were adjustable and highly practical. In 1929 he joined Le Corbusier to found the UAM (Union des Artistes Moderne) and opened his own company, Société des Ateliers Jean Prouvé, in 1931. His designs were ideally suited for industrial mass production and were used in schools and other public buildings throughout France.

A carpet, designed
by Paul Follot c.1938.
£6,650–£8,000/
$10,000–$12,000

A "Transat" chair, designed
by Eileen Gray c.1925–6.
£70,000–£90,000/
$105,000–$135,000

A pair of chairs, Model number 300,
designed by Jean Prouvé c.1947 and
produced by Les Ateliers Jean Prouvé.
£3,000–£4,000/$4,500–$6,000

# Le Corbusier, Pierre Jeanneret, Charlotte Perriand

From left to right: Pierre Jeanneret (1896–1967), Le Corbusier (1887–1965), and Charlotte Perriand (1903–99).

The Swiss born Le Corbusier (1887–1965), whose real name was Charles-Edouard Jeanneret, is arguably the most important and influential architect and designer of the 20th century. His introduction to early Modernism and its use of new technology to produce goods probably came in 1910–11 when he worked in Berlin in the offices of Peter Behrens. Le Corbusier's furniture designs have become highly collectable today, with original prototypes particularly in demand. His concept of standardized, mass-produced housing, which he believed would transform the way we live, was perhaps his biggest contribution to architecture. He was also one of the first architects to sing the praises of high-rise living blocks.

He moved to Paris in 1917, and in 1922 he established an architectural practice with his cousin Pierre Jeanneret (1896–1967), who was also an architect. When the two cousins began to work with Charlotte Perriand successes such as the "Grand Confort" armchairs and the "B306" chaise longue were produced by all three designers.

Le Corbusier designed the Pavillion de l'Esprit Nouveau for the 1925 Paris Exposition, which highlighted his ambition to create furniture and fittings that would be part of a unified decorating scheme for a building's interior. He described the house as a "machine for living", where each room would have a particular function and this functionalist concept had a huge influence on Modernist designers and architects across Europe. He also took up the Modernist ideal of furniture being both

The"B306" chaise longue ("LC1"), designed in 1928–9 for Thonet & Embru. This is a later example, manufactured by Cassina.
**£1,500–£2,000/$2,250–$3,000**

The "LC2" couch, designed in 1928, and later manufactured by Cassina.
**£3,000–£4,000/$4,500–$6,000**

functional and aesthetically pleasing. Le Corbusier is best known for his architectural commissions from the late 1920s onwards and the effects of his theories on urban housing and office spaces are still felt today.

Charlotte Perriand (1903–99) studied at the Ecole des Arts Decoratifs in Paris from 1920 to 1925 during the height of the French Art Deco movement. She rejected this style however, and produced a design for a minimalist bar at the Salon d'Autumne in 1927 complete with extensive use of chrome tubing and aluminium. By 1927 her aluminium and chromed-steel furniture attracted the attention of Le Corbusier. In the same year she began designing furniture, lighting, and interiors with him and Jeanneret, and this collaboration lasted for the next ten years. Memorable designs include the "LC2" lounge chair and the "B301" chair.

The trio first exhibited together at the 1929 Salon d'Autumne in a display called "Equipping a Living Space". Pieces of furniture were never designed on their own; they were always made to fit into an entire living environment. Perriand's contribution to the work of Le Corbusier has been somewhat overlooked in the past

A "B301" chair, designed in 1928, and later manufactured by Cassina.
**£150–£250/$225–$375**

An "LC2" Grand Confort lounge chair, designed for Thonet in 1928 and later manufactured by Cassina.
**£400–£600/$600–$900**

but her leading role in International Style furniture design is now being reappraised.

Two of the most memorable and collectable furniture designs to come out of the Perriand/Le Corbusier collaboration were the "Grand Confort" armchair and the two-seater chairs designed in 1928–9. This former was a reinterpretation of a traditional English leather club chair. It is both geometrically precise and extremely stylish with its use of a polished tubular steel frame left outside the chair as an integral part of the design.

Modernism had moved on by the time the "Grand Confort" armchair was designed, and its designers set out to make sure it lived up to its name. Whereas early Modernist designers such as Ludwig Mies van der Rohe and Gerrit Rietveld concentrated more on the form of a piece of furniture, the "Grand Confort" is actually a chair that people would take great pleasure in sitting in. Versions of the chair were produced with black and tan leather upholstery. Original examples are rare and extremely collectable, but as with many Modernist pieces they were expensive to make and were never originally mass-produced. Be particularly wary of non-licenced reproductions. The Italian furniture company Cassina are still manufacturing this chair today.

Perriand, Le Corbusier, and Jeanneret also designed the "B306" chaise longue, which is probably one of the most famous pieces of 20th century furniture and epitomizes International Style. It encapsulates everything about the style, particularly the use of chromed tubular metal to make the frame, its functionalism, and beauty. The "B306" was ergonomically designed to fit the sitter's body, and was also adjustable so it could be used flat. This piece has also been reissued by Cassina and is available today with a range of coverings including leather and animal skins. Several original variations of the "B306" chaise were produced, including examples with leather, cowhide, and canvas over the frame. The frame itself was left unpainted in some of the chairs and painted in others.

A pair of stools from Maison du Brésil,
Paris, designed by Le Corbusier
in 1957–9.
**£3,000–£4,000/$4,500–$6,000**

Virtually anything designed by Le Corbusier and Perriand has a value to collectors today, and as a general rule the earlier the piece the better. Even relatively unassuming furniture such as stools are collectable, particularly if they were designed for a famous commission or show innovative use of materials such as tubular steel and chrome.

Perriand continued to design in the Modernist style into the middle of the 20th century when she worked in Japan with the designer Sori Yanagi, returning to France in the late 1940s. Her work became much more organic at this point, and she left behind the sleek and functional forms of the earlier chrome furniture to work in wood and explore the use of space in new ways.

A good example of a piece of furniture from this date is the "Tokyo" bench in ash designed c.1953–4. The rectangular, angled top consists of slatted ash strips on three wooden supports and the example shown here is complete with its original cushion. Her commissions in the 1950s included a prototype kitchen for Le Corbusier's housing block in Marseille, perhaps the most logical conclusion of about twenty years of designing furniture for interiors, and the Air France office in London in 1957.

A revolving stool, model number "B304", designed in 1929.
**£1,500–£2,500/$2,250–$3,750**

A steel wall light, designed by Le Corbusier in 1950 for the Cité Universitaire, Paris.
**£2,000–£3,000/$3,000–$4,500**

An ash "Tokyo" bench, designed by Charlotte Perriand in 1953–4.
**£6,000–£8,000/$9,000–$12,000**

# British Modernism

At the end of the 1920s, steel and metal furniture was viewed by the public in Britain as primarily fit for office furniture and not really suitable for domestic interiors. Perceptions began to change when the Viennese firm Gebrüder Thonet set up showrooms in London in 1929 and began to import their successful tubular steel furniture to Britain.

British firms quickly began to see a gap in the market and started to produce tubular steel furniture in the early 1930s. The work of Alvar Aalto (*see pp.32–5*) was first shown in Britain in 1933 and this probably heightened and influenced experiments with plywood furniture in particular. British plywood and tubular steel furniture from the 1930s that was created by key designers is now very collectable, with Gerald Summers' and PEL's (Practical Equipment Ltd.) pieces particularly in demand.

International Style furniture came to the country through progressive retailers and new companies, foremost of which was Isokon, who produced and promoted modern architecture and furniture in Britain and operated from 1932 to 1939. Isokon was named after Isometric Unit Construction, which was an architectural term for a drawing that utilized an isometric view of a house. The company was founded by the furniture manufacturer Jack Pritchard (*b.*1899) and the architect Wells Coates (1895–1958), who worked together on the designs for the Modernist Lawn Road apartments in north London. The design of these apartments reflected the teachings of Le Corbusier and the Bauhaus, as they were both functional and uniform in their construction.

The Lawn Road apartments became a commune of avant-garde intellectuals and artists in the 1930s and were one of the first expressions of architectural Modernism in Britain. Key Modern movement architects and designers actually lived at Lawn Road, including Walter Gropius (*see pages 22 and 24*) and other avant-garde German designers who fled Germany when the Nazi party came to power. This enabled a rich interchange of ideas between Bauhaus and British designers.

Isokon set out to sell pieces of modern design furniture including chairs, tables, and stools that were standardized and used new materials such as aluminium and plywood. Work was commissioned from Gropius, Marcel Breuer, and others and the company only ceased trading when furniture materials from Europe became in short supply with the advent of World War II.

In 1929 Gerald Summers (1899–1967) founded Makers of Simple Furniture in London to manufacture a range of unusual furniture to his own specifications. This small but successful firm also produced innovative new furniture in the International Style and some of Summers' own designs, which were distributed by Isokon. Summers used plywood for his pieces right through the 1930s until imported supplies began to dry up from Eastern Europe at the beginning of World War II and he gave up furniture production. As a result only a few of his designs were actually produced, hence their rarity today.

Summers' early work hit the British market at the same time as Aalto's plywood chairs came to Britain in 1935. Summers' work was also marketed abroad, with advertisements appearing in American magazines and selling in stores such as Marshall Field in Chicago. Summers was one of the first designers of the 20th century to be interested in how a single sheet of plywood could be moulded into a piece of furniture, and it is his innovative ideas and designs that make his work popular among collectors today. His early work includes a three-tier serving trolley formed out of a piece of plywood bent into an S-shape, which was distributed by Isokon.

Summers' masterpiece, however, was his ground-breaking plywood armchair of 1933–4, which was designed for the export market. This was a beautifully

## Heal & Sons

Heal & Sons was particularly influential in bringing Modernist furniture design to the discerning middle classes in Britain from the 1920s onwards. The company began trading in 1810 and quickly gained recognition for retailing fine quality furniture. Heal's is still situated on Tottenham Court Road in London in the building which was designed in 1914 for Ambrose Heal, who was the grandson of the store's founder.

Ambrose Heal (1872–1959) joined the family business in 1893 after studying at the Slade School of Art in London and serving an apprenticeship at Messrs Plunketts in Warwick, where he learnt cabinet-making. He began to design furniture for Heal's from 1895 onwards, and his early pieces were typified by their use of plain oak in simple, unadorned styles following the teachings of the Arts and Crafts movement. In 1913 Ambrose became chairman of Heal & Sons, and by the 1930s the store was retailing designs by PEL and other modern furniture manufacturers and designers, including key British Modernist designer Gordon Russell (1892–1980). His furniture won a gold medal at the 1925 Paris Exposition and is now becoming very popular with collectors.

A PEL chromed tubular steel lounge chair, model number "SP7", manufactured c.1932.
**£300–£400/$450–$600**

A rare curved back chair, designed by Gerald Summers in 1935.
**£1,600–£1,800/$2,400–$2,700**

A plywood armchair, designed by Gerald Summers in 1933–4.
**£13,350–£20,000/ $20,000–$30,000**

# British Modernism

Modernist and highly functional piece of furniture, but it was expensive and time consuming to make so wasn't a great commercial success. This highly unusual one-piece plywood armchair was cut from a single piece of plywood and contains no joinery, hence its very simple yet effective construction. Parallel cuts were made in the plywood and the legs separated from the arms and seat, these elements were then bent in opposite directions into their fluid shapes. The impetus for this design came from a commission for furniture to be used in the tropics, and by eliminating joints which would be weakened by humidity and having no upholstery on the seat Summers created a chair that would withstand damp and rot in tropical conditions. These chairs are extremely popular today and their value comes from the originality of their design and because they were made in such limited numbers.

Some of Summers' other furniture designs were more suited to the British climate and were made for outdoor use. In c.1935 he designed a plain, functional dinner wagon for Makers of Simple Furniture Ltd. as well as a beautifully proportioned five-drawer chest of drawers. He was also interested in the concept of modular furniture, an idea that was pretty radical at the time. This can be seen in the set of five number 796529 book display units illustrated opposite. These cleverly designed, geometric shelves become a moveable work of art when placed together in different combinations and look forward to the designs of modular furniture that became popular in Europe in the 1960s.

PEL was perhaps the most successful company manufacturing modern chairs and other furniture in Britain in the 1930s. It began when Tube Investments, a firm based in Oldbury, near Birmingham, registered a new company name, PEL, in July 1929. It operated from part of an existing factory, run by Accles and Pollock, and had just eighteen employees. Tube Investments provided all the raw tubular steel materials for PEL to make its furniture ranges, which included chairs, desks, and tables.

A key early designer was Oliver Bernard (1881–1939) and he produced stunningly elegant tubular steel furniture that quickly attracted a following in artistic circles. PEL showrooms opened in London towards the end of 1931 and a range of bedroom, living, and dining room furniture was put on display in specially designed room settings.

One of PEL's first important commissions was to produce furniture for the BBC's Broadcasting House in London. The corporation's policy was to only use British goods for the furnishings of its headquarters. This job really brought PEL to public attention and commissions grew from then on, including more from the BBC, which led to PEL furniture appearing in their buildings throughout the world.

Nine months after the firm began production a catalogue was produced and in April 1932 PEL exhibited at the *Ideal Home Exhibition* in London. This led to commissions for the furnishings for the new *Daily Express* building in Fleet Street and furniture for hotel interiors including the Savoy and Claridges. Heal's also sold PEL furniture, which helped to bring its products to a wider audience. PEL became popular with an avant-garde clientele, including the graphic and textiles designers Marion Dorn, Betty Joel, and Edward McKnight Kauffer. Wells Coates of Isokon fame designed furniture for the company and PEL also began to export to India and receive commissions from the English Royal Family.

PEL's success lay in its innovative, user-friendly furniture style. Its patent method of construction and the use of telescoped steel tubes meant that many of its models could be packed flat. Three of PEL's most popular products were the standard stacking chair "RP6", the chromed tubular steel lounge chair "SP7", and the "SP43" chair. All of these reflect the European International Style through their use of tubular steel and are excellent illustrations of how Modernism was spreading throughout Europe at the time.

By 1935 PEL had a large production run and its furniture was available at reasonable prices. Public commissions grew, including designs for British Railways, hospitals, and schools. But by the end of the 1930s the political climate and the threat of World War II began affecting production at the factory and during the war normal work was suspended and items produced for the war effort.

Denham McLaren is another collectable designer who worked in Britain in the 1930s. He was an interior and furniture designer known for his exotic style using animal skins, chrome, and glass much in the style of Eileen Gray (*see pp.*38–9). He gained recognition when his interiors were published in the *Architectural Review* at the time, and his work is bound to increase in value in the future.

A chest of drawers, designed
by Gerald Summers c.1935 for
Makers of Simple Furniture Ltd.
£1,500–£2,500/$2,250–$3,750

A dinner wagon, designed by
Gerald Summers c.1935 for
Makers of Simple Furniture Ltd.
£1,600–£1,800/$2,400–$2,700

A set of five number 796529
book units, designed by Gerald
Summers c.1935 for Makers of
Simple Furniture Ltd.
£2,000–£3,000/
$3,000–$4,500

A high–backed chair,
designed by Gerald Summers
c.1938 for Makers of
Simple Furniture Ltd.
£6,650–£10,000/
$10,000–$15,000

# CERAMICS

A slipware dish, designed by Bernard Leach, c.1928.
£8,000–£12,000/
$12,000–$18,000

People have been collecting studio pottery fanatically since the early 20th century. It was traditionally sold in galleries and often direct from the artist's studio, but since the early 1980s the auction market has offered the best of the historical pieces and values are soaring. Bernard Leach's (1887–1979) work was always very popular in Japan where the appreciation of ceramic art is much more widespread. In the early days of the Leach Pottery much of his best work was sent to Japan, where it was sold more readily.

The beauty with collecting ceramics is that the pieces are often functional as well as beautiful. As in other areas of collecting, condition is important as chips, cracks, and any other damage will dramatically affect the value of a piece. Ceramics are actually remarkably resilient, and apart from the obvious damage from impact you do not have to worry about light or moisture damaging them as you might with so many other collectables.

The Bauhaus had a pottery workshop, as did all of the major Modernist schools of the early 20th century. Running in parallel with these schools was a group of individuals like Leach and Michael Cardew (1901–83) who were interpreting the traditional styles and techniques of anonymous craftsmen potters from around the world.

Studio potters created handmade rather than machine-made pieces and believed in functionalism, truth to materials, and meaningful surface decoration. Leach's work is all about surface decoration – resolving a surface design within a form. Studio potters were committed to the social power of design, believing that the creation of beautifully designed, hand thrown pots was somehow truthful and would benefit society as a whole.

Britain was at the forefront of studio pottery design in the 1920s and 1930s. This was partly due to an already strong and well-established ceramics industry going back to Staffordshire, Worcester, and Derby in the 18th centuries through to the Arts and Crafts movement art potters of the late 19th and early 20th century. There were also some very important exhibitions of Chinese work at this time, which exposed artists to new forms and glazes previously unseen in the West.

The 1920s saw the beginnings of a trend that would occur in ceramic design throughout the rest of the 20th century – a fusion of Oriental ceramic styles and techniques with the Western ceramics tradition. Orientalism had begun in England in the 1870s with the Aesthetic movement, when artists and collectors began importing Chinese pottery into Britain in great quantities.

"Tree of Life" dish, designed
by Bernard Leach in 1923.
**£18,000–£25,000/
$27,000–$37,500**

It was not until the 20th century, however, that Eastern
traditions were really taken up by British potters.

Leach fused these two strands together, and his many
students, collectively known as the "Leach" school,
created their own distinctive wares but often continued
the Leach tradition, coupled with mass production and
affordability. Other potters such as Cardew were inspired
by traditional English country styles. Norah Braden
(b.1901) and Katharine Pleydell-Bouverie (1895–1985)
were both prominent early students of Leach. The two
women shared a studio from 1928 to 1936 and are known
for their experimental use of ash glazes which they made
from plants and wood from the Bouverie estate.

In 1919 Leach went to Tokyo with the idea of funding
his travels by teaching etching, a technique that he learnt
at the Slade in London and took to Japan. Soon after this
he developed his growing interest in all types of Oriental
ceramics. Many Japanese and Korean forms are evolved

An ovid vase, designed
by Katharine Pleydell-Bouverie,
c.1928.
**£3,000–£4,000/$4,500–$6,000**

A flared bowl,
designed by Norah Braden
in 1935.
**£2,000–£3,000/$3,000–$4,500**

A "Bird" dish, designed
by Michael Cardew c.1930.
£5,000–£7,000/$7,500–$10,500

A stoneware vase, designed
by Shoji Hamada, c.1955.
£30,000–£40,000/
$45,000–$60,000

from items used in the Japanese "tea ceremony" and these might include teabowls of various forms, water pots for holding the water used to make the tea, and vases for Ikebana (the Japanese art of flower arranging) used to decorate the teahouse. Leach first discovered ceramics at a "Raku" party. Raku is a technique which allows the artist to decorate and fire a pot very quickly. The theme of the party was for guests to decorate a piece of ceramic, fire it, and take it home. Leach became a student of the great art potter Ogata Kenzan VI and quickly established himself. He began to develop one of his key design ideas, that the design on a pot should work in the round and enhance the form. In his treatise on ceramics, *A Potters Book,* he outlined his belief that "a pot in order to be good should be a genuine expression of life".

Leach moved to St Ives in Cornwall in 1920 along with Shoji Hamada (1894–1979), a Japanese potter inspired by his work in Japan. They built a traditional Japanese three-chambered climbing kiln called an Anagama, which was the only one of its kind in the West. Kiln building is a difficult thing to get right and many of the early firings suffered from flaws of one kind or another, yet these pieces are now among the most sought after of both artists. They held their first exhibition in London in 1921.

The majority of the work produced in the 1920s in St Ives is slipware and some stoneware – the large chargers produced at the time are the most collectable of Leach's work (see pp.108–10).

Hamada was 26 years old when he arrived in England for four years, although he did return later in his career. Despite his short stay, he had a huge influence on studio pottery design of the 20th century. Hamada trained at the Tokyo Technical College and met Leach in 1918. He was an artist in his own right and although Leach introduced Hamada as his assistant, Hamada's pieces were never derivative of Leach's. When the pair began working together at St Ives their work progressed in tandem. Hamada produced mainly bowls with carved designs and vases with painted floral motifs from the Chinese tradition. The pieces that Hamada made in Britain are all marked, making them easy to date to a specific time period.

Hamada and Leach's early work is similar, but later Hamada developed a less pictorial approach pouring abstract splashes of glaze that are less controlled and very expressive. After 1923 Hamada didn't sign his pieces, partly because of his belief in Zen philosophy, which advocated humility and non-recognition for the individual, but a trademark design of Hamada's is the bamboo spray

A vortex bowl, designed
by William Staite Murray c. 1929.
**£4,000–£6,000/$6,000–$9,000**

A stoneware flattened vase,
designed by Kanjiro Kawai c. 1935.
**£12,000–£18,000/$18,000–$27,000**

and this appears on many of his items. He believed that, by repeating a design over and over, making a piece became an almost automatic process; more expressive and somehow from within. Like Leach, Hamada believed in honesty to materials and usefulness of purpose. He returned to Japan in 1925 and a young potter called Michael Cardew joined Leach.

Cardew was one of Leach's most famous students to come out of the St Ives studio in the 1920s. He arrived there with a knowledge and love of North Devon slipware, one of the few remaining regions in England where local age-old crafts still flourished. Cardew worked with Leach until 1926 when he set up his own studio in a traditional pottery at Winchcombe in Gloucestershire.

The relationship between Leach and Cardew was fairly reciprocal – Leach introduced Cardew to the world of Eastern ceramics and Cardew taught Leach how to incorporate pulled handles on his pots. Cardew produced pots, bottles, plates, cups, teapots, and other more traditional forms like oil jars and cider flagons and exhibited in London during the 1930s. His work was also sold at Heal's. His pieces should bear an impressed "MC" seal and his Winchcombe pieces should also be marked

## Potter's marks

Examples from the 1920s are rare but can still be found and will bear impressed marks, and this marking occurred throughout the century. Many pieces will have both the monogram of the artist that made it and of the kiln that it was fired in. For example, you will find pieces fired in the 1920s with the St Ives monogram next to a "BL" (Bernard Leach), the Japanese character for Shoji (Shoji Hamada), or "MC" or "MAC" (Michael Cardew). This also happens with other kilns, such as Michael Cardew's Winchcombe kiln mark being seen next to an "MC" (Michael Cardew) or "S.T." (Sidney Tustin). The "Leach pottery" is the term used for the St Ives kiln. Leach marked virtually everything that he had a hand in producing, but if the piece has an impressed "BL" seal then it is generally accepted that he threw and decorated the piece himself whereas if it has a painted or incised monogram then the piece was probably thrown by one of his apprentices and Leach himself decorated it. The St Ives monogram appears only on the pieces fired in this kiln so you can find pieces with only Leach's mark which may have been made elsewhere.

A stoneware pot, designed
by William Staite Murray in 1923.
**£2,000–£3,000/
$3,000–$4,500**

with an impressed Winchcombe Pottery seal – a combined
"W" and "P". The most collectable of Cardew's pieces
from this period contain animal motifs, birds, and stags.

William Staite Murray (1881–1962) enrolled on a
pottery course at the Camberwell School of Arts, London,
and between 1915 and 1918 he worked with the artist
Cuthbert Fraser Hamilton at his Yeoman's Row studio.
Murray had a strong interest in Orientalism and became a
Buddhist. In 1919 he set up his own studio at his brother's
engineering works in Rotherhithe, London, and his pots at
this time are very much influenced by Sung wares, the early
Chinese ceramics. He produced characteristic tall,
stoneware vases, pots, and bowls, all bearing elegant
monochrome decoration. He also utilized natural plant and
flower motifs, and terracotta glazes.

In 1924 Murray constructed an oil-fired kiln in his
garden at Wickham Road, London. Most pieces of this
period were almost totally devoid of decoration – he was
concentrating on developing special glazes for use in oil-
fired kilns (a relatively unknown technique). From 1924
his pieces will bear a seal-mark rather than an incised
mark. He exhibited every year throughout the 1920s until
1929 at Patterson's gallery and attracted the attention of
several well-off patrons.

A slipware vase, designed
by Thomas Sam Haile c.1946.
**£2,000–£3,000/$3,000–$4,500**

Murray believed that beauty in a ceramic pot came from
resolving form, colour, and surface as a single entity, thereby
connecting the arts of painting and sculpture. He didn't
place as much emphasis on functionalism as Leach and
Hamada. In 1927 he became a member of the 7 + 5 society
of avant-garde painters, critics, and sculptors that included
Barbara Hepworth, Henry Moore, and Christopher Wood.

In 1929 he moved house to Bray in Berkshire and
acquired a larger kiln, and began to make much bigger
pieces. He gave most of his major items a name, which
helps in identification and classifying his work today. He
exhibited up until 1936 at the Lefèvres Gallery, but his
works tended to become prohibitively expensive and
available only to the very affluent. This was the major
distinction between Leach and Murray – Leach believed
that his work should be affordable and produced in great

A Vienna period black teapot,
designed by Dame Lucie Rie
in 1928.
£8,000–£12,000/$12,000–$18,000

quantities, Murray sold through fine art galleries in small quantities and asked high prices for his work.

Murray too, as well as Leach, proved to be a very influential, if somewhat unconventional teacher. One of his most well known students was Thomas "Sam" Haile (1909–48) who had a short but distinguished life. He entered the Royal College of Art in 1931 to study painting then transferred to ceramics under Staite Murray. He was an accomplished surrealist painter and his work is characterized by exceptionally vivid and characteristic figurative, often surreal decoration, working primarily in stoneware. Haile married the potter Marianne de Trey (b.1913) in 1938 and moved to the USA where he became highly influential in the late 1940s. He worked at Ann Arbour in America for a time, making him internationally recognized and collected.

Dame Lucie Rie (1092–95) was born Lucie Gompertz in Vienna. In 1917 she enrolled at art school to study drawing but switched to ceramics after she tried out a potters wheel, describing how she was "lost to the wheel" after this. By the 1930s Rie's work was receiving attention in Vienna and she began exhibiting to great acclaim. In 1937 Josef Hoffman (1870–1956), the great Viennese designer, created the Austrian pavilion for the 1937 World Exhibition in Paris and built a glass corridor to house seventy of Rie's pots. Vienna pots will be marked "LRG Wien (Lucie Rie Gompertz)".

When Hitler annexed Austria in 1938 Rie left and came to England. When she arrived in London she began to mark her pieces with a "RIE" or "LR". She worked in a lens factory in Camden during the war and also made ceramic buttons from a workshop in Paddington, which helped to fund her experiments in more artistic pottery. Rie was naturalized in 1945 and soon after this Hans Coper (1920–81), then an aspiring sculptor, arrived at her studio. They worked together for over a decade and remained close friends until Coper's death.

Rie's earthenware Vienna pieces are characterized by their elegant and finely potted forms and the warmth of their surfaces, despite a lack of conventional surface ornament. Where glaze is used, it complements the intrinsic beauty of a piece, which is effortlessly achieved through the shape of the vessel itself. Functionality was also important, as can be seen in the beautifully simplistic, yet highly practical design of this important Vienna period teapot. Rie's work is all "once-fired", which is a technique born out of necessity as in her early days in Vienna she had to carry all her unfired pots across the city to be fired.

# GLASS

A green flower dish, designed by Alvar Aalto in 1939 and produced in 1949 by Karhula.
**£2,000–£3,000/$3,000–$4,500**

Glass has become a very popular area of collecting with an array of different factories and styles available from throughout the 20th century. The work of some factories and designers is already more collectable than others and can fetch high prices, yet pieces from lesser-known factories are still very affordable today.

As with other areas of design, the Modern movement had an effect on glass. The late 19th and early 20th century saw highly decorative and colourful pieces in the Art Nouveau style (typified by Tiffany in the USA, Loetz in Austria, and Galle and Daum in France). Although Lalique was mass-producing high quality, stylized, naturalistic pressed glass in the 1920s and 1930s the influence of Modernism was being felt on glass design elsewhere. New simple shapes, often with restrained geometric decoration, were beginning to become influential.

The start of the process can be traced to the English designer Dr Christopher Dresser (1834–1904) who took the first steps towards Modernism with his organically-shaped Clutha glass, produced by James Couper and Son, and the functionalist metal and glass tableware he designed for Hukin and Heath in the late 19th century.

It was Joseph Hoffman (1870–1956) within the Wiener Werkstätte and the Deutsche Werkbund who

A "Paris" vase, designed by Wilhelm Wagenfeld in 1936.
**£600–£700/$900–$1,050**

A clear glass vase with stylized figurative cutting,
designed by Richard Süssmuth in 1928
and manufactured by the artist.
**£180–£220/$270–$330**

The work of the secessionists and the Wiener Werkstätte anticipated the Modernist pieces coming out of the Bauhaus by some twenty years. The most prominent exponent of Modernist glass at the Bauhaus was Wilhelm Wagenfeld (1900–90). He trained at the Weimar Bauhaus and believed firmly in the school's teachings of functionalism and truth to materials. Wagenfeld produced some iconic designs, including the "MT9" table lamp in 1923–4 and a range of moulded glass-stacking storage jars in the 1930s. His designs were an excellent fusion between Bauhaus Modernism and industry. The "Paris" vase illustrated here exhibits all the properties of the Bauhaus edict and dates from 1936.

The German glass designer Richard Süssmuth (1900–74) combined traditional finishing with modern forms and production processes. The vase shown here encapsulates these factors with its simple form and restrained, stylized cut figurative decoration and was mass-produced in his factory at Penzig, Germany.

The influence of the Wiener Werkstätte and the Bauhaus designers was felt in other countries. In Sweden the work of Simon Gate (1883–1943) and Edward Hald (1883–1980) successfully combined functionalism and modernity while still exhibiting a sense of the organic form.

In Finland, Alvar Aalto (1898–1976) was designing glass at the same time as developing his ideas on modern furniture design. His first success in glass was the "Flower of Riihimaki" in 1933. The most famous of Aalto's glass designs is the "Savoy" vase (*see p.*35). His designs are usually soft organic forms blown with the use of wooden moulds. The flower dish (*see opposite*) is a typical example of Aalto's organic glass.

In 1914 Andries Dirk Copier (1901–91) was at the beginning of his long career as a designer with the Leerdam Glassworks in Holland. His versatility included Rietveld-inspired designs such as his primary coloured cactus pots set on a black tray, through to Modernist vases and tableware.

The only real exponent of Modernist glass in England was Keith Murray (1892–1981), a New Zealand born architect and designer who was influenced by the Paris 1925 Exhibition as well as the Swedish Exhibition in 1930. His work includes simple, minimalist, symmetrically blown pieces and cut and engraved items, the best known of which are his series of "Cactus" vases. These pieces were all made by Stevens and Williams, Royal Brierley, and are occasionally marked with a facsimile signature. While it is possible that the mark may be faint, it is a common misconception that all these pieces are marked.

heavily influenced modern glass design, initially with his geometric and restrained floral "broncit" designs produced by J. & L. Lobmeyr. This was a process taken up by Lobmeyr and it involved etching away the outer coating of bronzite on a piece, so leaving a raised design with a matt background, often in black, or red over white.

The glasses which Otto Prutscher (1880–1949) designed for the Wiener Werkstätte are among the most stunning and memorable pieces of glass produced at this time. They are typified by their slender stems and cylindrical bowls in clear glass, having a coloured overlay that has been cut away in a geometric, grid-like pattern. The design has a very architectural feel.

Along with Peter Behrens (1868–1940) Hoffman also produced simple designs. His were typified by graceful, blown forms for J. & L. Lobmeyr and facet-cut forms for Moser of Karlsblad, while Behrens combined colour and form in his glasses produced by Rheinische Glashütte.

# TEXTILES

A wall hanging, designed by Gunta Stölzl in the 1920s. (Reproduced in a limited edition in 2000.)
**£8,000–£9,000/ $12,000–$13,500**

The 1920s and 1930s saw a resurgence in textile design in Europe. This was partly a continuation of the revival of handcrafted textile design that began with the English Arts and Crafts movement in the late 19th century, but also because Modernist interiors and furniture needed Modernist fabrics to match. The work of some textile designers is already commanding premium prices, but examples by anonymous designers or those that have yet to be recognized are an excellent way to begin a collection or furnish your home. You can collect rugs, embroideries, wall hangings, and even blankets.

The Bauhaus produced two of the most famous and original textile designers of the 20th century, Anni Albers (1899–1994) and Gunta Stölzl (1897–1983). Both women taught at the Bauhaus and believed in creating good design that could be mass-produced. Other collectable textile designers from the School are Gertrud Arndt, Otti Berger, Léna Bergner, Marli Ehrman, Dörte Helm, and Margaret Leischner.

The weaving workshop at the Bauhaus was the only workshop in the school to run from its foundation in 1919 to its closure in 1933. It was also commercially successful. When the Dessau Trade Union inspected the Weimar Bauhaus in 1925 they commented, "The weaving workshop seems to be better than others. Its products clearly demand recognition." Women designers were directed here when they enrolled at the Bauhaus because textile design was traditionally seen as the preserve of women. Many of the designers had already studied fine art, hence their flair for colour and composition. Students learnt about looms and weaving techniques, as well as materials. In addition, they studied embroidery, knitting, crochet, sewing, and book keeping in preparation for professional life.

Bauhaus textile designers experimented with new materials such as Lurex, leather, and cellophane. They also created original textures by juxtaposing new materials with traditional ones such as cotton or jute, and even made pieces that were light reflective or could be reversed. This was an important consideration because houses had less and less servants so designers tried to produce textiles that were easy to look after and would last, aiming at a cross-section of society. New technology also allowed them to design pieces that had double and triple weaves, and the Jacquard Loom (which featured a system of punched cards for the automatic selection and weaving of cords into a particular design), allowed more elaborate designs to be created.

*left* A tufted rug, designed by
Edward McKnight Kauffer
in the 1930s.
£5,000–£7,000/$7,500–$10,500

Stölzl initially studied painting and ceramics in Munich. In 1919 she joined the weaving workshop at the Bauhaus (it was the only workshop open to women at the time). Undeterred by this restriction, by 1927 she was running it and was the only woman to head one of the Bauhaus departments. She was an expert weaver and combined technical skills with an instinct for good design. She believed that "Weaving is an aesthetic whole, a unity of composition, form, colour and substance."

Her wall hangings and tapestries combine bold and dynamic use of colour with abstract patterns, very much influenced by the painter Wassily Kandinsky who taught at the Bauhaus. Stölzl's favourite motifs include stripes of pure colour, squares, and circles. She also spent time in the furniture workshop at the Bauhaus and produced several designs with Marcel Breuer, such as the "African" chair of 1921 with its abstract tapestry seat and back, and a side chair in the same year which featured a De Stijl-inspired seat and back.

*right* A wall hanging, designed by Gunta Stölzl
in the 1920s (reproduced in a limited
edition in 2000).
£8,000–£9,000/$12,000–$13,500

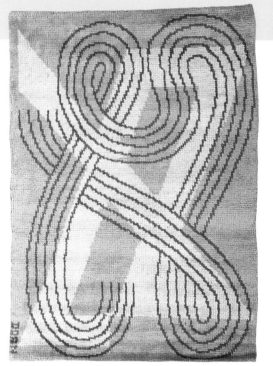

A tufted rug, designed by
Marion Dorn in the 1930s,
bearing the "Dorn" monogram.
**£3,000–£4,000/$4,500–$6,000**

A rug attributed to
Marion Dorn, c.1930.
**£2,000–£3,000/**
**$3,000–$4,500**

Stölzl was a prolific designer in the 1920s but very few of her watercolour designs were produced as textiles at the time because of material shortages, so original examples are rare. However, selected designs are being reproduced today and are a good way to acquire her work. They will probably hold their value in the future as they are limited editions. The best way to spot an original textile from a reproduction is through signs of natural aging (colours may be faded, threads may be coming loose, or patches of the textile may be worn) and provenance. As a general rule, period textiles that are in good condition will always attract the best prices.

Anni Albers was another central figure in the Bauhaus weaving workshop. She is particularly known for her wall hangings and one-off weavings. Albers studied and taught at the Bauhaus before emigrating to the USA with her artist/designer husband Josef in 1933, where she taught textile design and exhibited her pieces to great acclaim. Like Stölzl's work, her textiles are instantly recognizable for their use of bold, abstract colour and form, particularly inspired by the painter Paul Klee who taught at the Bauhaus.

Bauhaus textile designs have been poorly recorded and documented so many of the designs are anonymous, such as the example illustrated here (*see opposite*). Original Bauhaus textiles are very rare, as the school itself bought and catalogued most of the students' designs and were the official owners of the work. On relocation to the Weimar Bauhaus the workshop was spilt into two, the "experimental" and the "production" and the latter concentrated on designs that were intended for mass production. In 1930 the weaving workshop joined with Polytextil, a commercial textile company that wanted to produce and market reasonably priced, yet artistically brilliant Bauhaus upholstery and curtain fabrics. These pieces are relatively rare but examples do turn up, and they will be labelled "bauhaus-dessau".

Textiles in Britain took on a distinctly Modernist flavour after the 1925 Paris Exposition. Rugs in particular became extremely stylish overnight. Marion Dorn (1896–1964) produced some of the most vibrant textiles of the period, and these can be seen in her brightly coloured, geometric rugs in the Modernist style.

Dorn was a design pioneer who succeeded in a male dominated industry, and it is for these reasons that Dorn has become one of the most collectable British textile designers of the last century. Dorn continued to design in the bold, cubist-inspired style right into the mid 1930s

An anonymous woven
Bauhaus textile fragment.
£800–£1,200/$1,200–$1,800

when she produced rugs for the interior of Claridge's Restaurant in London in c.1935.

Dorn was married to the artist and graphic designer Edward McKnight Kauffer (1890–1954), who also produced Modernist, geometric, brightly coloured textiles and rugs. Kauffer was born in the USA and came to England in 1914. He worked with the artist Wyndham Lewis, who was part of the Omega workshops in London that made a range of ceramics, textiles, screens, and furniture in the Modernist style before World War I. This short-lived workshop also produced memorable graphic art for the London Underground.

Both Dorn and Kauffer created cubist-inspired designs and also pieces with abstracted figural and naturalistic motifs. From 1928 their designs were handwoven at the Wilton Royal Carpet Factory, Wiltshire, England. Their work can be characterized by strong use of colour, plain backgrounds, and, in most cases, the absence of borders. The monogram "KK" will usually be woven into McKnight's work and "Dorn" into Dorn's pieces.

## Displaying and caring for textiles

Keep antique textiles away from sunlight and strong artificial light, which will fade the colours and detract from the beauty and value of the piece. The best way to protect delicate textiles is to frame them. One way to do this is to stitch the textile to a fabric-covered, acid-free board before framing it to give it extra protection.

If you intend to store your collection, it is best to roll textiles or keep them flat rather than folding them, as this can lead to splitting along the fold line. Use sheets of acid-free tissue paper (available from specialist suppliers) as extra protection between each item. Storing your collection in this way will also keep your textiles safe from moths and carpet beetles.

It is generally safe to vacuum antique rugs if you do so very carefully, taking care not to catch any loose threads in the vacuum cleaner. For extra protection, cover the nozzle of the vacuum cleaner with a small piece of net as you clean each area of the rug.

# METALWARE

A lacquered sheet steel desk set, designed by Marianne Brandt in 1930–2, and manufactured by Ruppelwerk GmbH, Gotha.
**£1,200–£1,500/$1,800–$2,250**

Bauhaus and Bauhaus-inspired metalware is arguably the most stylish of the 20th century. It combines functionalism with understated elegance in a way that was completely new and influenced metal designers throughout the century. Traditional materials such as brass were combined with nickel and chrome to create a machine tooled aesthetic that remains one of the Bauhaus's strongest legacies.

Marianne Brandt (1893–1983) is perhaps the best-known designer working with metal in the late 1920s and early 1930s. She produced a host of stylish everyday objects ranging from electroplated brass tea infusers to chrome desk sets, as well as ceiling and bedside lamps, utilizing new and traditional materials. Brandt joined the Weimar Bauhaus in 1924 as an apprentice in the metal workshop, which was supervised by László Moholy-Nagy at the time. She went on to become deputy director of the workshop and one of the most successful female Bauhaus designers, despite encountering initial hostility from her fellow male designers.

One of her most striking designs is an abstract brass and nickel-plated ashtray (see p.257) that was produced for the Bauhaus metal workshop in 1924. This superbly designed piece, combining spherical and semicircular shapes, turns an everyday household object into a work of art and encapsulates the key Bauhaus ideals of functionalism and beauty. Examples were also made in silver and bronze. This ashtray was handmade, but the design was perfectly suited for mass production. It is produced today by the Italian manufacturer Alessi, under licence from the Bauhaus Archive in Berlin. It is easy to tell these reproductions from a Brandt original because new examples are made in stainless steel and do not bear the signature "Bauhaus" on the foot of the ashtray.

Brandt went on to design a host of other functional items and from c.1927 onwards produced metal and nickel-plated desk lamps, which were a great commercial success. She remained head of the metal workshop until 1929, when she worked for a brief period in Walter Gropius's office in Berlin and at the Ruppelwerk manufacturing factory in Gotha, where she continued to produce desk sets and other domestic items before becoming a teacher and painter for the rest of her career.

Christian Dell (1893–1974) designed a range of metal jugs, tea infusers, and lighting while master of the metal workshop at the Bauhaus from 1922 to 1925. Like Brandt, he believed in creating functional metalware suitable for mass production but looked back to the past

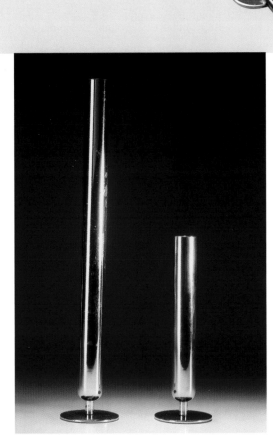

An electroplated brass tea infuser, designed by Christian Dell in 1934.
**£600–£800/$900–$1,200**

Two white metal cylinder vases (model number BR24), designed by Fritz August Breuhaus in 1928 for WMF.
**£700–£900/$1,050–$1,350**

much more than his Bauhaus contemporaries and this historicism is reflected in his designs. He also utilized more expensive materials such as ebony and silver.

The two white metal cylinder vases illustrated above were designed by Fritz August Breuhaus in 1928. They were produced for the German manufacturer WMF (Württembürgische Metalwarenfabrik) and represent a stark contrast to the company's previous output of extremely ornamental metalware in the Art Nouveau style. Their highly abstracted, attenuated bodies rest on a single cylindrical foot to create a stark yet beautiful design. These vases are an excellent illustration of how the principles of the Bauhaus were spreading into industrial production by the late 1920s. They are stamped with the WMF makers' mark.

# LIGHTING

Model number 6580 "Super" desk lamp, designed by Christian Dell in 1933–4 and manufactured by Kaiser and Co.
**£1,350–£2,000/$2,000–$3,000**

A black painted metal and steel adjustable table lamp, designed by Karl Trabert c.1932–4 for G. Schanzenbach.
**£1,000–£1,500/$1,500–$2,250**

The 1920s and 1930s were the decades in which mass-produced electric lighting came into its own, particularly with the emergence of the desk lamp. Some of the best examples of lighting came out of the Bauhaus metal workshop at the same time as Marianne Brandt's metalware, but there were also some outstanding new designs from France and Scandinavia.

Desk lamps were especially innovative, having functional shapes with minimal decoration, but table lamp design also broke new ground. One example, the brass and glass "PH" table lamp (*see opposite*) designed by Poul Henningsen in 1925 for the Danish firm Louis Poulsen was to prove extremely influential and has inspired many similar designs right through to the present day. The beauty with Modernist lighting is that it can be used in the home, although most examples that appear on the market still have their original Bakelite plugs and cable and will need to be rewired to meet modern safety standards.

Poul Henningsen (1894–1967) was one of Scandinavia's most prolific lighting designers, producing hundreds of different types of lights during his long career. He originally trained as an architect and then turned to journalism before beginning to design in 1924.

The prototype of his "PH" lamp, with its innovative three-tiered shade designed to produce a soft and directional light, was exhibited at the 1925 Paris Exposition and was an immediate success, winning a gold medal. The lamp soon went into mass production and was exported to Central Europe, North America, and Africa until the outbreak of World War II. Production continued after this and the lamp is still manufactured today. The rare example illustrated here was produced in 1927 and has a tiered copper shade on a brass shaft. Early models will have a "patent applied" mark under the shade, in this case dated to the first series of production c.1927. Slightly later examples are marked "patented".

The chromed metal and glass table lamp manufactured by Desny is a superb example of how glass and metal can work together to produce a functional, yet highly beautiful object. The unusual design of a section stem intersected with plates of glass makes this lamp particularly appealing. Its geometric, cubist shape is typically modern and also reflects modernist styling that originated in France after the 1925 Paris Exposition. La Maison Desny was an interior furnishings and decorating store in operation from 1927 to 1933. It was founded by two designers, Desnet and René Nauny and they

A chromed metal and glass table lamp, manufactured by Desny c.1935.
**£2,000–£3,000/$3,000–$4,500**

An early "PH" table lamp, designed by Poul Henningsen in 1927 for Louis Poulsen.
**£5,000–£7,000/$7,500–$10,500**

produced a wide variety of exclusive furniture, textiles and metalwork including vases, bowls, lamps, rugs, and aluminium chairs.

Christian Dell (1893–1974) was one of the foremost metal designers at the Bauhaus. He was head of the Weimar Bauhaus metal workshop between 1922 and 1925, and it was here that he developed extremely modern designs for lighting as well as producing metal household objects such as wine jugs and tea infusers. Dell continued to design Modernist metalware in the 1930s before turning to jewellery manufacture in the early 1940s. The model 6580 "Super" desk lamp (*see opposite*) was designed in 1933–4 and manufactured by the German company Kaiser and Co. The combination of Dell's elegant, functional styling and the fact that this is a double desk lamp and as such more unusual than single examples, makes this piece particularly collectable today.

## Desk Lamps

Single and double desk lamps are becoming increasingly popular among modern design collectors, particularly those by recognized designers such as Christian Dell from the Bauhaus and Karl Trabert. Many lamps were made in painted metal and steel and were adjustable according to the needs of the user. The Trabert example illustrated opposite is way ahead of its time and looks forward to 1950s styling with its domed shade and elegant shape.

You will be able to tell a genuine desk lamp from a reproduction if it hasn't been refitted for present day use because it may still have its original flex and plug. If you don't want to get it converted to use in your home, a desk lamp will be a decorative addition to a collection nevertheless. Condition is important and lamps that have scratched metal shades or dents will generally be worth less than pristine examples, unless they are by a particularly important designer or are one-off prototypes that were never mass produced.

# GRAPHICS

*Keeps London Going*, a poster
designed by Man Ray in 1932.
**£40,000–£60,000/$60,000–$90,000**

Artwork for *Speed*, a poster concept
by Alan Rogers dating from 1930.
Not for commercial sale.

One of the best examples of Modernist graphic art is the work that was undertaken for the London Underground in the 1920s and 1930s, and this has become a popular collecting area in its own right. Rare images by famous artists and designers of the time can now command five-figure prices. Today, the walls of the London Underground have become an exhibition space for posters advertising everything from theatre shows to books. But in the early years of the 20th century London Transport had to advertise its own product and enlisted some of the greatest modern artists and designers of the day to help get its message across to passengers.

London Railway services ran on steam until 1890 when the City and South London Railway developed the first electric underground railway in the world. It quickly became known as "the tube", due to its circular-shaped tunnels. By the late 1920s London Underground had developed its iconic bar and circle logo, which itself came to symbolize London for the rest of the 20th century. The Underground's purely stylized and abstracted grid map was produced by Henry C. Beck in 1933 and is still in use today due to its timeless and ground-breaking design.

Colour lithographic posters came into their own in France in the 1890s, and by 1910 the London Underground was utilizing this new medium for its advertising campaigns to encourage customers to use what was still a relatively novel way to travel. Modern design reached the public through something they would have seen everyday – the Underground poster.

Frank Pick was appointed publicity officer for London Transport in 1908 and it was his design vision that brought modern art into the everyday lives of thousands of Londoners. Pick commissioned some of the most creative avant-garde artists of the time to design posters including Edward McKnight Kauffer, Laura Knight, László Moholy-Nagy, and Man Ray. By the end of the 1930s Bauhaus-, Vorticist- and Russian Constructivist-inspired posters decorated tube stations across London, with up to forty new designs appearing every year. Some of each print run were available for sale to the public, hence the reason why they appear in the collector's market today.

Edward McKnight Kauffer (1890–1954) was first commissioned in 1914 and went on to become one of the Underground's leading designers, producing over a hundred posters. His early posters are very traditional and featured images of naturalistically painted English landscapes to encourage Londoners to experience the delights of the countryside. By the time he had created

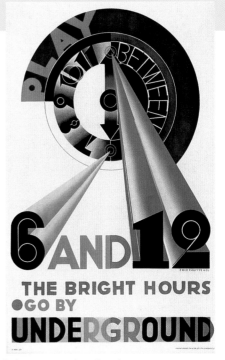

*Power*, a poster designed
by Edward McKnight Kauffer
in 1931.
£15,000–£20,000/$22,500–$30,000

*Play Between Six and Twelve*,
a poster designed by
Edward McKnight Kauffer in 1930.
£8,000–£10,000/$12,000–$15,000

one of his most famous images, *Play Between Six and Twelve* in 1930, his work reflected European and American Modernism, with its attenuated, streamlined numbers rushing towards the viewer and solid blocks of colour influenced by Bauhaus graphics. A year later he produced *Power*, an extremely powerful image which echoes Russian Constructivist graphics of the preceding decade. The same influence can be seen in Alan Rogers's poster *Speed*, with its bold use of geometric shapes.

One of the rarest London Underground posters is *Keeps London Going*, designed by the pioneering avant-garde photographer and artist Man Ray (1890–1976) in 1932. Man Ray was born in America and found fame through his paintings, drawings, photographs, films, and sculptures. He was a member of both the Dada and Surrealist groups in the 1920s and it was at this time that he developed his "rayographs" or "photograms", which were photographs produced without a camera by placing objects directly onto light sensitive paper and exposing them to light. *Keeps London Going* is the only image that Man Ray produced for London Transport, hence its value and desirability. It is an imaginative, witty, and completely modern image, unlike anything that would have been seen before on the Underground.

## László Moholy-Nagy

The Hungarian-born designer László Moholy-Nagy (1895–1946) arrived at the Bauhaus in 1923 and taught firstly in the metal workshop before taking over the preliminary course at the school. He began his career as a sign painter and graphic/typographic artist. Moholy-Nagy's work was heavily influenced by Constructivism in Russia, and this can be seen in the work he did for London Transport.

Moholy-Nagy was a self-taught artist (he had received a war wound in 1917 and took up painting while recovering from it). His dynamic, bold graphics are representative of the Bauhaus style and early Modernist graphics and are characterized by straight lines, geometric shapes, and abstract compositions in primary colours. Moholy-Nagy's graphics also reflect his interest in the machine age and industrialization.

# MID-CENTURY DESIGN

# MID-CENTURY DESIGN

From the mid 1940s to the end of the 1950s, designers began to move away from the stark lines of early Modernism towards a more organic style, epitomized by the coffee table (*above*) by Isamu Noguchi (1904–88) with its sculptural, biomorphic legs. It was also a time of convergence in design, when British, Scandinavian, and Italian styles began to merge with the work of a new generation of designers and artists coming from the USA. In the mid 20th century, cutting-edge Modern design finally moved from galleries and limited edition pieces to mass production, particularly in the USA and Scandinavia.

International exhibitions continued to be a dominant force in the dissemination of the new organic style, particularly those held at the Museum of Modern Art in New York and the Triennials in Milan. New materials continued to be popular, with plywood, laminates, and, by the end of the 1950s, plastics in general use (polythene was first used in the USA in 1949).

In Britain, the first signs of a new, post-war design came at the *Britain Can Make It* exhibition held at the Victoria and Albert Museum, London in 1946. Devised as an exercise to boost public morale in British design and industry after the devastation of the war, the exhibition attracted over one and a half million visitors. It contained wonders of modern technology including air-conditioned beds, labour saving devices, and modern home furnishings, and saw the first public appearance of new furniture by designers such as Ernest Race and glass by the Whitefriars factory. One of the most memorable exhibits was a Spitfire plane set against a backdrop of bomb-damaged London, with aluminium prams, saucepans, and other everyday articles placed in front of it to show the public how materials developed during the war could be applied to domestic goods. The newly created Council for Industrial Design chose exhibits from manufacturers across the country. But the *Britain Can Make It* exhibition was only a taster for the delights that would appear at the Festival of Britain in 1951, which launched the careers of several mid-century British designers and showcased the best new textiles, furniture, ceramics, and domestic goods in a themepark-like setting on the South Bank in London.

In the USA, young designers such as Charles and Ray Eames, Eero Saarinen, and Harry Bertoia had been inspired by pre-war Modernism developments, particularly the use of plywood in furniture and its possibilities for mass production. The Museum of Modern Art's exhibition *Organic Design in Home Furnishings* in 1940 brought the organically styled, plywood chairs of Eames and Saarinen to public attention for the first time. By the early 1950s, both these designers were firmly established as contemporary successes, producing some of the most classic designs of the century and architectural commissions to match, supported by major manufacturers and retailers such as the Herman Miller Co. and Knoll.

The same developments were happening in Scandinavia, but as these countries were not as affected as the rest of Europe by World War II, traditional furniture, glass, and ceramics manufacture continued in parallel with the introduction of new laminate woods, metal, and plastics in furniture design. The new organic style had spread through Scandinavia by the end of the 1950s, typified by the glass of Timo Sarpaneva (*b*.1926) and Tapio Wirkkala (1915–85), and Arne Jacobsen's (1920–71) "Egg", "Ant", and "Womb" chairs.

The 1950s saw the start of the nuclear age; atomic styling also became popular in Britain and the USA, with everything from table legs to clocks reflecting the shapes of atomic structures.

An ebonized birch and glass coffee table, designed by Isamu Noguchi and manufactured by Herman Miller Co., c.1950s.
£2,650–£4,000/$4,000–$6,000

# Festival of Britain

An aerial view
of the Festival
of Britain South
Bank Exhibition.

The late 1940s was a time of great economic expansion for Britain after World War II. Britain was an optimistic, blooming nation and its most successful public relations event, both for the morale of people in Britain and abroad, was the 1951 Festival of Britain, dedicated to the very best of new British industry and design. A hundred years previously, the Great Exhibition of 1851 had celebrated the best design and architecture of the British Empire. But the 1951 festival was much more than this. It represented a break from the past and a look forward to an optimistic future. Gerald Barry, the festival's director, described it as a riot of "fun, fantasy and colour".

The festival was set up in collaboration with the Arts Council of Great Britain and was held over five months at London's South Bank on 11ha/27 acres of bomb-damaged land. Eight million people visited the site with its vibrant gardens, cafes, and open-air displays and saw futuristic exhibits such as the rocket-shaped Skylon and the Dome of Discovery, and pavilions including "The Land of Britain" and "The People of Britain". The centrepieces were the South Bank Exhibition, which aimed to show the world how far Britain had developed in the arts, sciences, and industry, and the newly-built Royal Festival Hall, designed by the architects Robert Matthew and Dr J. L. Martin with seating by Robin Day.

The festival had a huge impact, not just on people's perception of design but on design itself, and its effects were felt in Britain right through the 1950s. Some of the leading designers of the decade such as Robin and Lucienne Day (whose Calyx textile was designed specifically for the event), Sir Terence Conran, and even a young Mary Quant were involved in designing objects and the exhibition itself. There were very high levels of quality; no piece was put on display unless it met the strict standards for good design set by the Council of Industrial Design. New furniture was seen for the first time and introduced modern design into Britain, as during the war government restrictions meant that only plain Utility furniture using easily available material was manufactured. For the first time, British people could see furniture that

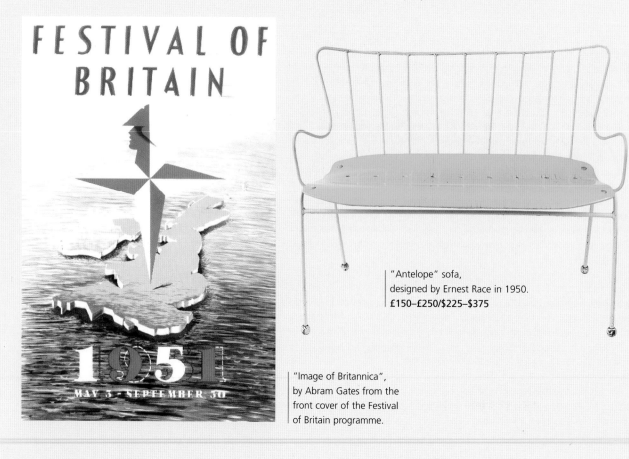

"Antelope" sofa,
designed by Ernest Race in 1950.
**£150–£250/$225–$375**

"Image of Britannica",
by Abram Gates from the
front cover of the Festival
of Britain programme.

was made of new materials such as plywood and had metal rods instead of traditional wooden chair legs. It is difficult to imagine just how innovative this was at the time.

Ernest Race (1913–64) provided the seating for the exhibition and these chairs have become very collectable. They are a good investment because, as well as their use of new materials and new design, they will always be associated with the festival, itself a collectable field in its own right. His "Antelope" chairs were made in both single and double versions with tables to match. The frames were constructed of enamelled welded steel rods, which made the chairs ideal for outdoor use as they were rustproof. Plywood was used for the seats and they had white ball feet. "Antelope" chairs came in a riot of colours including blue and red. They were one of the first mass-produced chairs in Britain to reflect atomic styling, which influenced the design of masses of items throughout the 1950s. The slightly splayed steel legs of "Antelope" chairs became a characteristic of many tables, chairs, and hall stands produced in Britain during the 1950s.

A length of "Calyx" textile, designed by Lucienne Day in 1951.
£300–£500/$450–$750

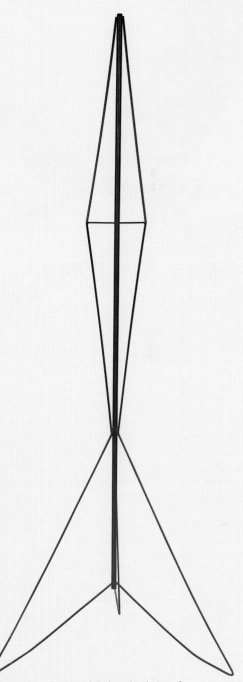

A metal lamp base modelled on the design of the futuristic Skylon at the Festival of Britain.
£150–£200/$225–$300

# FURNITURE

A folding and stacking "Neptune" deck chair, designed by Ernest Race in 1953 and made by Ernest Race Ltd. for P&O Ltd.
**£1,000–£1,500/$1,500–$2,250**

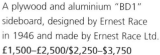

A plywood and aluminium "BD1" sideboard, designed by Ernest Race in 1946 and made by Ernest Race Ltd.
**£1,500–£2,500/$2,250–$3,750**

The main development in furniture design in the mid 20th century was the rise of organic styling, which was evident across Europe and in the USA. Modernist functionalism remained but shapes became much softer and more curvaceous. Machine production enabled designers to create these fluid new designs (the early plywood chairs of Charles and Ray Eames in the USA, for example, simply would not have been possible without the aid of machinery). Molecular and atomic styling also began to appear in furniture, but not to the extent that it emerged in other areas of design.

Another important development was that modern design began to move into the private and commercial spheres in the early 1950s, with young designers receiving commissions for offices, libraries, people's homes, and cruise ships – furniture was finally being made to be used in all walks of life. It was also the time when forward-thinking stores and manufacturers such as Heal's in Britain and Herman Miller in the USA began to sell the work of modern designers, although it wasn't really until the 1960s that modern design was brought to the British high street by Habitat. The marketing of new design through homes and interiors magazines, as well as the more traditional exhibitions also helped spread modern design

to a wider audience throughout the decade. New materials and techniques were increasingly important, for example there was a widespread use of screenprinting patterns and pictures onto chairs, coffee tables, and screens, which is typified in the work of the Italian designer Piero Fornasetti and the British couple Robert and Dorothy Heritage. By the mid 1950s Britain, Scandinavia, and Italy were firmly back on their feet after the war and were leading the way for new design, which would continue in the Pop revolution in the 1960s.

In Britain, Ernest Race carried on the work he had begun at the Festival of Britain and continued to produce radical new furniture. Race was born in Newcastle-upon-Tyne in 1913 and studied interior and textile design at the Bartlett School of Architecture in London in the 1930s. He opened a shop in London in 1937 to sell his own hand-woven textile designs, but this closed two years later when he was called up to serve in World War II. Ernest Race Ltd. was formed in 1945 by Race and the engineer J. W. Noel Jordan, to manufacture furniture from new materials because of Utility manufacturing restrictions on traditional woods. They aimed to create a range of furniture that could be mass-produced at low cost, utilizing materials from the

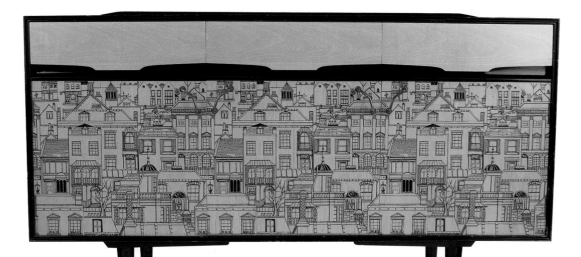

Sideboard, designed by Robert and Dorothy Heritage in 1954 for A. G. Evans and Co.
£1,300–£1,800/$1,950–$2,700

war effort, including plywood and aluminium. Race found fame after the Festival of Britain (his "Antelope" chairs from the festival won a gold medal at the 1954 Milan Triennial) and by the mid 1950s he was firmly established as one of Britain's best new designers, particularly when he was made a Royal Designer for Industry in 1953.

In the same year he designed a range of mass-produced folding and stacking "Neptune" deck chairs for P&O cruises' Orient Line, which utilized pre-formed plywood, beech laminates, and fabric in their construction. Essentially a redesign of traditional Victorian deck chairs, the "Neptunes" show a remarkably economical use of materials and simplicity in their overall construction and were also very comfortable as they could be adjusted to the sitter's needs. In addition they solved a practical design problem, as they were made to fold up without the use of metal hinges, which would have rusted at sea, and the plywood was bonded with a waterproof adhesive.

Race also produced furniture for private use, for example the "BD1" sideboard, which was designed earlier in his career in 1946. It demonstrates a relaxed elegance with its graceful proportions and striking early use of plywood for the body and doors with aluminium decoration, and would sit well in any modern home today.

## The Sideboard

The 1950s was the decade in which the sideboard became a very popular storage solution in many homes, with natural wood Scandinavian examples imported into Britain and British designers producing their own versions of this style. Mid-century sideboards are now becoming all the rage again and fine examples are already fetching premium prices, but good quality, mass-produced Danish and English examples are still available to buy in second-hand or antique shops for between £150/$240 and £300/$480. The Robert and Dorothy Heritage sideboard illustrated above is a supreme example of a 1950s sideboard, as it demonstrates key elements of Mid-Century styling. Its low-slung shape is similar to the many Danish examples that were appearing in Britain at the time. It has a solid wood body, ebonized top and sides, and pale birch veneer on its drawers. The door panels are covered with a dense screenprint of buildings drawn by Dorothy Heritage reminiscent of Fornasetti's work in Italy.

# Robin Day

Robin Day
(*b*.1915).

Robin Day is one of the most successful post-war British designers. He was born in 1915 and trained at the Royal College of Art in London. His furniture has been popular since the 1950s when he established himself as one of the key figures in the Mid-Century design movement in Britain. Day still designs furniture and his work went through a renaissance in 1999 when Habitat reissued two of his most popular and innovative designs – the "Polyprop" chair and the "Forum" sofa. This introduced Day's work to a new generation and these pieces will no doubt become collectable themselves in the future.

In the 1950s, Day's design philosophy and working practices were very similar to those of the American designer Charles Eames. Charles and his wife Ray worked closely together as did Robin and his wife, the award-winning textile designer Lucienne Day. The couple became media celebrities in the early 1950s when their home was featured in magazines such as *House & Garden* and the *Ideal Home* book. The social context of design and the importance of producing good quality furniture were crucial to Day. He believed in the use of new materials such as polypropylene and plywood to create unconventional, stylish, and affordable items for the home. Day's designs are very practical and they are becoming increasingly collectable.

His career began in 1948 when he opened a design office in London, specializing in exhibition signage and graphic design. Like many of his contemporaries, his first big break came in 1949 through an international competition entry. He entered a series of plywood and aluminium-framed modular storage units (co-designed with Clive Latimer) for the *Low Cost Furniture* competition at the Museum of Modern Art in New York. The units' functional, innovative design coupled with the clever use of new materials won him first prize out of 3,000 entries and gave his furniture international recognition.

Day went on to collaborate with the British company Hille Ltd., producing a dining room suite for the British Industry Fair. The partnership was a great success and Day became design director in 1950. At this time he produced the highly practical and cost effective "Hillestack" chair, with a one-piece seat and a bent plywood back on a tubular steel base. Its unusual shape, seen as very radical at the time, is a fusion of Scandinavian Modernist influences and British tubular steel furniture of the 1930s.

Further success came in 1951 when Day won a gold medal for a room interior at the Milan Triennial Exhibition. Lucienne produced textiles to accompany his furniture for the competition. Day also helped design the visitor

An F12 single convertible
bed settee, designed in 1957
for Hille Ltd.
**£800–£1,000/$1,200–$1,500**

signage and furnished two rooms in the *Homes & Gardens* pavilion at the 1951 Festival of Britain.

In 1962, Day produced the first commercial polypropylene stacking chair, known as the "Polyprop". This went into mass production and quickly became a feature of schools, canteens, and other public areas, including Heathrow airport. Polypropylene was invented in 1953 and Day's chair marked the first commercial success of the new material in British furniture design. Thousands were produced and exported worldwide and the "Polyprop" became one of the bestselling chairs of all time, so much so that an armchair version went on sale in 1964. The utilitarian chair was cheap to produce, strong, easy to clean, and stacked neatly for storage. A contemporary review in the *Architect's Journal* announced that the chair "would prove to be the most significant development in British mass-produced design". "Polyprop" chairs are not particularly appealing to collectors because so many were produced, but examples in their original packaging are now becoming sought after. Day also designed radios and televisions for Pye and furniture schemes for interiors, including seating for the Barbican Arts Centre.

An F1 and F2 "Hillestack" table and chair, designed in 1950.
**Table: £200–£300/$300–$450**
**Chair: £40–£60/$60–$90**

A Hille seating leaflet, 1953–4.
Not for commercial sale.

An F4 chair, designed in 1951 for the Royal Festival Hall, London, produced by Hille Ltd.
**£400–£500/$600–$750**

# French and British Style

Although Britain, Italy, Scandinavia, and the USA led design in the mid 20th century, other countries also produced key designers whose work is collectable today. For example, furniture in France at this time was dominated by the work of Jean Prouvé and Jean Royère.

In the 1940s French furniture was of very high quality and was often commissioned by wealthy patrons, not mass-produced. Wood, including oak and fruitwood such as pear and cherry, was popular, as was the use of decorative wrought iron in furniture and modern patterns and fabrics for upholstery.

Today prices are still reasonable for some of the unknown designers of the period, particularly if you are willing to visit Paris and explore the famous flea markets to find a bargain. The market for Mid-Century French furniture is particularly strong in the USA. It's not just pieces by named designers that will grow in value, if you look for good quality materials and appealing style your investment will continue to increase.

Jean Royère became a decorator at the age of 29 and his first major commission came in 1933 when he was asked to decorate the bar of the Carlton on the Champs-Elysées in Paris. Soon after this he began to design original and very high quality furniture. After the war his business expanded to take in Egypt, Syria, and other countries, and he became particularly famous for his decorative commissions in the Middle East. His work is characterized by its bold forms and somewhat daring use of materials, both of which are represented in his "Bear" armchairs, which have already become Modern design classics.

The "Bear" armchairs date from 1951 and were originally part of a suite that also included a sofa. This range of furniture was primarily called "boule" or "haricot" but before long it was nicknamed the "Bear" because of its furry upholstery and large proportions, which made the armchairs resemble a bear's paw. These chairs are very rare and this is reflected in their price today.

Jean Prouvé (1901–84) was another extremely prolific French designer, working both on his own and in close collaboration with Charlotte Perriand (see pp.40–3) during his long career. He began as a metalworker in the early 1920s and went on to design tubular metal furniture in the International Style during the 1930s. In 1944 he became Mayor of Nancy and c.1947 he opened his own factory/workshop called Les Ateliers Jean Prouvé. This venture produced several notable designs but in 1954 he resigned as director to open his own studio in Paris. Following this he founded Les Constructions Jean Prouvé in 1956, where he worked until 1966.

Prouvé's work in the late 1940s and 1950s included many architectural projects in which he celebrated industrial processes and production. The table shown here is crafted in oak and illustrates the way Prouvé embraced new technology and new processes of material production, as in this case bent steel is combined with natural wood.

Mathieu Matégot (b.1910) is another increasingly collectable designer from the early 1950s. Several landmark designs were issued from his workshop, which was known as Societe Matégot. His work is characterized by its use of moulded and flattened metal and clean, almost stark shapes – a complete contrast to the upholstered work of Jean Royère. The "Nagasaki" chair (named after Nagasaki, the Japanese port that was hit by an allied atomic bomb in 1945) dates from 1951 and shows how Matégot made use of perforated metal for the seat and back, and a painted tubular metal frame. Its design is simple yet effective, with the use of a single tubular steel rod supporting the back and a gracefully curving seat. Other versions of this chair can be found, and have wider perforations in the metal seats and back, and squarer bodies.

Matégot is also famed for a range of light portable metal trolleys with organic shapes, which are similar in style to Alvar Aalto's plywood trolleys (see p.32) from earlier in the century. Matégot also worked in cane and steel and was particularly interested in the juxtaposition of materials and textures in his work. In addition to this he produced large-scale abstract carpets and decorative tapestries for public and private buildings.

The pared down minimalism of the "Nagasaki" chair can also be seen in this later dining chair by William Plunkett. Aluminium has been used to support and suspend the seating elements in mid-air, giving the chair a wonderfully sculptural feel which, although dating from the early 1960s, reflects the Mid-Century French style. Single dining chairs such as this are worth collecting simply as one-off pieces, but an original set of four is much more appealing and will attract a higher price.

"Nagasaki" chair, designed by
Mathieu Matégot in 1951.
£3,000–£4,000/$4,500–$6,000

Dining chair,
designed by William Plunkett c.1960,
for William Plunkett Ltd.
£200–£250/$300–$375

A pair of "Bear" armchairs,
designed by Jean Royère c.1915.
£50,000–£70,000/$75,000–$105,000

Oak table,
designed by Jean Prouvé c.1945,
produced by Les Ateliers Jean Prouvé.
£15,000–£20,000/$22,500–$30,000

# East meets West

The mid 20th century brought a fusion of Eastern and Western furniture style and technology that had already occurred in the ceramics of Bernard Leach and Shoji Hamada in the 1930s. Improving international design exhibitions, world communications, and the invitation from the Japanese government for the designer Charlotte Perriand to advise the Ministry of Culture of the interest of Japanese design and products to the West, meant that design ideas from the West were filtering into Japan and vice versa. At the same time, Japanese students who had trained at the Bauhaus were returning to Japan. Thus, Japanese designers such as Sori Yanagi would have been aware of the developments in new materials and technology that were happening in the West and combined these with their traditional Japanese aesthetics to create a dynamic fusion of Eastern and Western styles.

Isamu Noguchi (1904–88) was born in Los Angeles but his work is firmly rooted in the Japanese tradition, as his initial training in cabinet-making took place in Japan c.1917. He returned to the USA and trained to become a doctor at Columbia University but also studied sculpture. By 1947 he had abandoned medicine altogether to concentrate on design. He won a Guggenheim Fellowship in 1927 and worked in Paris for two years as an assistant to the Modernist sculptor Constantin Brancusi. He visited Japan and Beijing (Peking) in the early 1930s and in 1932 returned to New York, where he practised as a sculptor.

In 1937 Noguchi created the "Radio Nurse" for the Zenith Corporation (see pp.30–1), which was a nursery monitor shaped like a Samurai, to look like a guarding force in a child's room. By the early 1940s he was working extensively in furniture, glassware, and industrial product design. He designed household furniture for the Herman Miller Co. and Knoll, and became a consultant designer for Herman Miller after his work was brought to their attention by George Nelson (see pp.82–3).

The rare, collectable birch sofa shown opposite was designed and made to order for the Herman Miller Co. in 1948. Its simple yet comfortable construction is a good example of the fusion of East and West traditions; its low body like a Japanese futon and upholstered seat like a Western sofa. Noguchi's designs no doubt helped Miller stay at the forefront of progressive Mid-Century design. He produced a range of organically inspired Japanese-style paper lamps, the "Akari", fusing sculptural qualities with industrial production techniques, and helped bring this popular Japanese lighting style to the West. Today, descendants of these lamps are available in high street shops, as well as original versions.

The furniture of George Nakashima (1905–90) marks the revival of craft in America. His day bed with a free-shaped back, illustrated opposite, dates from 1963 yet typifies many of the classic design trends in Mid-Century modern. Nakashima trained as an architect at the Massachusetts Institute of Technology and the University of Washington. In 1936 he worked for an architectural practice in Tokyo, returning to the USA in 1940, where he established a traditional furniture making workshop in Seattle. Between 1942 and 1943 he was interned due to his Japanese ancestry, but after this he began another furniture workshop in Pennsylvania. His work was very exclusive as it was mostly handcrafted and many of his pieces were made as individual commissions for patrons. He did, however, design some furniture for Knoll in 1946 and won the Craftsmanship Medal from the American Institute of Architects in 1952. The day bed has a simple, yet elegant form with its handcrafted rough wooden back set off by a plain upholstered cushion. It is an example of classic Nakashima style, where he celebrates the soul of the tree through his use of natural material to express his message.

Sori Yanagi was born in Tokyo in 1915. His long career has seen many successful solo and collaborative projects. He has worked in all mediums including ceramics, furniture, and architecture and he also designed the Olympic torch for the 1964 Tokyo Olympics. Yanagi studied painting and architecture at the Tokyo School of Fine Arts and after graduation became an assistant to Charlotte Perriand when she was working in Japan as an adviser to the Japanese Ministry of Culture in the early 1940s. It is probable that he learnt about functionalist aesthetics from her and his Mid-Century designs are an attempt to blend the theory of Modernist functionalism with traditional Japanese design. In 1951 he won the first Japanese competition for Industrial Design and in 1952 he founded the Yanagi Industrial Design Institute.

Yanagi's most famous design is arguably the "Butterfly" stool designed in 1954 and manufactured by Tendo Mokko. This beautifully proportioned, light, and elegant stool was inspired by the movement of a butterfly's wings. Its construction is effortlessly simple, being two pieces of moulded plywood held together by two screws and stabilized by a brass stretcher. The "Butterfly" stool was particularly popular in the USA, where it was sold in progressive shops such as Herman Miller. Reissues of this stool are now available in rosewood and birch, and there are European and Japanese manufactured versions.

"Butterfly" stool,
designed by Sori Yanagi
in 1954 for Tendo Mokko
(this is a later model).
**£550–£800/$825–$1,200**

A table, designed
by Isamu Noguchi
for Knoll in 1950.
**£1,200–£1,800/$1,800–$2,700**

Birch sofa and stool, designed by
Isamu Noguchi and manufactured
c.1948 for the Herman Miller Co.
**Sofa: £53,350–£66,650/
$80,000–$100,000
Stool: £13,350–£20,000/
$20,000–$30,000**

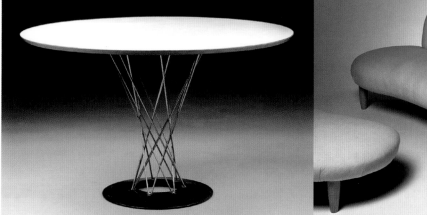

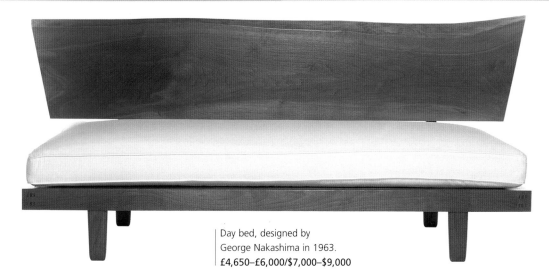

Day bed, designed by
George Nakashima in 1963.
**£4,650–£6,000/$7,000–$9,000**

# America

The Americans Frank Lloyd Wright (1867–1956) and Eero Saarinen (1910–61) were working at the same time as each other, but interpreted Mid-Century modern design in two completely different ways. Saarinen embraced new materials and organic, often futuristic shapes while Wright continued with more traditional methods of furniture manufacture and architectonic forms that reflected the angular lines of his building commissions. This is perfectly illustrated by the Frank Lloyd Wright chair shown here, which was designed in 1955 as part of a private commission for the house of Dr Turkel in Detroit, Michigan.

Eero Saarinen is perhaps best known for his futuristic Trans World Airline Terminal at John F. Kennedy airport in New York (1956–62) and for the design of the "Tulip" chair which sold in great numbers and was copied extensively in the 1960s. His father was the Finnish architect Eliel Saarinen (1873–1950), who was the first president of the Cranbrook Academy of Art, in Bloomfield Hills, near Detroit, Michigan, and it was here that Eero Saarinen met Charles Eames when they were both teaching at the institute in the 1940s.

One of Saarinen's first successes with Eames was their design for a group of chairs with single-form moulded plywood seats, which they produced for the 1940 *Organic Design in Home Furnishings* exhibition held at the Museum of Modern Art, New York. These chairs launched their careers, and in 1950 Saarinen opened his own office in Michigan called Saarinen & Associates. He continued to produce inspired examples of organic architecture and design until his untimely death in 1961.

Saarinen collaborated with the manufacturer Knoll to produce the "Womb" chair in 1947–8 (also known as the number 70 chair). This chair (see opposite) consists of a fabric upholstered fibreglass shell supported by a tubular steel frame. It became known as the "Womb" chair because its generous and supportive proportions encouraged the sitter to curl up in a ball. The "Womb" range included a chair, sofa, and matching ottoman, and it was produced by Knoll in New York from 1948 to 1993.

Saarinen's "Tulip" chair (see opposite) was completely revolutionary and way ahead of its time when it was first produced in 1957, looking more like a piece of 1960s Pop design. Saarinen was trying to produce an item of furniture in one piece with no added fixtures and fittings. He originally wanted to create a chair that was made totally of moulded plastic, but was prevented from doing so by a lack of suitable technology in the plastics industry at the time. Instead, he designed the "Tulip" chair, which

had a plastic-coated aluminium base supporting an upper fibreglass shell, complete with upholstered cushions that came in a range of colours. The "Tulip" chair was one of the first chairs to be supported by a single pedestal base.

Versions of the "Tulip" chair include examples with arms (model number 150) and without arms (model number 151). These chairs are still produced by Knoll today. The matching tables were made in four different sizes ranging from dining tables to side tables with marble or formica tops, and of these the marble examples have a greater value to collectors today.

Wright's early architectural projects included functional, unified buildings where the building's interior and exterior were designed to harmonize with each other for the benefit of those who lived and worked in them. A notable early commission was the Imperial Hotel in Tokyo (1915–22). In the 1930s Wright received two more important commissions – the Johnson Wax Administration Building (1936–9) and Fallingwater (1935–9), the residence of the important American retailer Edgar J. Kauffman. Between 1943 and 1946 Wright created the visionary Guggenheim Museum in New York, which still looks futuristic today.

## Frank Lloyd Wright (1867–1956)

Although primarily known for his Modernist architecture, Frank Lloyd Wright was also a celebrated design theorist and an extremely versatile furniture, textile, and ceramic designer. His pioneering Modernist work is of great interest to collectors, and good pieces can attract high prices.

Wright grew up at a time when traditional architecture was giving way to early Modernism. Although often categorized as an architect and designer of the late 19th century Arts and Crafts movement, Wright's work matured throughout the early 20th century to include streamlining in the 1930s and organic design in the 1950s. Throughout his career, however, he remained close to the principles of truth to nature and the spiritual value of furniture and architecture.

Wright originally studied engineering, but by 1893 had turned to architecture and set up his own studio in Chicago. He was inspired and influenced by Japanese architecture and design, and his early buildings are a fusion of natural wood, man-made materials, and angular lines and simplicity. His early work is similar to that of Charles Rennie Mackintosh in Britain, who was also influenced by Japanese design and architecture.

A mahogany lounge chair,
designed by Frank Lloyd Wright in 1955.
**£4,000–£5,000/$6,000–$7,500**

A "Womb" chair and ottoman,
designed by Eero Saarinen
in 1946–8 for Knoll.
**£1,500–£1,800/$2,250–$2,700**

A "Tulip" chair and side table,
designed by Eero Saarinen
in 1956 for Knoll.
**Chair: £60–£80/$90–$120**
**Table: £100–£150/$150–$225**

# George Nelson

George Nelson (1908–86).

The work of George Nelson (1908–86) and his design team has become extremely collectable and his furniture in particular is now attracting premium prices. His work was popular both in the USA and Europe and his archetypal office and domestic furniture, lighting, clocks, and industrial design, are still influential to young designers today. He also wrote perceptive and visionary books on interior design and architecture.

Nelson studied architecture at Yale University from 1924 to 1931. He won the prestigious Rome Prize and was in Italy between 1932 and 1934, where he was introduced to the work of key early Modernist designers, such as Le Corbusier and Ludwig Mies van der Rohe. When he returned to the USA, Nelson took up writing about architecture and design and became assistant editor of *Architectural Forum*. In 1946 he collaborated with fellow designer Henry Wright to write a book called *Tomorrow's House*, which helped bring Modernist architecture and design to a wider American audience.

In 1936 Nelson set up his own architectural practice in New York along with William Hamby. He then joined the Faculty of Architecture at Yale University, where he developed many impressive ideas such as pedestrianized shopping malls and clever storage solutions, which were typified in his "Storage Wall" of 1944.

Between 1946 and 1972 he was director of design at the Herman Miller manufacturing firm. He brought his vision of modern design to the company immediately, and by encouraging the other directors to support the early work of designers including Charles Eames and Isamu Noguchi, Nelson revitalized the firm's somewhat traditional output and helped to make it a commercial success. The "Coconut" chair (*see opposite*) is an excellent example of a successful design from this period.

In 1947 he set up his own design office, George Nelson & Co., in New York. The office's most famous designs date from the late 1940s and 1950s and include the "Atom" clock (*see opposite*) (1949), the "Marshmallow" sofa (1956), and the beautifully organic and highly original "Coconut" chair (1955). In 1964 Nelson produced one of his most innovative design concepts – the "Action Office System", which changed the concept of office space by combining storage panels with space dividers.

A walnut, leather, and steel "Home Office Desk", designed for the Herman Miller Co., c.1946.
**£10,000–£16,650/$15,000–$25,000**

Nelson had been interested in office design earlier in his career, as can be seen in the "Home Office Desk", designed in 1946, which helped revolutionize the way desks were manufactured for domestic use. Lightweight and practical, it is economical in its use of space. Its thin, attenuated steel legs are extremely graceful, yet provide a sturdy support for the body of the desk above. The piece was designed for comfort and ease of movement while the sitter is working, and features a flip-open typewriter table on the left-hand side and a pull-out metal mesh file drawer on the right. Clutter is stored away in the compartmentalized area above the desk.

The Nelson office designed the "Atom" clock for the Howard Miller Clock Co. in 1949. This clock is an early example of atomic style, where the shapes of scientific atomic and molecular structures were applied to domestic and commercial design. The "Atom" clock is a supreme example of this style, which is why it is so desirable to collectors today. The clock is made from steel, brass, and wood with an electric movement, and the design was freely copied throughout the 1950s in a host of less expensive imitations.

An "Atom" or "Ball" wall clock, designed in 1949, for the Howard Miller Clock Co.
**£600–£800/$900–$1,200**

A rosewood and metal jewellery cabinet, designed for the Herman Miller Co., c.1955.
**£4,000–£5,350/$6,000–$8,000**

A "Coconut" chair, designed for the Herman Miller Co. 1955–78, reissued by Vitra from 1988.
**£4,000–£5,000/$6,000–$7,500**

# Knoll International

A new generation of American designers found fame in the 1950s supported by forward-thinking manufacturers such as Knoll. Many of them studied at the same art schools and set up networks that allowed them to try out new ideas and influence the work of each other, both consciously and subconsciously. All experimented with new materials and techniques in their work, and what they produced is collectable today.

Harry Bertoia (1915–78) was born in Italy and moved to the USA with his family in 1930. He studied at the Cranbrook Academy of Fine Arts, in Bloomfield Hills, near Detroit, Michigan, where he met Charles and Ray Eames, and eventually became head of the metal working department at the academy. Bertoia was primarily interested in sculpture and this is reflected in his futuristic wire mesh chairs from the early 1950s. The wire mesh "Bird" lounge chair (model number 423LU) was designed in 1951–2 for Knoll and is very similar to the "DKR-1" chair (see p.90) made by Charles and Ray Eames at about the same time. Bertoia spent three years working in the Eames Office from 1943–6 before leaving to pursue his own sculptural furniture designs and more commercial pieces for Knoll. He also made Ray Eames's wedding ring.

Bertoia created a sense of space through the diamond-shaped grids on his chairs, which include "Diamond" lounge chairs. Bertoia chairs demonstrate a masterful use of materials and space, and are extremely sculptural, particularly the "Bird" chair which looks more like a piece of sculpture suspended in space than a chair. The chairs were made through moulding a sheet of metal mesh into shape and then welding this on to wire legs. The chairs were then mass-produced, but mainly by hand rather than by machine.

The "Bird" chair came with a matching ottoman and both can be found with or without upholstered cushions. Examples were either plastic-coated or chrome-plated. Although these chairs were mass-produced at the time and are still in production today, the value of original examples in good condition will probably continue to increase. Many chairs will have rusted over time through neglect or those that were used in offices will have been discarded. Perfect examples are worth investing in, even more so if they still have their original cushions.

Warren Platner (b.1919) also designed characteristic chairs in metal, and his model number 1725A remains true to the style set by Bertoia even though Platner produced most of his designs in the early to mid 1960s. He studied architecture at Cornell University, Ithaca, New York. After graduating he worked in Raymond Loewy's design office and for Eero Saarinen & Associates in Michigan, before setting up his own office, Warren Platner Associates, in 1965. The number 1725A chair dates from 1965 and does not reflect the Pop style but instead stays close to Mid-Century styling. It was manufactured by Knoll.

Florence Knoll (b.1917) was not only a great furniture designer and architect but also a businesswoman, founding Knoll with her husband Hans Knoll. They were particularly instrumental in introducing modern European design into America. She studied architecture at the Cranbrook Academy of Art and worked for Marcel Breuer and Walter Gropius in their American offices. The design of the credenza illustrated here looks back to early Modernism and the stark yet beautiful works of Le Corbusier and Charlotte Perriand. Florence Knoll's designs can be recognized by their understated elegance and truth to materials. She seldom used decorative effects and let the natural beauty of the materials speak for themselves, as can be seen in the conference table shown here, designed in 1961.

## Knoll International

Knoll International was one of the biggest manufacturers of modern design furniture in America in the 1950s. Hans and Florence Knoll formed the company in 1946. Hans Knoll (1914–55) set up his first furniture company in England with his German cousin and Tom Parker, an English businessman. Parker-Knoll produced sofas and armchairs and has remained a household name ever since. But the furniture was not particularly innovative and so in 1937 Knoll moved to the USA, aiming to introduce the work of Modernist designers to a new audience. He founded the Hans G. Knoll Furniture Co. in New York in 1941 and Knoll Associates in 1946. In 1948 Mies van der Rohe gave the company production rights to his early "Barcelona" chairs, and it was also given rights to produce Marcel Breuer's designs for the American market. At the same time, the company began to commission new designers such as Isamu Noguchi.

When Hans Knoll was killed in a car accident in 1955 Florence continued to run the business, but it was eventually taken over by Art Metal and later by General Felt in the 1970s while retaining the Knoll International name. Today the company specializes in office furniture.

A model number 1725A chair,
designed by Warren Platner
in 1965 for Knoll.
**£500–£700/$750–$1,000**

A wire mesh "Bird" lounge chair,
designed by Harry Bertoia
in 1952 for Knoll.
**£500–£700/$750–$1,000**

A model number 2080 conference table,
designed by Florence Knoll
in 1961 for Knoll.
**£800–£1,200/$1,200–$1,800**

A credenza, designed by
Florence Knoll c.1960 for Knoll.
**£1,200–£1,600/$1,800–$2,400**

# Charles and Ray Eames

Ray Eames
(1912–88) and
Charles Eames
(1907–78).

Charles Eames (1907–78) and Ray Eames (1912–88) were one of the most dynamic and multi-talented design partnerships of the 20th century and their work is now extremely collectable. The sheer scope and range of their design is astonishing, taking in architecture, furniture, textiles, films, graphics, and even children's toys.

The couple were much more than designers, they were humanitarians, described by their friends as witty and generous/ They believed firmly in the Modernist tenet that new technology would lead to good design that would improve people's lives both functionally and intellectually. Over forty furniture ranges and designs were produced in the Eames Office until Charles's death in 1978. The work of Ray Eames has been overlooked in the past, but it is now being reassessed and recognized in its own right as essential to the output of the Eames Office.

Charles was inspired by the work of the designers Alvar Aalto and Frank Lloyd Wright, particularly their love of natural, organic forms and Aalto's early Modernist work in experimental moulded plywood furniture. Eames studied architecture at Washington University before starting his own architectural office in 1930. He received a fellowship to the Cranbrook Academy of Art in Michigan, USA, where he became head of the design department. It was here that he met Ray Kaiser, who had trained as a painter and illustrator. She became his wife in 1941 and the couple moved to California, where they began their pioneering work in mass-produced moulded plywood furniture.

In 1942 Ray was working to illustrate the capabilities and dynamics of three-dimensional moulded plywood.

A plywood sculpture designed in 1943.
£240,000–£265,000/$360,000–$400,000

She created two known examples of these organic plywood sculptures (*see opposite*) which illustrate her artistic background and show her interest in the 1940s avant-garde movement.

The Eames' first major joint project was their own house at Pacific Palisades, Santa Monica. It was designed and built between 1945 and 1949 as part of the Case Study House programme in the USA, which encouraged architects and designers to create high quality, well-designed living spaces after World War II. The house was constructed from standard prefabricated industrial components and finished with brightly painted steel panels that reflected the style of the Dutch painter Piet Mondrian and De Stijl. It is a perfect example of an economically built, well thought-out space for living and working in, reflecting how the Modernist ideas spread by De Stijl and the early Bauhaus designers came to fruition after 20 years in the USA. The interior relates to the exterior and it is a fully co-ordinated, functional home as well as being a masterpiece of modern architecture.

Charles first came to public attention with his winning competition entry (along with Eero Saarinen) for the 1940 *Organic Design in Home Furnishings* exhibition at the Museum of Modern Art, New York. They created a series

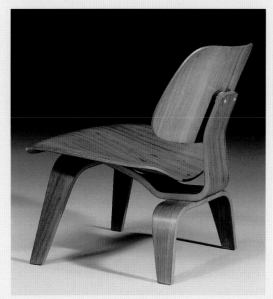

An early "LCW" (Lounge Chair Wood), designed in 1946, and manufactured by Evans Products Co. in early 1946.
**£6,000–£8,000/$9,000–$12,000**

A set of "DCM" (Dining Chair Metal) chairs, designed in 1945, and manufactured by the Herman Miller Co.
**£1,200–£1,600/$1,800–$2,400**

of prototype chairs that were designed for mass production, but industrial processes were not developed enough to enable them to go into production. When Charles and Ray moved to California they experimented with a machine they created called the "Kazam" to try to find the solution to producing comfortable, low-cost, compound curved plywood furniture.

In December 1941 they began work on their first commercial enterprise, a plywood leg splint that was used by the US navy from 1942. In the Spring of 1943 they opened an office called the Plyformed Wood Company and the rights to produce and distribute their leg splints were bought by Colonel Evans, a forest owner. The Eames operation then became the Moulded Plywood Division of Evans Products Co. Later that year Charles and Ray moved into their office at 901 Washington Boulevard in Venice, California and this was to remain the Eames Office for the next 45 years.

By 1945 Charles and Ray had renewed their quest to make well-designed, mass-produced plywood chairs utilizing technology developed during the war. One of their early commercial projects was a moulded plywood

child's chair and stool, and these are incredibly desirable to collectors today. Their major commercial breakthrough came, however, with the "Plywood" series that included the "DCW" (Dining Chair Wood), "DCM" (Dining Chair Metal) and "LCW" (Lounge Chair Wood), all of which are collectable today. Examples from the "Plywood" series were first shown in prototype form to the public in the winter of 1945 and exhibited at the Museum of Modern Art, New York, in March 1946. The chairs were both beautiful and functional, as Ray often explained, "What... works is better than what looks good." Later that year Evans Products produced a series of one thousand plywood "LCW" chairs and these have now become rare.

"Plywood" series chairs have a moulded plywood seat and back with various finishes, including black aniline, red or black paint, plain leather, and skunkskin. The two parts of the chair were attached to a solid rod chrome-metal frame by rubber shock mounts. By 1951 2,000 of these chairs were sold every month, including some examples with wooden legs, but these were not as popular, which makes them more collectable today as examples are much rarer. They were available in both dining and lounge chair

Lounge Chair and Ottoman,
designed in 1946, and manufactured
by Herman Miller, and later by Vitra.
**£1,800–£2,200/$2,700–$3,300**

sizes, and a table and folding screen were designed in the same range. Collectors today seek to find the earliest versions of these pieces (with "Evans Evans" appearing on very early models and variations including "Herman Miller and Charles Eames" among others) in order to show the evolution of the chairs. All early examples of Eames furniture are collectable today, especially the developmental prototypes.

In 1946 the American manufacturer Herman Miller began to market Eames plywood furniture, describing their work in his catalogue as "not only the most advanced part of the Herman Miller collection, but the most advanced furniture being produced in the world today". Miller was already committed to high-quality modern design furniture, thanks to the directorship of George Nelson, and the company went on to work with other Mid-Century pioneers such as Isamu Noguchi.

A moulded plywood ten-panel folded screen, designed c.1952 for the Herman Miller Co.
**£6,650–£10,000/$10,000–$15,000**

"E5U421-C" storage units in plywood, steel, and Masonite, designed c.1951 for the Herman Miller Co.
**£13,350–£20,000/$20,000–$30,000**

A moulded birch plywood child's stool, designed c.1945 for Evans Products.
**£1,350–£2,000/$2,000–$3,000**

Charles and Ray Eames designed the Herman Miller showrooms in Washington Boulevard, California, and in 1948 the company took over the manufacturing of Eames furniture as well. In 1957 Vitra International were licenced by Herman Miller to produce Eames furniture in Europe, and continue to do so today. The more contemporary, licensed examples by Vitra will bear a facsimile of Charles Eames's signature on each chair.

In 1946 Charles created yet another masterpiece. The Lounge Chair and Ottoman, which consists of a three-piece moulded plywood shell with leather upholstery. A hundred thousand of these chairs were eventually sold throughout the world and they are eagerly sought after by collectors today.

In the early 1950s the couple began to work with fibreglass and metal to create a series of armchairs and sidechairs, including the "DAR" (Dining and Desk Chair Rod Base) series in 1950–3. These chairs had a fibreglass shell, manufactured by Zenith Plastics of California, and were offered for sale with several different interchangeable supports, including wood or metal legs, a rocking base or a wire strut base (known as the Cat's

Cradle or Eiffel Tower base). The chairs came in a variety of colours, including yellow, black, and red and were a great commercial success. Original examples will have a white, black, and red chequer label on the underneath of the chair saying "Miller Zenith" and these are particularly collectable. Early chairs also have an embedded cord around the rim of the chair. Rarer models are the wooden dowel legged versions and examples with "bikini" pad upholstery (a two-piece seat cushion) covered in original fabric upholstery.

Charles and Ray also created bent wire furniture in the early 1950s. They believed that wire was an ideal metal for use in furniture construction because it was light, modern, and could be manufactured easily utilizing existing production techniques. The "DKR-1" chair was designed in 1951 and produced between 1951 and 1967 by Banner Metals for Herman Miller. The example illustrated here dates from 1951 to 1953 and consists of a wire rod shell on a black Eiffel Tower base with rubber and metal feet. It has a single removable cushion pad stamped underneath "made by Herman Miller Furniture Company". These chairs were popular in homes and in

A set of "DAR" chairs, designed in 1950–3,
and manufactured by the Herman Miller Co.
Left: Eiffel Tower base with arms **£500–£700/$750–$1,000**
Centre: Eiffel Tower base without arms **£250–£300/$370–$450**
Right: Rocker **£1,400–£1,600/$2,100–$2,400**

public buildings, and the chair's double wire edging received the first US mechanical patent for design. The "DKR-1" chair is very similar to the wire mesh chairs designed by Harry Bertoia in 1952 (see p.85).

The Aluminium Group chairs were launched in 1958 and were initially produced as an indoor and outdoor series of furniture. They have aluminium frames with a swivel base. Another desk chair, the Soft Pad range, was designed in 1969 and came complete with soft, leather cushions. Charles and Ray also produced several sofa designs, and the rarest of these is the Wire Sofa, which dates from 1951 and for which only four known prototypes were produced. They also created a range of original, practical, and beautifully designed storage units.

The Sofa Compact illustrated below dates from 1954, and is still in production today. The couple wanted to solve practical design problems, so they created this sofa which could be folded down for storage or easy transportation. It consists of a metal frame covered in foam pads and came in leather, vinyl, or fabric covering, with leather or period textiles by Alexander Girard being the most valuable in today's collectors' market.

Sofa Compact, designed in 1954 for the Herman Miller Co., with upholstery by Alexander Girard.
**£3,000–£4,000/$4,500–$6,000**

Soft Pad lounge chair, designed in 1969 for the Herman Miller Co.
**£400–£600/$600–$900**

# Italy

Furniture development in Italy in the mid 20th century matched that of Britain, with these two countries undergoing a period of recovery after the devastation of World War II. There was a need for new housing and domestic goods, and the Italians rose to the challenge of rejuvenation by embracing the new modern style to inject a fresh look into interiors and architecture. They quickly began to lead European design, particularly in Milan, where the Milan Triennials offered a showcase for up-and-coming designers to launch their work. The Italians joined in the trend for organic styling, but some reintroduced ornament into their work.

Many Italian designers worked across several disciplines. Pier Giacomo Castiglioni (1894–1967) and his brother Achille Castiglioni (b.1918) were talented lighting designers as well as furniture makers and Osvaldo Borsoni (b.1911) was primarily an architect but was employed by manufacturers to design up-to-date furniture. While the overall output of Italian design in the middle of the century shared the common themes of functionality, use of new materials, and innovative styling, the end results were often very different. Piero Fornasetti (1913–88) produced surreal screens, magazine racks, chairs, and a host of other items in a playful, decorative style utilizing colourful graphics and repeated patterns. In contrast, the architect Gio Ponti (1891–1979) created elegant chairs without surface decoration where functionality was placed above the decorative aspects of a piece of furniture.

Other designers, particularly the Milanese architect Marco Zanuso (b.1916), began to experiment with materials such as foam rubber that had not been used in furniture manufacture before, and this was only possible with the aid of increasingly sophisticated technology. Foam rubber opened up a host of new design possibilities, especially since it could be shaped, moulded, and upholstered to produce soft, curvaceous forms.

In 1948, the tyre company Pirelli, which went on to be involved in furniture production in Britain in the 1960s and 1970s, commissioned Zanuso to explore the possibilities of using foam rubber in furniture design. They were impressed by his original prototype designs and formed a separate company called Arflex, which still produces furniture today. The result was the "Lady" armchair, completed in 1951. It was made from a light wooden frame covered in elastic webbing and foam rubber, and marked a clear break from the springs and horsehair stuffing traditionally found in armchairs. The "Lady" chair won a gold medal at the 1951 Milan

Triennial and has now become a design classic, although it is rare to find examples in a completely original state as many have been recovered in leather or fabric (as in the example illustrated here). Those that are in original condition come in a variety of coloured fabrics including red, white, and blue and will attract a higher price.

A highly experimental armchair from the end of the 1950s is the "San Luca" chair, designed by the brothers Castiglioni in 1959–60. This design still looks radical today, so it must have been received with amazement and probably bewilderment when it first appeared in the offices of the furniture manufacturer Dino Gavina. No attempt has been made to disguise the inner structure of this chair, a design concept which goes right back to Gerrit Rietveld's "Red-Blue" chair (see p.19) from 1918. A sketch for the "San Luca" chair shows how the ergonomically designed elements fit together – curved sections for the headrest and the back, two sections for the sides, and a separate seat. The accentuated curves of the "San Luca" make it more like a piece of sculpture than a chair. The Italian firm Bernini reissued the chair from 1990 onwards so be aware of later versions, although as with many other reissues of classic models the quality of the newer versions will still be very good.

## Gio Ponti (1891–1979)

Some Italian designers in the mid century worked in a much more conservative style, and this is particularly well represented in the work of the architect Gio Ponti. He is perhaps best known for his architectural design and ceramics but he was also a great design theorist, founding the prestigious journal *Domus* in 1928.

His famous "Superleggera" ("Superlight") chair was designed in 1957 for Cassina. It lived up to its name and was very light and easy to move around. Ponti thought that a chair should be light, slim, and convenient. The 1950s side chair illustrated opposite is similar in style to the "Superleggera" chair and shows the influence of Gio Ponti's designs on furniture at this time. The unusual attenuated top section adds flamboyance to a traditional design.

Ponti was a prolific designer and teacher as well as an architect, working with Piero Fornasetti on furniture in the 1950s and teaching at Milan Polytechnic from 1936–61. He also worked in glass, producing a range called "a canne" for the Italian factory Venini. These pieces are highly sought after by collectors today.

An enamelled wooden magazine rack, designed by Piero Fornasetti in the mid 1950s.
£100–£120/$150–$180

A "Lady" armchair, designed by Marco Zanuso in 1951 for Pirelli.
£1,000–£1,500/$1,500–$2,250

An ebonized side chair, designed in the 1950s (maker unknown).
£125–£175/$175–$250

A brown leather "San Luca" armchair, designed by the Castiglioni brothers in 1959–60, and manufactured by Dino Gavina.
£1,000–£1,200/$1,500–$1,800

# Scandinavia

By the early 1940s design had become increasingly international in scope, with the work of the Bauhaus in particular spreading across Europe through exhibitions and avant-garde journals. But the new wave of design in Scandinavia was to prove a contrast to the machine-tooled, polished chrome products designed in Germany. Scandinavian designers were aiming for a much warmer style, creating pieces that would fit into any interior. They wanted to put quality furniture within the economic reach of all, and believed that this would lead to a happy and fulfilled society.

Traditional methods of manufacture were paramount to Scandinavian designers in the late 1940s and early 1950s. Sweden, Finland, and Denmark had a centuries-old workshop system and refused to submit entirely to the Modernist machine aesthetic (although there were exceptions, such as Verner Panton who went on to use plastics in his mass-produced furniture).

Scandinavian designers chose to continue their craftsman-based manufacturing tradition while at the same time embracing new technologies and retaining a strong national identity in their work. Poul Kjaerholm, for example, produced some stunning pieces in leather and chrome, including these "PK22" lounge chairs which date from 1957 (see opposite). Key collectable designers today include Nanna Ditzel, Arne Jacobsen, Grete Jalk, Finn Juhl, Kristian Vedel, and Tapio Wirkkala.

By the mid 1950s, a younger generation of designers had begun to experiment with new technology, particularly Arne Jacobsen, whose teak-faced plywood "Ant" chair (1951–2) was the first mass-produced Danish chair. Jacobsen's famous "Egg" chair was originally designed for the SAS Royal Hotel in Copenhagen in 1957–8 and later retailed by Fritz Hansen. Its sculptural qualities reflect the organic shapes produced in the late 1940s and early 1950s, but instead of hardwood, Jacobsen chose plywood for the body of the chair and steel tubing for the frame and legs. The "Egg" chair's innovative design quickly lifted it to iconic status, where it has remained ever since.

Another key designer was Hans Wegner (b.1914) and his work is extremely collectable today. One of his most innovative and desirable chairs is the experimental "Flaginstolen" lounge chair (see p.106) which dates from 1950 and combines traditional materials (flag halyard) with newer materials (a steel frame). Its wonderfully futuristic shape looks forward to the space exploration vehicles designed in the 1960s. Two versions of this chair are available, with a back pillow in orange or green.

Finland is the exception among the Scandinavian countries in that it did not have such an established craft tradition and embraced new technology faster than its sister countries. Finnish glass was particularly innovative, especially the work of Tapio Wirkkala and Timo Sarpaneva, who designed for the firm Iittala from 1946 to 1950. Both designers produced glass vases and bowls that reflected the natural Finnish landscape through their ice-like, clear, and pure forms. Wirkkala also designed furniture, and the table illustrated here is a wonderful example of his intuitive use of natural wood combined with a beautifully fluid form. The Finnish designer and architect Alvar Aalto was also working in glass at the same time as developing his ideas on modern furniture. He led the plywood revolution from the early 1930s onwards and his work, notably early examples, is highly collectable today.

## Wood in Scandinavian design

The abundance of natural materials in Scandinavia, particularly wood, had a direct effect on its design output. Wood was freely available throughout World War II as a natural home resource and made an ideal material for furniture production.

Scandinavian furniture is typified by its widespread use of wood. Many pieces have sculptural qualities reflecting natural, organic forms. They can also be recognized by their lack of ornamentation, as excessive surface decoration was thought to spoil the natural beauty of the wood. A good example of this can be seen in this child's chair (see opposite) by Danish designer Kristian Vedel (b.1923) with its restrained yet effective use of decorative cut-outs. Danish furniture is well known for its use of teak, which appeared on the world market in great quantities after the Indo-China War (1946–54).

New machine-processed wood, especially bent plywood, meant that designers could create new forms in furniture manufacture for the first time. Finnish designer Alvar Aalto was an exponent of plywood in furniture design from the 1930s onwards.

A table, designed
by Tapio Wirkkala
c.1955, for Asko.
**£1,000–£1,500/$1,500–$2,250**

A child's chair,
designed by Kristian Vedel
in 1957, for Torben Ørskov.
**£400–£500/$600–$750**

A "PK22" lounge chair,
designed by Poul Kjaerholm in 1957,
and manufactured by E. Kold Christensen.
**£700–£900/$1,000–$1,350**

# Finn Juhl

Finn Juhl
(1912–89).

Finn Juhl (1912–89) was working in the Mid-Century Scandinavian style but in a more personal way than fellow designers such as Arne Jacobsen. Juhl shared their love of organic, natural forms and materials but his work relied even more on traditional cabinet-making techniques to create his complicated designs.

He was also influenced by non-European primitive art, particularly African sculpture and artefacts, and this gave him a very individual and easily recognizable style which is extremely sculptural, especially in the arms of his chairs which have a characteristic, graceful shape.

Juhl began his career in the office of the architect Vilhelm Lauritzen, and here he started working with Niels Vodder, a master cabinet-maker, on the construction of his furniture designs. His success in furniture design was certainly due in part to his special relationship with Vodder, whose skills enabled Juhl to realize his ideas. By the late 1940s Juhl had opened his own design office and was also teaching at the Fredericksburg Technical School. By the mid 1950s Juhl was recognized as a designer of international importance when he won gold medals at the 1957 Milan Triennial. His work was highly influential

and many critics today ascribe the success of teak in Mid-Century and later Danish furniture to Juhl's love of the new material and the wonderful forms he created from it.

One of Juhl's most collectable designs is the "Chieftain" armchair, which was constructed by Vodder in 1949. The chair gets its name because King Friedrich IX was said to have sat on an example of the chair at the Cabinet-maker's Guild Exhibition in 1949, and because its sheer bulk and presence make it look like a throne. The African connotations of the name stem from of the chair being of a similar construction to ancient African chairs. The ingenious design consists of turned wooden vertical supports at the front and back, and supporting flat strips of wood at the sides. The inner workings of the chair are therefore revealed to the viewer as an intrinsic part of the design, and this trend can be traced back to Gerrit Rietveld's "Red-Blue" chair (see p.19) from 1918. Examples of the "Chieftain" are very rare as no more than 78 were originally made and most were purchased for use in Danish embassies across the world ,and only a few of them were bought by museums. Its rarity gives the "Chieftain" its value today.

*Above*: A mahogany NV-45 armchair, designed in 1945 and manufactured by Niels Vodder.
£1,200–£1,600/$1,800–$2,400

A teak NV-48 armchair, designed c.1948 and manufactured by Niels Vodder.
£1,200–£1,500/ $1,800–$2,250

Juhl's "Easy" chair is similar in shape to the "Chieftain" but lacks its imposing presence. Instead, it has a more relaxed, graceful design with the beauty of the wood set off by upholstered contemporary fabric. This chair seems much more lightweight and it has a simpler construction, as the body of the chair seems to float in space away from the frame. Its beautifully slender, curvaceous arms are one of the reasons why this chair appeals to collectors today.

Juhl also produced upholstered settles in conjunction with Vodder, again designed to express the beauty inherent in their natural materials. His sofas reflect the overall look of his chairs and display his distinctive, sensual style through their wide, curving backs and comfortable padded seats on teak frames.

A "Chieftain" chair,
designed in 1949 and
manufactured by Niels Vodder.
**£700–£900/$1,000–$1,350**

A sofa, designed c.1945
and manufactured by Niels Vodder.
**£3,000–£4,000/$4,500–$6,000**

An upholstered sofa,
designed c.1950 and
manufactured by Niels Vodder.
**£2,000–£3,000/$3,000–$4,500**

# Scandinavia

The Danish designer Verner Panton (1926–98) launched his career in the 1950s. His startlingly original work spanned four decades, and he revolutionized seating not just in Scandinavia but also throughout the world. Panton was a powerful and charismatic designer and theorist and broke new ground in chair construction in particular, starting with his wire chairs in the 1950s and culminating in his foam towers and room installations in the 1960s.

Most Scandinavian designers working in the Mid-Century style continued to use wood and other natural materials for many of their products, but Panton was keen to explore the possibilities of newer materials. He designed his zinc-wire "Cone" chair in 1960 and it shows a masterful use of this new material, which was also favoured by Harry Bertoia in the USA (*see pp.*84–5). The original version of the "Cone" chair was produced for the manufacturer Plus-Linje and these examples have a greater value than later models manufactured by Fritz Hansen. In 1960 Panton created his adjustable "Peacock" chair (designed to resemble the outstretched tail of a peacock), which is similar in style to the "Cone" chair but has a flatter and rounder body and came complete with seven circular upholstered cushions.

Panton had already designed an upholstered version of the "Cone" chair in 1958 for use in the interior of the Komigen Inn on the Danish island of Funen, and Fritz Hansen also manufactured this chair. Both the "Cone" chair and the "Heart" chair (created a year later in 1959) were Panton's first attempts to challenge people's preconceived notions of what form this piece of furniture should take. These chairs are constructed from sheet metal with a metal base and upholstered in fabric-covered foam. The "Heart" chair is particularly organic in its styling, but its name and light-hearted design look forward to the mid 1960s and Pop style.

Denmark and Sweden tended to dominate design in the mid 20th century but Finland's contribution should not be overlooked. Finnish design was brought to Britain in a joint exhibition of Finnish art and design called *Modern Art in Finland, An Exhibition of Paintings, Sculpture, Graphic and Applied Arts* in 1953–4, which helped bring the country international recognition and encouraged furniture exports.

The pine and ebonized dining suite shown here was created by the Finnish designer Ilmari Tapiovaara (1914–99) and its use of natural materials contrasts completely with the futuristic styling of Panton's zinc-wire "Cone" chair. This is probably because in Finland more than Denmark nature continued to be the leading source of inspiration and creativity to many designers. A contemporary critic wrote of Finnish designers, "their sense of form does not stem from classical antecedents, nor is it based on shapes developed by man over the millennia. Their archetype is the primitive nature around them." Finnish designers also believed that purity and function were paramount in design, and this is evident in Tapiovaara's dining room suite as it is extremely functional and has no excess decoration.

Tapiovaara began his career in the late 1930s as a designer of Modernist-inspired, inexpensive plywood chairs for Asko, Finland's largest furniture manufacturer. But although these chairs were made up in the factory, Asko's retailers thought that Tapiovaara's furniture was too modern for their customers so early pieces were never retailed and would no doubt be collectable today if examples came on the market. Tapiovaara left Asko soon after this and went on to design for the manufacturing company Keravan Puuteollisuus Ltd. He became the company's artistic and commercial director in 1941.

Tapiovaara's most famous chair design is probably the stackable "Domus" armchair, which was produced c.1946–7. After some success in Finland, the chair was sold in Britain under the name "Stax" and in the USA by Knoll as the "Finnchair". Made out of moulded plywood with an organically-shaped back, the "Domus" chair was inexpensive to make and was packaged in easy-assembly parts, making it one of the earliest flat-packed chairs. The success of this chair led Tapiovaara to form his own design company in 1951 and he became a consultant for Asko, where he had previously been art director, between 1938 and 1941. In the 1950s he employed the young Eero Aarnio, who went on to find fame in the 1960s through his iconic "Ball" or "Globe" chair. Tapiovaara is also known for his lamps and lighting fixtures, both of which are collectable today.

## OTHER KEY SCANDINAVIAN DESIGNERS:

| | |
|---|---|
| Karen Clemmensen (*b.*1917) | architecture, furniture |
| Jørgen Ditzel (1921–61) | furniture |
| Peter Hvidt (1916–86) | furniture |
| Edvard Kindt-Larsen (1901–82) | furniture |
| Poul Kjaerholm (1929–80) | furniture |
| Kaare Klint (1888–1954) | furniture |
| Henning Larsen (*b.*1925) | furniture |
| Mogens Lassen (1901–87) | architecture, furniture |
| Ole Wanscher (1903–85) | furniture |
| Helge Vestergaard Jensen (1917–87) | furniture |

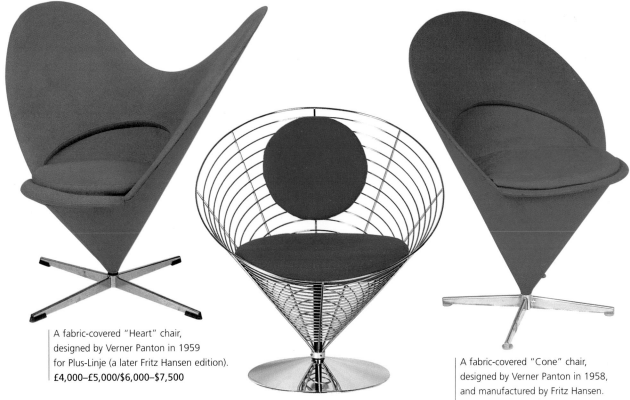

A fabric-covered "Heart" chair,
designed by Verner Panton in 1959
for Plus-Linje (a later Fritz Hansen edition).
**£4,000–£5,000/$6,000–$7,500**

A zinc-wire "Cone" chair,
designed by Verner Panton in 1960
for Plus-Linje (a later Fritz Hansen edition).
**£700–£1,200/$1,000–$1,800**

A fabric-covered "Cone" chair,
designed by Verner Panton in 1958,
and manufactured by Fritz Hansen.
**£400–£500/$600–$750**

A pine and ebonized
dining room suite, designed
by Ilmari Tapiovaara in the
late 1950s, for Asko.
**£700–£1,000/$1,000–$1,500**

# Arne Jacobsen

Arne Jacobsen
(1902–71).

Arne Jacobsen was born in Copenhagen in 1902 and ran his own design practice until his death in 1971. He has become one of the most sought after 20th century designers among collectors today, thanks to his iconic designs such as the "Egg" chair, "Ant" chair, and "Swan" chair, which are archetypal representations of the Mid-Century modern Danish style, as well as startlingly original and timeless in their own right.

Jacobsen also designed lighting for Louis Poulson, cutlery for Georg Jensen, and metalware for Stelton, all of which are increasing in rarity and value today. Jacobsen's furniture is much in demand and prices have rocketed since the mid 1990s, particularly for his most popular designs. Original pieces of furniture are becoming increasingly hard to find and some items now command several thousand pounds as his work, and modern design itself, has become even more collectable.

Jacobsen embraced new technology and believed in truth to materials, just like Charles Eames in the USA at the same time. He was committed to the Danish tradition of using natural materials, but by the late 1950s had embraced new technology that enabled him to create the wonderfully sculptural organic shapes of his furniture. In this way Jacobsen differs from other designers such as Hans Wegner and Finn Juhl, who still relied very much on traditional cabinet-making techniques. In fact, Jacobsen was one of the first Danish designers to whole-heartedly embrace new technology and materials. All Jacobsen's pieces can be recognized through their organic forms and lack of excess decoration, so his work also reflects early Modernism from the 1920s and 1930s.

Jacobsen originally trained as a mason but switched to architecture, graduating from the Royal Danish Academy of Fine Arts in 1927. By the early 1930s he had founded his own design office specializing in architecture and interior design. He was influenced by the early Modernists such as Le Corbusier and Ludwig Mies van der Rohe to create functional, practical, and elegant buildings. Perhaps his best known building commission was for the SAS Royal Hotel in Copenhagen in 1956–60 and this is now one of the most outstanding surviving Mid-Century expressions of Scandinavian style. He created everything from textiles to furniture for the hotel, including several of his most desirable chair designs.

A "Drop" chair,
designed in 1958–9, and
manufactured by Fritz Hansen.
**£3,000–£4,000/$4,500–$6,000**

An "Egg" chair, designed in 1958,
and manufactured by Fritz Hansen.
**£2,000–£2,500/$3,000–$3,750**

The "Egg" chair was designed in 1958, and is arguably the most famous chair of the 20th century, thanks to its overtly organic form and innovative style. These chairs were used in the reception area of the SAS Royal Hotel and were later manufactured by the firm Fritz Hansen (founded in 1872). The "Egg" chair sparked a host of copies worldwide and its influence can still be seen in furniture design today. Consisting of a foam-covered fibreglass shell with made-to-order fabric or leather upholstery, the chair has a swivelling aluminium base and moveable cushion. Its sculptural, rounded shell supports the sitter either in an upright position or curled up. The style and name of the "Egg" chair relates to Eero Saarinen's "Womb" chair of 1946 (*see p.81*). Leather is the most desirable covering among buyers today but condition is important as scratches or rips in the upholstery will affect the value. A similarly shaped organic ottoman is also available, and the "Egg" chair will attract a greater price today if it is offered with an ottoman.

The "Drop" chair was designed in 1958–9 and also manufactured by Fritz Hansen. It is even more organic-looking than the "Egg" chair, following the pear-shaped

A "Swan" or model number 3320 chair, designed in 1957–8 and manufactured by Fritz Hansen.
**£600–£800/$900–$1,200**

An "Ant" chair, designed in 1951–3 and manufactured by Fritz Hansen.
**£60–£80/$90–$120**

form of a raindrop. This chair was upholstered in leather and has splayed legs that reflect the general trend in the 1950s for atomic styling. It was used in the SAS Royal Hotel but is less known than the "Egg" chair today. Its design is similar to the "Pot" lounge chair opposite.

The "Ant" chair was designed in 1951–3 and won a Grand Prix at the 1957 Milan Triennale. It was extremely successful once it was mass-produced by Fritz Hansen from 1962 to the present day. Its organic form and splayed, insect-like legs gave the chair a real personality, and its sinewy shape with a head support and waist-like effect made it much more than just a chair. The oldest and most original examples were made from a single piece of moulded teak finished plywood with tubular steel legs and these are rare. Both three- and four-legged versions were made. Original examples are more desirable to collectors and will be in unpainted plywood, as later versions were made in different colours including blue, red, orange, and black.

The "Swan" or model number 3320 chair (*see p.101*) was designed for the SAS Royal Hotel in 1957–8 and manufactured by Fritz Hansen from 1958 to the present day. It too has an overtly organic form, in this case

reflecting the shape of outstretched wings. The "Swan" has a very similar construction to the "Egg" chair but is more lightweight, having a foam-covered one-piece fibreglass shell with fabric upholstery and an aluminium swivel base. In addition Jacobsen designed a "Swan" sofa of similar form and these are also collectable today. The first full scale version of the "Swan" chair had four laminated wooden legs and an example of this model would be very rare and valuable today.

Jacobsen continued to design famous furniture and interiors well into the 1960s, including the interior for St Catherine's College, Oxford University, between 1960 and 1964. He also became a Professor of Architecture at the Royal Danish Academy of Fine Arts. He carried on experimenting with organically-inspired furniture forms right through to the late 1960s and early 1970s, for example the "Seagull" or model number 3108 chair was created in 1970 and manufactured by Fritz Hansen in

Aj stainless steel flatware,
designed c.1957 and
manufactured by Georg Jensen.
**£500–£700/$750–$1,000**

1971. Designed to reflect the outstretched wings of the sea bird, original examples of this chair will be marked under the seat, "Made in Denmark, 1971 by Fritz Hansen."

Jacobsen's lighting and other household designs are also collectable today. Lighting was seen as an integral part of how new Mid-Century interior furnishings and designs could work together. Jacobsen created lights for Louis Poulson, one of Scandinavia's leading firms, and also made a range of stainless steel wall clocks.

He produced cutlery and other metalwork utilizing stainless steel, one of the most important new materials to be used in metal design in the 1950s. Stainless steel was suitable for moulding into new, organic shapes and was ideally suited for mass production. One of Jacobsen's most popular ranges was the "Cylinda" line, made in the late 1960s for Stelton. This range included stainless steel tea and coffee pots, and organically formed cutlery.

A Synkronar steel wall clock, designed in 1955 and manufactured by Lauritz Knudsen.
**£300–£400/$450–$600**

A "Pot" lounge chair, designed in 1959, and manufactured by Fritz Hansen.
**£700–£900/$1,050–$1,350**

A "Seagull" or model number 3108 chair, designed in 1970 and manufactured by Fritz Hansen.
**£1,200–£1,600/ $1,800–$2,400**

# Scandinavia

By 1951 Scandinavian design was becoming more and more popular throughout the world, thanks to wider promotion through exhibitions and critical acclaim in the press. Tapio Wirkkala's "Leaf" platter appeared on the cover of the catalogue for an exhibition called *Design in Scandinavia,* which toured the USA and Canada between 1954 and 1957 and introduced Scandinavian design from Norway, Finland, Sweden, and Denmark to a new audience. America as well as the rest of Europe quickly came to appreciate Scandinavian Modernism's fine, traditional craftsmanship and the abundance of natural materials used in its products. The USA is a particularly strong market for Scandinavian design today, whether from private collectors or from museums and institutions.

Tapio Wirkkala (1915–85) is perhaps best known for his work in glass, but he also created lighting, furniture, and ceramics. At the end of the 1940s he began to create one-off sculptural forms in laminated woods, including leaves and shells and these are very rare. The "Leaf" platter was designed in 1951 and made between 1951 and 1954. It has become a modern classic. It was exhibited at the 1951 Milan Triennale and in 1952 *House Beautiful,* the American interior design magazine, chose it as "The most beautiful object of 1951." They commented, "You may call it a tray, or a piece of sculpture... here is a marriage between ancient craftsmanship and modern engineering", which just about sums it up. It is an exceptionally sculptural piece of work, reflecting the Finnish designer's love of nature and organic forms. Wirkkala stays true to his material and the delicate cross-cut wood laminations on the surface of the platter make the leaf appear to be alive. Leaf platters should be incised underneath with the initials "TW" and they are now selling for several thousand pounds.

A more affordable way to enjoy Scandinavian design is to invest in a set of chairs and a table by designers such as Hans Wegner (b.1914) and Carl Jacobs, whose stacking chairs can still be found for under £500/$750 for four. The set of stackable and low-cost "Jason" chairs shown here was produced in 1950 by the Danish architect Carl Jacobs for the London firm Kandya Ltd. These chairs are made of beech and have a shaped plywood seat on ebonized legs and bear a transfer label "Rg Design" underneath. They also came with metal legs and different coloured plywood seats. Jacobs designed a corresponding table in this range with similarly shaped ebonized legs. The "Jason" chair demonstrates a masterful ability to bring out the qualities of plywood, thanks to its delicately curved back with striking cut-outs in the wood.

Grete Jalk's 1963 oregan-pine "Laminate Lounge Chair" has become extremely popular with collectors and is one of the most desirable chairs in the current Scandinavian design collector's market. Jalk was born in 1920 and began her training as an apprentice joiner in 1940. Her work was exhibited at the 1951 Milan Triennial and she set up her own design studio in 1954, where her clients included Fritz Hansen and Poul Jeppeson. She was also a respected design theorist and critic, and was editor of the periodical *Mobilia* from the late 1950s to the early 1970s.

The Laminate Lounge Chair was manufactured by Jeppeson, and its simple two-part construction was secured by just two pairs of steel bolts. The chair was the result of experiments that Jalk had started the previous year in new furniture shapes and it is a most unusual organic design. It was made by Jeppeson in a variety of surface veneers but by the time it was produced in the early 1960s, buyers were losing interest in plywood in favour of plastics and Pop design. Ironically, Jalk designed the chair for mass production but it was considered much too radical to put into production so only about 150 were finally manufactured (they should be marked"PJ" underneath the seat). This makes it rare and of particular interest to collectors.

## Scandinavian lighting

LIGHTING

During the late 1940s and early 1950s, all the Scandinavian countries were moving forward in the field of good quality, affordable lighting design. Hanging lamps, pendant lamps, as well as more traditional styles were manufactured in new materials such as plastic and paper. Designers who experimented with lighting included Alvar Aalto, Arne Jacobsen, and Verner Panton, both for one-off pieces and designs to complement an entire interior commission, for example Jacobsen's light fittings for the SAS Royal Hotel in Copenhagen between 1955 and 1960.

In the 1950s Aalto produced lighting that was both modern and sculptural, and created innovative lighting solutions for private and public commissions, including the National Pension Institute in Helsinki in 1955.

The hanging lamp "Handgranate A 111" by Aalto illustrated here is made from white painted metal and brass, and can be identified by a Valaistustyö stamp at the top of the lamp shaft. The first version was made with a solid metal shade, and then Aalto developed it into the current version where the shade comprises a series of thin vertical rods between two horizontal bands.

A set of four "Jason" chairs,
designed by Carl Jacobs
in 1950, for Kandya Ltd.
(set) £500–£600/$750–$900

A hanging lamp "Handgranate A 111",
designed by Alvar Aalto c.1951,
for Valaistustyö.
£600–£1,000/$900–$1,500

A "Leaf" platter, designed
by Tapio Wirkkala in 1951,
for Soinne et Kni.
£1,000–£1,500/$1,500–$2,250

A "Laminate Lounge Chair",
designed by Grete Jalk in 1963,
and manufactured by Poul Jeppeson.
£15,000–£20,000/$22,500–$30,000

# Hans Wegner

Hans Wegner
(b.1914).

Hans Wegner is one of the most prolific Danish designers of the 20th century. His chairs have sold throughout the world and were even used by President John F. Kennedy in a televized presidential debate. Wegner began his career in 1931 when he was certified as a joiner. After this he enrolled at the Technological Institute in Copenhagen and graduated in joinery in 1938. Between 1943 and 1946 he ran his own furniture making office and made a name for himself in the 1950s, winning the prestigious Lunning Prize and a gold medal at the Milan Triennale in 1951. One of his longest collaborations has been with the Copenhagen furniture manufacturer Johannes Hansen, whom he first teamed up with in 1940. He also worked with Fritz Hansen and A. P. Stolen. Wegner is inspired by traditional furniture examples that he then updates with the use of newer materials such as teak and plywood. His Mid-Century furniture is exceptionally organic, with its widespread use of solid wood and natural forms, giving a complete contrast to the sleek metallic lines of early Modernist furniture.

One of his most characteristic early designs is the ash-framed "Peacock" chair, which he created in 1947.

It is based on the design of English Windsor chairs (c.1750–1850), except Wegner gave his chair a subtle twist by making the seat very low and the back wide and full, providing extremely comfortable support for the sitter. Teak was used for the armrests and the seat is made from paper cord. The designer Finn Juhl, a close friend of Wegner, christened the chair after the back's resemblance to the spread of a peacock's tail feathers. In 1953 Wegner reworked the design of this chair into an easy chair prototype, which retains the overall structure but adds solid arms and an upholstered back. Wegner often used the same basic furniture design again and explored all its functional possibilities.

The teak "Valet" or "Bachelor's" chair from 1952 is one of Wegner's more inventive designs, being a combination of a clothes hanger and a chair – a perfect example of Modernist furniture created for a specific function. The unusually shaped back can be used as a jacket hanger and the seat, when pulled upright at the front, serves as a trouser hanger. There is also a box under the seat for storing small items of clothing and accessories. The "Valet" chair utilizes solid pine for the

A "Flaginstolen" lounge chair, designed in 1950, and manufactured by Getama.
£1,600–£2,500/$2,400-$3,800

frame and teak for the seat. It was exhibited in 1952 at the *Danish Cabinet-maker's Guild Exhibition* and received great critical acclaim. King Frederick of Denmark placed an order for eight Valet chairs shortly after the exhibition.

The rare "Flaginstolen" lounge chair from 1950 is Wegner's most futuristic design, with its squat form and angular tubular steel frame. It resembles a spacecraft (some ten years before the space age really began). It had no clear historical precedent and is therefore extremely collectable. The seat, sides, and back are made from flag halyard and it came with a removable sheepskin cover and a pillow for a headrest. Despite its appearance the chair is comfortable and also ultra fashionable in today's interior design world.

The more spacious and solid "Ox" chair and its accompanying stool were designed in 1960 and manufactured by Johannes Hansen. The chair has a moulded plywood seat shell set on a chromed tubular steel base and its generous breadth allowed the sitter to move around freely.

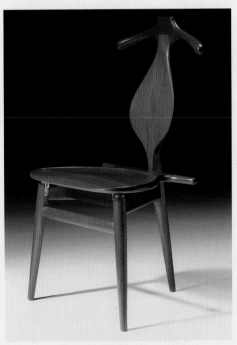

A "Valet" or "Bachelor's" chair, designed in 1953 for Johannes Hansen. **£1,500–£2,500/$2,250–$3,750**

A "Peacock" chair, designed in 1947 for Johannes Hansen. **£1,000–£1,500/ $1,500–$2,250**

An "Ox" chair, designed in 1960 for Johannes Hansen. **£800–£1,200/$1,200–$1,800**

# STUDIO CERAMICS

An "Oxblood" glaze vase,
designed by Axel Salto
c.1937 for Royal Copenhagen Porcelain.
£12,000–£15,000/$18,000–$22,500

There were several major developments in ceramic style during the Mid Century. While Bernard Leach's (1887–1979) approach and ethics remained relatively unchanged throughout his working life, Dame Lucie Rie's (1902–95) changed dramatically and new artists such as Hans Coper (1920–81) arrived on the scene. Outside of the Leach school and the Rie/Coper tradition, other artists, who had their own style and work ethic, began to emerge. Examples are James Tower (1919–88), Nicholas Vergette (1923–74), and Margaret Hine (1927–87), who all used a technique called "tin glazed earthenware" to dramatic effect. The new artists of the time were not looking backwards to the Orientalism of Leach and instead took their inspiration from other sources.

British designers including Leach, Rie, and Coper developed their existing styles. Leach continued producing a similar style of work throughout his life but introduced a range of production wares designed by himself but made by the apprentices at the pottery – this is known as Leach "standard" ware and is still relatively affordable. It was made in vast quantities and it is a very rugged and useable type of dinnerware – most items from this range can be picked up for as little as £10/$15 or £20/$30 today, with a full dinner set costing several hundred pounds.

A "Solfatara" glaze vase,
designed by Axel Salto in 1945
for Royal Copenhagen Porcelain.
£18,000–£25,000/$27,000–$37,500

The St Ives pottery (see pp.50–1) operated throughout World War II and Leach continued to develop his craft and produce outstanding designs, all of which are collectable today. Other potters joined him in the 1950s and 1960s (including his wife Janet Leach, née Darnell), and his son David. Janet Darnell was a Texan who had spent time working with Shoji Hamada (see pp.50–1) before meeting Leach. The Leach studio became internationally renowned, due to Leach's tours, exhibitions, writings, and lectures – people, including some from abroad, came to work with Leach and to learn how to make "Leach school" pots. Young British potters and local apprentices

A stoneware "Tenmoku" cut-sided vase, designed by Bernard Leach c.1961.
**£3,000–£4,000/$4,500–$6,000**

also worked at St Ives and some then left to form their own studios, taking Leach's teachings and stylistic influence with them.

By the early 1950s the Leach studio potters were producing over 70 different glazed stoneware items with hand-decorated surfaces for the retail market. More standardized pieces were cheaper to make and helped finance the pottery's experimental, one-off studio pieces. The more expensive and rarer pieces will always be more desirable among collectors, for example the stoneware cut-sided vase (*see above*) and classic forms such as the "Leaping Salmon" vase (*see p.*110). This is an example of one of Leach's designs that occurred at various points

during his career and it is difficult to say when it was first produced. It is one of his most famous designs and as such is extremely collectable today. Leach was also producing beautifully crafted bowls at this time, for example the porcelain celadon bowl (*see p.*110), with its delicate, incised thistle motif.

Leach's seminal work *A Potters Book* was published in 1940 and continues to exert its influence today. Despite becoming almost entirely blind, he continued working almost up until his death in 1979. His teachings remain highly influential and the Leach tradition lives on.

Rie came through a relatively unsuccessful period when she was trying to emulate Leach, but then she

A porcelain celadon
bowl, designed by
Bernard Leach c.1961.
**£2,000–£3,000/$3,000–$4,500**

developed her own distinctive style, apparently unrelated
to anything that came before. This was a highly influential
stylistic shift which has been emulated by potters ever
since. Her forms were uniquely hers and the incredible
control of glaze and balance of form that she achieved
has never been matched. The work of this new wave of
potters achieved great success and international
recognition. Due to the handmade process and the
vagaries of kiln firings no two pieces of experimental
pottery by these designers are ever the same, but Rie and
Coper, in particular, developed themes that re-occur
and evolve throughout their work.

Studio pottery was also developing in Europe. One of
Denmark's leading studio potters was Axel Salto
(1889–1961), and his naturalistically-inspired pottery work
is particularly popular in the Scandinavian and American
collectors' market at the time of writing.

Salto's ceramics really took off in 1923 when he began
working in enamel-glazed porcelain. It was these early
pieces that won a silver medal at the *Paris World
Exhibition* in 1937. By 1929 Salto was working in
conjunction with the Halier studio in Fredericksburg,
Germany, on high-fired stoneware and these pieces are
particularly collectable today, thanks to their beautiful,
organic forms and exquisite coloured glazes. The Halier
studio closed in 1930 and Salto went on to collaborate
with Nathalie Krebs at the Saxbo studio. In 1934 Salto
began producing designs for Denmark's leading
manufacturer, Royal Copenhagen Porcelain.

A "Leaping Salmon"
vase, designed by
Bernard Leach c.1970.
**£9,000–£12,000/$13,500–$18,000**

Salto's ceramics are highly expressionistic. His work is
mainly influenced by the natural world, including horse
chestnut burs, pineapples, and sea urchins. His vases often
have a "prickly" quality; they are highly tactile, and look
as if they are about to burst into life.§

Salto pieces are easy to identify because his style is so
characteristic, and his works were marked throughout his
career in a fairly consistent manner. Ceramic objects will
be incised underneath with an attenuated "Salto" name
and some pieces will also be dated, particularly those
produced in the early 1930s.

A large conical porcelain vase,
designed by Dame Lucie Rie c.1964.
**£18,000–£25,000/$27,000–$37,500**

A straight-sided porcelain
bowl, designed by
Dame Lucie Rie c.1964.
**£4,500–£6,000/$6,750–$9,000**

Both Rie and fellow potter Coper are remembered for their modesty, commitment to their art and materials, and their technical and often inventive brilliance, as they experimented with new glazes and firing techniques throughout their careers.

Rie was naturalized in Britain in 1945 and set up her own studio in Albion Mews, London, where she lived and worked for the rest of her life. Hans Coper literally turned up on her doorstep in 1946, having been interned during the war as an "enemy alien", and announced that he wanted to work with her. This collaboration at Albion Mews lasted for some twelve years and the pair remained close friends throughout their lives.

Rie took Coper in, his talents immediately impressed her and he began working with her on ranges of buttons. When Coper expressed an interest in making sculpture with clay, Rie sent him to Woolwich Polytechnic, London, to be taught how to throw on the wheel. Once he had learnt this technique, he began making domestic household and commercial ware for the Bendicks Coffee House in London and other clients. Umbrella handles, hatpins, and circular buttons survive from this period and are collectable today, although this work is usually attributed to Rie rather than Coper.

Both Coper and Rie exhibited at the *Festival of Britain* in 1951. Coper held his first solo exhibition in London at the Primavera Gallery in 1958 after he had won a Gold Medal at the Milan Triennale. He moved to his own studio at the Digswell Arts Trust in 1959. In 1962 he was commissioned to produce some monumental candlesticks for the new Coventry Cathedral. Coper continued to receive success throughout the 1960s and 1970s, particularly for his elegant sculptural ceramic forms. He taught first at Camberwell School of Arts, London, and then at the Royal College of Art from 1966. Coper moved to a farmhouse near Frome, south west England, with Jane Gate, who was an accomplished photographer. His work is well documented from the mid 1950s onwards through Gate's photographs. He had a degenerative disease called Amyotropic lateral sclerosis, which meant that towards the end of his life he was only able to work on smaller pieces and his last works from the mid 1970s, collectively known as the "Cycladics", are incredible essays in composition on a small scale. These are the most collectable of Coper's works today.

Each period in Coper's work is very definable – for example, the Albion mews pieces are very different to those produced at Digswell and Frome. His early work was

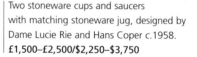

Two stoneware cups and saucers
with matching stoneware jug, designed by
Dame Lucie Rie and Hans Coper c.1958.
**£1,500–£2,500/$2,250–$3,750**

A stoneware bottle vase,
designed by Dame Lucie Rie, c.1958.
**£12,000–£16,000/$18,000–$24,000**

small scale, but in later years he created monumental-sized vases – for example, the "thistle" and "spade" shapes.

Rie and Coper visited the ancient artefacts at Avebury Museum, Wiltshire, in the late 1940s and were extremely impressed with the sgrafitto decoration that appeared on traditional pots (the pattern was scratched into the surface of the glaze with bird bones). Rie began to use this technique on her own pots by applying the decoration with a needle, and these pieces, decorated with finely hatched lines, appear from the early 1950s. Rie's ceramics from the early 1950s onwards will bear an "LR" seal. The seals changed over time and, as with many artists, it is possible to use the style of seal to give a piece a fairly accurate date.

On the early domestic wares that were collaborative pieces Coper threw the form and Rie decorated them. These pieces will have both artist's seals and are very

collectable. Coper was also influenced by abstract art and modern painting and sculpture, particularly the sculpture of the Italian artist Alberto Giacommetti and Ben Nicholson's abstract painting. Rie found more of her inspiration in the natural world and through natural objects such as feathers and leaves.

From 1948, when she installed an electric kiln at Albion Mews, Rie was able to high-fire pieces. This enabled her to work increasingly with stoneware and porcelain and to begin experimenting with new glazes and colours, including lead, dark blue, light blue, pinks, and uranium yellow. Rie mischievously called this "American yellow" because she found it very difficult to sell the idea of a piece with a uranium glaze to the American market at the time. Most potters dipped their work in glaze, and Rie was unusual in using a paintbrush to apply her glazes.

Rie began to sell her work to the USA and New Zealand and produced a range of work for Liberty & Co. and Heal's in London in the late 1940s and early 1950s. She had her first solo show at the Berkeley Gallery in

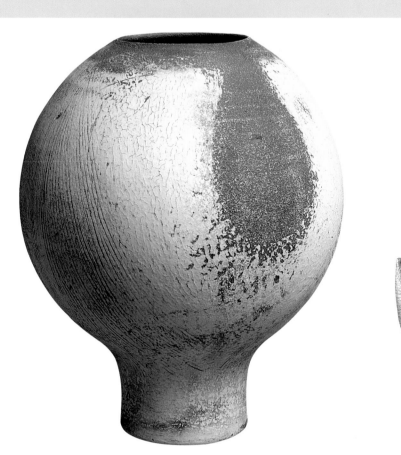

1949. In the late 1950s she developed even more dramatic and innovative glazes on the outside of her pots, coupled with decorative techniques including sgrafitto, inlay, and fluting. Sgrafitto is the term for a piece that has been covered in glaze with a design scratched through to the body. Inlay is effectively the opposite, as this involves scratching lines into the unglazed body, which is then covered in glaze. The excess glaze is wiped off, leaving glaze only in the scratches, then the whole piece is glazed again (usually in a different colour) and, when fired, the "inlay" appears as a coloured design on a different ground. Another technique that is particularly common in Rie's work is the mixing of two types of clay, as two lumps thrown together create a marbled effect, and during firing the glaze works differently with each sort of clay producing various colours on the surface. All of these techniques are typical of Rie's work and are frequently used by her followers.

*Above left*: A stoneware gobular pot, designed by Hans Coper c.1953. **£18,000–£25,000/$27,000–$37,500**

*Above*: A black "Cycladic" form, designed by Hans Coperc.1976. **£30,000–£40,000/$45,000–$60,000**

# GLASS

An "Iceberg" vase, designed by Tapio Wirkkala in 1950 and manufactured by Iittala, 1951–69.
**£1,500–£1,800/$2,250–$2,700**

An "Orchid" vase, model number 3868–540, designed by Timo Sarpaneva in 1953 and manufactured by Iittala, 1954–73.
**£400–£600/$600–$900**

Glass design in the mid 20th century moved towards exploring the sculptural possibilities of glass rather than the more functional pieces resulting from Modernism. Colour, too, became increasingly important and new techniques for glass manufacture continued to develop.

The 1950s saw the growth of new glass styles throughout Europe, with Italy and Scandinavia leading the way in modern glass design. There was a greater awareness of good, modern design in the post-war years and a call throughout the Western world for a fresh approach to living. In the field of glass this could be seen both in the demand for new styles in domestic ware and in the increased purchasing of art-based glass. Modern abstract art and sculpture also had an influence on 1950s glass, which can be seen in the new forms that were produced. It is possible to collect Mid-Century glass by designer, factory, or even by country.

In Scandinavia artists and designers were employed in conjunction with craftsmen at the major glasshouses, such as Orrefors and Kosta in Sweden and Iittala and Nuutajärvi Notsjö in Finland. This tradition can be traced at Orrefors from Simon Gate and Edward Hald during the years following World War I right through to designers working in the Orrefors studios today.

Finnish glass became influential in the late 1940s with the work of Tapio Wirkkala (1915–85) and later Timo Sarpaneva (b.1926). It was Gunnel Nyman (1909–48) whose instinctive grasp of the material first attracted attention, with her creative designs produced by the factories of Riihimaki, Nuutajärvi, and Iittala. Her styles varied from pliable-looking "folded" models through to restrained cutting techniques. There was also a series of vessels with bubbled decoration, where symmetrical

A "Fish" Graal vase, designed
by Edward Hald in 1937, for Orrefors.
**£350–£500/$520–$750**

patterns of tiny bubbles were used to internally decorate the item, as seen in the example shown here, a technique later imitated by others.

Much Finnish glass can be enjoyed for its own inherent beauty and for its simple everyday functionalism. Its clarity of line and simplicity of form is synonymous with Scandinavian design. However, many of the most memorable designs in Finland are based upon ice and icicles. All are deeply sculptural in nature.

Wirkkala and Nyman's success at the Milan Triennales of 1951 and later Sarpaneva's in 1954 confirmed both the quality of their work and its worldwide influence. From the 1950s Italian glass began to influence Finnish designers. Finnish glass appealed to an America audience through the influential *Design in Scandinavia* exhibition, which toured the USA between 1954 and 1957.

Wirkkala designed sculptural glass of exceptional quality and originality, reflecting his background as a sculptor. Ice-like, crystal-forms, as in the "Iceberg" vase shown here, and naturalistically inspired shapes reflecting the rugged Finnish landscape make his work instantly recognizable. He was inspired by nature, leaves, seashells, ice formations, and the natural movement of water and birds. In 1959 Wirkkala began to work for Venini

A "Bubbled" vase,
designed by Gunnel Nyman
in 1947, for Nuutajärvi Notsjö.
**£300–£400/$450–$600**

and by then he was already designing for Iittala and Rosenthal. He continued to work for all these companies until his death in 1985.

Sarpaneva studied at the Central School of Applied Arts in Helsinki between 1941 and 1948, joining Karhula-Iittala in 1950. His early work was deeply sculptural, relying on purity of line and the quality of the material, with occasional use of milky colour - for example, in the "Lancet" series. His major designs of this period are seen as sculptures and not utility items. The famous "Kayak" of 1953 is rare and desirable, and the "Orchid" vase shown here is now regarded as a design icon.

From 1951 Kaj Franck (1911–89) worked for Nuutajärvi Notsjö, initially in a reductive style. His designs

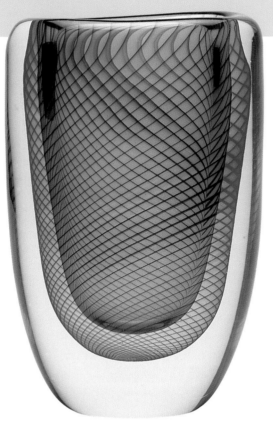

An "Ariel" bowl, designed by
Ingeborg Lundin and manufactured
by Orrefors, Sweden, c.1966.
**£600–£800/$900–$1,200**

A clear cased green and threaded
vase, designed by Vicke Lindsrand and
manufactured by Kosta, Sweden, c.1955.
**£300–£380/$450–$570**

were simple, strong, often angular, and sometimes had flat polished sides. In the late 1950s, when there was a move away from post-war austerity, he designed more curvilinear pieces, the most notable being the "Kremlin Bells", which was inspired by Russian architecture.

The Swedes led the world with innovative techniques such as Graal and Ariel by Orrefors prior to World War II. Orrefors extended this lead with the work of Edvin Ohrstrom (1906–94) and his Edvinglass, an extension of Ariel which is cased and has a smooth finish, whereby the air trap becomes raised above the surface while still being cased. Nils Landberg (1907–91) introduced the "Serpentina" collection and Edward Hald (1883–1980) developed "Aquagraal" in collaboration with Heniz Richter.

Edward Hald and Simon Gate designed together during the formative years of Orrefors between the wars. While Hald's work on the "Sandvik" range exhibits a house style, his Graal designs became heavier by 1937 when his "Fish" Graal vase was introduced. This heavily cased design foresaw the 1950s and was so successful that it stayed in production in various forms until 1980.

In 1937 the Swede Sven Palmquist (1906–84) began designing for Orrefors, but his initial work was fairly pedestrian by company standards. After much experimenting he introduced Kraka ware in 1944 and Ravenna in 1948. Both techniques demonstrated a maturity of design and style. With Kraka the blank, a partially formed vessel, left to cool and then worked on, is covered with a fine mesh, sandblasted, clear cased, and then blown out to reveal a net-like pattern of trapped air bubbles. Ravenna is constructed by sandwiching clear and coloured glass, sandblasting a geometric pattern to the surface, and then dusting pigments into the recesses before a clear casing is added, finally blowing out the shape. These pieces are highly collectable today.

The "Tulip" series introduced by Landberg harnesses the elasticity of the material to form the elegant designs of his vases. Much of his work makes use of elongation, as can be seen with the "Tulip" series, his "Hourglass" vases, and the "Prydnadsglas" stemware from 1960.

Ingeborg Lundin (b.1921) was the first female glass artist at Orrefors and joined the company in 1947. Her work is quirky, often humorous, and is skilled in the use of line and form, as demonstrated by her "Hourglass" stemware of 1954 and the famous "Ariel" bowl of 1966. She also continued the Orrefors tradition of Ariel, often using geometric patterns, as can be seen in the bowl shown here. Her engraved and cut-glass work is fun and innovative.

Sandblasted dishes,
designed by Ladislav Oliva, c.1957–60
and manufactured by Borské Skio.
(each) **£3,000–£4,000/$4,500–$6,000**

Although Vicke Lindsrand (1904–83) worked for Orrefors until 1940, producing stunning Ariel, Graal, and engraved work, he has become synonymous with the firm of Kosta, which he joined in 1950. His work is extremely collectable today, thanks to its fine workmanship and simple but dynamic forms. Lindsrand's Mid-Century work is beautifully sculptural with a restrained, organic feel and subtle use of colour, which often relies on linear patterns within the glass (*see* opposite). His work usually bears the incised factory mark, including his two-letter code to the base of the item. Occasionally there is his full name inscribed, or else there may be a rectangular, acid-etched mark with his name.

Orrefors can be identified by the incised marks on the base of the object. First there is "Orrefors" or "Of", then the designer letter code followed by that of the type of glass (cut, engraved, blown, etc) with the model number and finally the date – which is in code after 1938.

Czechoslovakia's glass industry was totally changed in 1948 after the political revolution. The huge numbers of glassworks, decorator, and teaching institutions were put into one enormous body under the auspices of the State. To enhance the inter-relationship between artists, designers, and industry the Creative Glass Centre was opened in 1952 in Prague. Much of the work was varied and imaginative and developed upon the traditional forms at which the Czechs excelled, namely cutting, engraving, and enamelling.

There are many names associated with Czech glass that are already recognized internationally by collectors: Jaroslava Brychtová, Jirí Harcuba, Pavel Hlava, Stanislav Libenský, and René Roubíček being just a few. All bar Brychtová and Libenský worked with cut glass, whether exclusively, such as Vladimir Zahour, or as part of a much larger repertoire like Roubíček, who also worked in blown glass (both functional and art), painted glass, and decorative panels. While the Czechs carried on producing commercial, traditionally-cut glass, it was the modern designers who made both restrained and complex patterned items with a fresh style, utilizing the abilities of the craftsmen to their fullest. Some, like Harcuba, designed and executed their own work. Ladislav Oliva specialized in cut or sandblasted pieces, usually of geometric patterns.

In 1954, Brychtová and Libenský began a 40-year partnership working on their main interests of sculptural and architectural designs. Libenský originally felt himself an artist and Brychtová a sculptor. Both found themselves orientated towards the medium of glass and together they produced monumental works. They married in 1963.

The economic boom in Italy after World War II led to an increased output in all fields of design. Italian glass manufacture centred on specialist factories making art glass for use as decorative objects, rather than functional vessels. The finest pieces came from Murano, a small island near Venice that has been at the centre of Venetian glass making for centuries.

The leading Murano manufacturer was Venini, founded by Paolo Venini (1895–1959) in the 1920s. With an innovative design approach, combined with new methods of working, Venini produced some of the most desirable and collectable glass of the period. While Venini introduced his own designs, such as "Zanfirico" and the "Murrine" series and excelled in light fittings and window or screen designs, he also employed other designers.

It was Fulvio Bianconi (1915–96) who produced some of the foremost designs for the company. Bianconi won prestigious awards at the Milan Triennales of 1963 and

*Above left*: A "Spicchi" vase, designed by Fulvio Bianconi in 1951 for Venini & Co.
**£3,000–£4,000/$4,500–$6,000**

*Above:* A "Patchwork" jug vase, designed by Ansola Fuga c.1955 for AVEM.
**£3,000–£4,000/$4,500–$6,000**

1964. His work for Venini was initiated by the series of figurative pieces, such as clowns and musicians, known as Commedia dell'Arte, followed by the well-known "Handkerchief" ("Fazzoletto") vase in collaboration with Venini. The "Patchwork", or "Pezzato" series, with its brilliant use of a controlled grid of colour, was introduced in 1950. It is highly desirable today, but one has to be careful since some of the designs are still being produced. Originals can be identified by the period acid-etched marks

*Right*: A "Valve" sidrale vase,
designed by Flavio Poli
*c*.1952 for Seguso Vetri.
**£8,000-£10,000/$12,000-$15,000**

*Below*: A "Neolitici" vase,
designed by Ercole Barovier
*c*.1954 for Barovier and Toso.
**£1,500–£1,800/$2,200–$2,700**

and there is a tendency for the earlier pieces to be of lighter construction. The "Bianconi "vase shown here is from the "Spicchi" series and is a simplified version of the "Patchwork" range, whereby transparent, vertical panels of coloured glass are cased together to form the item.

The "Patchwork" vessel, designed by Ansolo Fuga (1915–98) for Arte Vetraria Muranese (AVEM), is typical of the designs he produced for them with contrasting opaque white and transparent colour. It is charcteristic of the sculptural forms produced in Italy at the time.

Flavio Poli (1900–84), who worked with the firm of Seguso Vetri d'Arte, was another of the formative Italian designers of the post-war period. Poli trained as a ceramic designer, but is most famous today for his sculptural glass vases. The "Valve" pieces from the "Conchiglie" ("Shell") designs, first introduced in 1951, are the best known and most highly prized of his work. Even more successful was the "Valve Siderale", shown here, with a front plate consisting of a murrhine of concentric circles.

The Italian designer Ercole Barovier (1889–1974) produced many and varied designs, styles, and finishes, often using gold and always exploiting the ductility of the material. From 1930, he specialized in the use of chemicals to colour glass, discovering in particular a technique of decorating the surface of an item with unmeltable materials. The range "Barbaric", produced from 1951, was one example of this. Like other Italian designers he used murrhines, however the use of paired murrhines of glass pieces was synonymous with him. The Graffito style vase shown here is a variation of the ancient Fenicio technique where air is trapped in the spiral.

The mid 20th century saw a move in the English glass industry to employ resident designers in line with the general policy of the government, who saw design as the way ahead. The *Britain Can Make It* exhibition in 1946 and the Festival of Britain in 1951 (*see pp*.70–1) witnessed the design ideals that would go on to influence development that can be traced through to the present day. The Stourbridge companies largely developed through cut glass. While producing traditional, but commercial cut wares they began manufacturing work with far more restrained and simplified patterns. Irene Stevens (*b*.1917) worked for Webb Corbett, John Luxton (*b*.1920) for Stuarts, and David Hammond (*b*.1931) for Thomas Webb. In America Steuben continued production of quality wares, especially in clear lead glass. They also carried on the successful practice of commissioning artists to design for limited edition engraved glass series.

# TEXTILES

The fabric designs of Lucienne Day typify the spirit of exuberance and playfulness in design in the early to late 1950s. The work she created for the British retailer Heal's is particularly sought after today. Thanks to innovations such as screenprinting, well-designed textiles could be mass marketed for the first time in Britain at a reasonable cost. Before the 1950s, textiles were very expensive and tended to be made of traditional materials such as velvet. Day often stated that she wanted to bring good design into the home and textiles proved to her to be an excellent way of doing this.

Day was born Désirée Lucienne Conradi in 1917 to a Belgian father and an English mother. She initially trained at the Croydon School of Art, Surrey, between 1934 and 1937 after displaying an early talent for design, specializing in industrial art. In 1938 she entered the Royal College of Art, London and it was here that she met Robin Day in 1940. They were married in 1942. During the war she spent some time in the Fire Service but was invalided out and found a teaching job.

One of her first commissions as a fabric designer was for Cavendish textiles, suppliers to the John Lewis partnership, and she also worked for the Edinburgh Weavers Co. Some of these early designs were noticed by

Lucienne Day at work in her studio.

Heal's, a furniture store committed to marketing the work of good young designers. In 1947 Day became a full-time freelance designer. Around this time she and Robin visited Scandinavia and this made a deep impression on them. Lucienne's early work is clearly inspired by Scandinavian Modernism, with its use of natural motifs such as leaves and plant forms.

Her first high profile designs were the fabrics that she produced for Robin Day's room interiors at the 1951 *Festival of Britain*. She designed "Calyx" (*see p.*71) especially for the exhibition and also fabric to cover the auditorium seating in the Telekinema at the South Bank. "Calyx" won a gold medal at the 1951 Milan Triennale and was also successfully exported to the USA. The fabric was produced on linen because cotton was still in short supply after the war. It proved to be a commercial success, staying in production for over ten years.

"Calyx" is particularly desirable among collectors today, because it is an example of an extremely original textile design. Day's vibrant, limited use of colour, and abstracted plant forms are very much in the style of Miró and the Bauhaus teacher and artist Paul Klee. These artists

"Herb Anthony",
designed in 1956 for Heal's.
**£150–£200/$225–$300**

*Above left*: "Linear",
designed in 1953 for Heal's.
**£150–£200/$225–$300**

*Above*: "Fall",
designed in 1952
for the Edinburgh Weaver's Co.
**£150–£200/$225–$300**

were particularly important to Day. She said, "What I was really interested in – the Bauhaus, painters like Klee, Kandinsky and Miró – they gave me heart and made me feel that I could do the same sort of thing for textiles."

Day worked in partnership with Heal's from 1950 to 1974, producing around five new designs a year. The company commissioned two more designs immediately after "Calyx", including "Flotilla", which used screenprinting technology. Other patterns including "Allegro", "Small Hours", "Herb Anthony", and "Strata" are increasing in value today. Some of the more popular designs such as "Calyx" were used in home furnishing as well as in public buildings. They all exhibit Day's use of abstract forms, limited colour, and natural shapes like leaves and trees – a breath of fresh air in contrast to the chintzes and heavy brocade of some English fabrics.

Day's designs sparked a host of contemporary copies, but it is easy to identify an original because both her name and the pattern were printed on the selvedge (the piece of unpatterned material that forms a border around the patterned area of the fabric when it is the roll).

In the 1960s, Day embraced Pop style and adopted a much less restricted colour palette and even bolder abstract motifs. In 1962 she was elected a Royal Designer for Industry and went on to design wallpapers; ceramics for the German manufacturing company Rosenthal, especially their 1950s Studio Line; carpet designs for the British company Axminster, and a range of textiles called silk mosaics, which were large enough to hang on the wall. She still designs today.

# JEWELLERY AND METALWARE

A silver bracelet, necklace, and earrings set,
designed by Henning Koppel in 1947
for Georg Jensen.
**£1,500–£2,500/$2,250–$3,750**

Mid-Century jewellery, particularly that produced by the Georg Jensen company in Denmark, has become extremely collectable. The Jensen name is synonymous with style, technical quality, and innovation. Henning Koppel and Nanna Ditzel are probably the best-known Scandinavian designers who worked in the Mid-Century style but others to look out for are Torun Bülow-Hübe, Bent Peter Gabrielsen, Erik Magnussen, and Magnus Stephensen.

Georg Jensen was born in 1866. He established his own firm of silversmiths in 1904 and collaborated with young designers to give his company its distinctive style. He died in 1935 but left a strong and productive company that was open to new design ideas, ethics, styles, and production. By the 1950s the Jensen company was commissioning new, avant-garde designs from Mid-Century designers including Ditzel and Koppel and it continues to work with talented young designers today.

Henning Koppel (1918–81) trained as a sculptor at the Royal Danish Academy of Fine Arts during the 1930s. His work was fresh and modern and nothing quite like it had been seen in jewellery design before. His jewellery can be identified by its strong use of organic, biomorphic forms – very much part of Mid-Century modern design.

Koppel's silver bracelet of 1947 is one of his first and still most revered designs. It clearly displays his organic Modernist style with its fluid use of silver in an abstract, sculptural form. Although complex-looking, its construction is deceptively simple, made from only two basic links that create a multifaceted piece. Koppel said, "Silver demands rhythm, I like the shape to be vigorous and alive with movement." Koppel's jewellery for Jensen will be marked with the Georg Jensen stamp.

Koppel always had a desire to push the limitations of silver and this can be seen in his range of hollow ware. He teamed up with the silversmiths at Jensen, who worked with him from his clay models and tested the properties of his material. This tuition led to the swollen, round forms seen in this innovative and beautifully moulded pitcher. Its style and shape had never really been seen before in silversmithing and it is one of the best recognized pieces from the Jensen studio. The company still only makes a handful each year, which makes them highly collectable.

A "Teardrop" necklace, designed by Nanna Ditzel in 1954 for Georg Jensen.
Silver: £800–£1,000/$1,200–$1,500
Gold: £3,000–£3,500/$4,500–$5,200

A silver arm cuff, designed by Nanna Ditzel in 1955 for Georg Jensen.
£500–£600/$750–$900

A silver pitcher, designed by Henning Koppel in 1952 for Georg Jensen.
£6,000–£7,000/ $9,000–$10,500

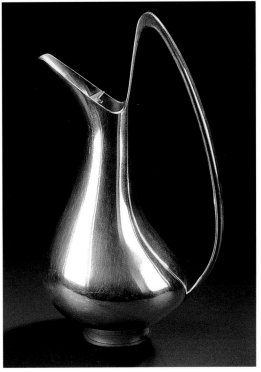

Another key collectable jewellery designer working in the Mid-Century Scandinavian style is Nanna Ditzel, who was born in 1923 and studied at the Danish School of Arts, Crafts and Design in Copenhagen during the 1940s. She met her husband, the designer Jørgen Ditzel (1921–61), here and they married after graduation. The Ditzels were a close and inspirational team who collaborated on every element of product design, like their contemporaries Charles and Ray Eames in the USA. Their education taught them the Modernist doctrine that there was no need for excessive or frivolous ornament on jewellery. They believed in truth to design and materials appropriate to the needs of an individual commission.

Following a recommendation from Finn Juhl, the Ditzels were invited to collaborate with the Jensen company in 1954. Their designs became popular across the world and Nanna's arm cuff and necklace were produced in her first range for Jensen and won the prestigious Lunning Prize in 1956. Both pieces have strong, sculptural forms and demonstrate a keen understanding of spacial awareness and geometry. The arm cuff is still in production today.

# POP AND RADICAL STYLE

The 1960s was the decade of flower power, psychedelia, the moon-landing, The Beatles, and the mini skirt. Youth culture asserted itself for the first time through fashion, music, and fun. There was optimism and an air of freedom and a belief in change – from student uprisings in Paris to mass protests against the Vietnam War. In April 1966 *Time* magazine ran the headline "London: The Swinging City", which put the King's Road and Carnaby Street at the centre of the 1960s style revolution. Pop style emerged out of this colourful backdrop, with the spirit of the age very much reflected in its products.

Pop design established itself in the 1960s but had really begun a decade before in the mid 1950s when young artists and designers began to react against mainstream conservative tastes in the USA. Pop was a celebration of mass popular culture, as its followers believed that art could be created from everyday objects. It was brash, gaudy, and fun but it could also be subversive and satirical. Pop took its inspiration from advertising, television, comic book art (particularly seen in the work of Roy Lichtenstein), and packaging (such as Andy Warhol's iconic images of Campbell's Soup tins).

The key material of Pop furniture design was plastic – the more colourful the better. Materials of Pop-inspired furniture often reflected the vibrant reds, blues, yellows, and greens of psychedelic art. Although plastics had been used in furniture manufacture for some time, new methods of production such as injection moulding were available by the late 1950s. This meant that plastic furniture was inexpensive to produce and retail and was ideal for the

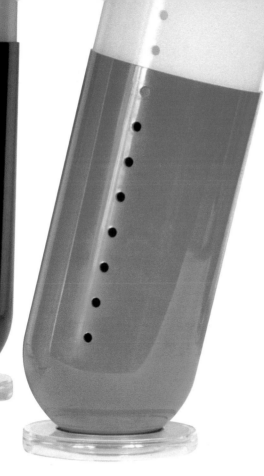

A set of five "Pillola" lamps designed by Italy's Cesare Cassati and Emanuele Ponzio, manufactured by Ponteur Plastics c.1968. Made of plastic with impressed marks on the underside. Each lamp with original carton:
**£3,000–£4,000/$4,500–$6,000**

growing youth market. Throwaway objects were also popular – ever more sophisticated mass-production techniques could replace products cheaply and by the mid 1960s, materials such as PVC were used in everything from furniture to coat hangers. De Pas, D'Urbino, and Lomazzi's PVC "Blow" chair was launched in 1967 and was quickly followed by cheap mass-produced copies. Fashion designers also exploited new materials, with throwaway paper dresses and transparent plastic dresses seen on the catwalks.

Another key development during the Pop era was the widespread availability of lithographic prints and posters. The 1960s saw the print trade flourish, with the work of British and American modern artists available to a mass market for the first time. Everyone could own a piece of Pop art, and many of the posters that come up for sale today from this period are typical examples of the style. Peter Blake, David Hockney, Richard Hamilton, and Allen Jones all worked in the Pop style. Posters and prints that combine icons of the decade with pop or psychedelic styling are particularly collectable, such as Richard Avedon's 1967 portraits of The Beatles.

Radical design developed in Italy in the late 1960s and early 1970s. It continued the tradition of using new materials and bold colours that began with Pop but also drew on historical styles such as Art Deco, Kitsch, and Surrealism. The main exponents of Radical design were small groups of architects and designers who questioned Modernism and rejected mass-consumer culture. Key groups and designers of the Radical style include Superstudio, Archizoom Associati, UFO, Gruppo Strum, and Ettore Sottsass, whose work went on to form the basis of Postmodernism in the 1980s. Like the early 20th century De Stijl and Bauhaus movements, Radical design had an underlying social purpose, which was to make people question their assumptions about design by taking everyday objects and architectural styles and reconfiguring them in new and surprising ways.

# FURNITURE

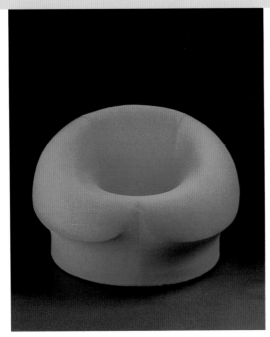

An "UP 3 Lounge" chair,
designed by Gaetano Pesce
in 1969, for C&B Italia.
**£4,000–£5,000/$6,000–$7,500**

A "Tulip" chair,
designed by Erwine and
Estelle Laverne c.1960.
**£1,800–£2,600/$2,700–$3,900**

Furniture manufacture was revolutionized in the 1960s, thanks to the availability of new materials including foam, and plastics such as polyethylene and vinyl. Plastic and foam could be moulded and shaped to fit the creative ideas of avant-garde designers and they opened up radical new possibilities for furniture design, as well as helping to create the style of the decade.

Plastic was discovered at the end of the 19th century and found its first mass practical application through Bakelite in the 1920s and 1930s. Bakelite was the first totally synthetic plastic and it was used for a host of domestic objects. Vinyl, polyester, and other petrol-based plastics were developed during the 1930s but it was not until after the war and its technological developments that designers began to work with plastics on a greater scale.

Designers including Erwine and Estelle Laverne were working with fibreglass by the late 1950s. Erwine (b.1909) and Estelle (b.1915) produced a range of moulded Perspex furniture that was already ahead of its time and in c.1960 they designed the "Tulip" chair. It has a fibreglass seat shell on a metal base and its wonderfully organic form reflects the natural shape of flower petals.

The development of foam in modern furniture design can be traced back to 1951 when Pirelli set up Arflex to experiment with rubber-based products in furniture construction. By the 1960s a range of newer, synthetic foams had been discovered and by the end of the decade designers were using it to create entire pieces.

The Italian designer Gaetano Pesce (b.1939) was immensely interested in the new design possibilities of foam. He trained as a graphic designer and architect and began working with avant-garde Radical design groups, such as Gruppo N, in the early 1960s. His interest in the growing Radical design movement (which aimed to challenge public notions of Modernism) was fully established by the late 1960s. His 1969 "UP" series of six chairs are organically formed, highly sensuous chairs based on male and female forms.

The "UP 3 Lounge" chair was made from moulded polyurethane foam and covered in coloured nylon jersey. The "UP 5 Donna" armchair and "UP 6 Ball" are even more voluptuous and they also made the political point that women were prisoners so the chair represents a woman with a ball chained to her foot. These chairs came vacuum-packed and when taken out of their PVC packaging expanded to ten times their normal size, a novelty that made them even more popular. The "UP" series was supported by a futuristic advertising campaign

An "UP 5 Donna" armchair with "UP 6 Ball", designed by Gaetano Pesce in 1969, and manufactured 1969–73 by C&B Italia, and by B&B from 1978.
**£12,000–£15,000/$18,000–$22,500**

and it was exhibited at the *Milan Furniture Fair* in 1969 to great critical acclaim. Pesce developed the possibilities of foam in furniture even further in the 1970s and 1980s.

Eero Aarnio's space-age "Ball" or "Globe" chair really captures the spirit and style of the 1960s. Aarnio was born in 1932 and studied industrial design in Helsinki, opening his own design office in 1962. His early work is in the Finnish Mid-Century style (relying on natural materials and traditional forms), but by the beginning of the 1960s he had discovered the possibilities of plastic. The "Ball" chair was designed in 1963–5 and made by the Finnish manufacturer Asko from c.1968. It was reissued by Adelta in 1992. It consists of a moulded fibreglass reinforced polyester shell on an aluminium base with soft foam-covered upholstery on the inside. Its original design made it a great success, as did the fact that it featured in the cult 1960s television show *The Prisoner* and in Mary Quant's London boutique. The "Ball" chair spawned several mass-produced variations in a similar style and while these do have a value they are not as desirable as an original example. Aarnio is also famed for his "Pastille" chair of 1968, which is an organic, pod-like ball of plastic with a moulded seat, and his "Bubble" chair of 1965, which is literally a suspended bubble of clear Perspex.

A "Ball" or "Globe" chair, designed by Eero Aarnio in 1963–5, for Asko.
**£1,500–£2,500/$2,250–$3,750**

# FURNITURE

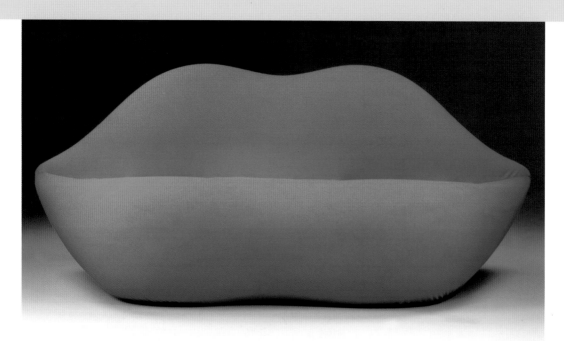

A "Marilyn" sofa, designed by Studio 65
and manufactured by Gufram in 1972.
This example was produced after 1986.
£2,000–£3,000/$3,000–$4,500

As 1960s society was undergoing a wave of counterculturalism, so was design. In the early years of the decade groups of avant-garde Italian architects and furniture designers were establishing themselves as radical and anti-designers. They were inspired by the work of revolutionary fine artists such as the surrealist Salvador Dali to challenge design in the same way that existing perceptions about art had been opposed by these artists earlier in the century. Radical designers played with people's views of what constituted a piece of furniture by introducing references from fine art and earlier 20th century design masterpieces into their work, and reworking early Modernist chairs and other furniture.

Much of their furniture looks like it has been created around an idea rather than to fulfil a functional purpose, so this challenged one of the main theories of Modernism. These designers saw modern design as nothing more than a marketing tool and believed that original Modernist ideas had now lost all their integrity. As a result they began to introduce kitsch into their work or reinterpret Modernist classics completely, such as the "Mies" chair by Archizoom (see pp.136–7) that reinterpreted the chairs of Ludwig Mies van der Rohe. Postmodernism in the 1970s and 1980s rose out of Radical design.

New materials, particularly plastic and foam, were ideal for radical design shapes as their malleable properties allowed designers to sculpt surreal, fantastic furniture shapes that would not have been possible in wood or metal. Watch out for condition of these pieces, though, as plastic can look awful when it is damaged and cannot be restored, and rips and scratches to the surface can adversely affect the re-sale value of an item.

Radical design groups included Studio 65, Superstudio (formed 1966), Archizoom (see pp.136–7), and Gruppo Strum (formed in 1966). One of the most famous designers was Ettore Sottsass (see pp.132–3). Sottsass worked with two of the 1970s most renowned groups, Studio Alchimia and Memphis, and he is still influential in design today.

Studio 65 produced the iconic and instantly recognizable "Marilyn" sofa in 1972. It is based on Salvador Dali's "Mae West" sofa from 1936, except this version is made in polyurethane foam and pays homage to Marilyn Monroe, the great screen icon of the 1950s and 1960s. The sofa was made by Gufram in Turin from 1972 to the present and is one of the best-known pieces of Pop furniture today, and as a result it is highly sought after by collectors.

A "Libro" chair,
designed by Gruppo Dam
in 1970, for Busnelli.
**£2,000–£2,500/$3,000–$3,750**

The "Libro" chair was designed in 1970 by Gruppo Dam (Designers Associati Milan) for Busnelli and produced by Gruppo Industriali in Italy. The chair is designed for reading – hence the name and witty shape – and each vinyl covered foam "page" can be turned to adjust to the needs of the sitter, so it becomes an interactive piece of art as well as a comfortable chair.

The "Capitello" lounge chair was designed in 1971 by Studio 65 for Gufram, and is modelled as a Greek Ionic capital. This provides an ironic comment that whereas Italy's architecture is long-lasting and solid, this chair, although looking the same, is actually made of foam rubber - so it is completely ephemeral in comparison. Its styling introduces neo-classical references which would be used by postmodern designers in the 1980s. Piero Gilardi designed the original prototype of this chair and Gufram is still making it today.

A "Capitello" lounge chair,
designed by Studio 65 in
1971, for Gufram.
**£2,000–£2,500/$3,000–$3,750**

# Ettore Sottsass

Ettore Sottsass (b.1917).

Ettore Sottsass (b.1917) is a radical and astonishingly inventive designer, and his huge output has included furniture, ceramics, and industrial design (particularly for the Italian firm Olivetti). He also explored the concept of total living environments in the 1960s in a similar way to Joe Colombo and Verner Panton. Sottsass used new materials, such as laminated plastics, in his furniture designs in the 1960s and this, coupled with his use of bold colour, symbols, and forms makes his work popular today.

In common with other great 20th century designers, Sottsass wanted to find his own style and solutions to design problems and this is one of the reasons why all his work is groundbreaking and he is such a favourite with collectors today. Much of his work was produced in very limited editions or as one-off pieces because many of the designs were experimental, and the rarity value makes them particularly collectable. As his work spans several decades, it is possible to collect pieces from different periods so you can trace its development, although his strong personal style is evident throughout his career.

During the 1930s, Sottsass developed an interest in painting, mainly in the strong geometric and brightly coloured canvases of De Stijl and other early Modernist groups and this love of colour is reflected across his whole output in design.

Sottsass began working in the Mid-Century style and produced fairly conservative pieces. By the late 1950s and early 1960s his more personal and radical style was appearing. His admiration of De Stijl and Japanese art can be seen in his works from the late 1950s, as they were geometric and often used square and rectangular forms and motifs. A good example of his style at this point is a brass mirror, designed for Poltronova in c.1959.

By the early 1960s Sottsass' work had developed a spiritual dimension, partly due to his travels around the world. He also became interested in Pop art as he admired its playful manipulation of mass media and other cultural images. Sottsass explored the meaning of objects in society by registering their symbols and signs and reinterpreting these in his own work.

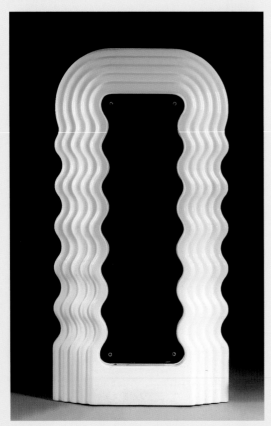

A painted metal chandelier, designed c.1956, and manufactured by Arredoluce.
**£5,350–£8,000/ $8,000–$12,000**

An Ultrafragola mirror, designed in 1970 for Poltronova.
**£800–£1,200/$1,200–$1,800**

During this decade Sottsass developed an interest in the tactile and visual possibilities of terracotta and this would come to fruition with his monumental "Totem" poles in 1966. In the "Totem" series, a giant earthenware, brightly coloured pole becomes much more than a decorative object. Its form consists of repeated elements, including circles and stripes, and it took on the importance of a piece of furniture in a room due to its size (over 2m/6½ft high). The "Totem" evokes prehistoric totems that carried spiritual as well as visual powers and Sottsass wanted people to be aware of its power when looking at it. The "Totems" were thrown and finished by hand in polychrome ceramics with white laminated wood bases and were made in limited editions over the years.

Sottsass first introduced plastic laminates into a range of furniture for Poltronova in 1965, such as the "Lotorosso" dining table shown below. With their bold primary colours, these laminates reflect Pop art and were a bright new concept in Pop and Radical furniture design.

An earthenware "Totem" from the large ceramic series, manufactured by Bitossi in 1966. This example was produced after c.1985 for a limited production.
**£3,000–£5,000/$4,500–$7,500**

A "Lotorosso" dining table, designed in 1965 for Poltronova.
**£2,000–£3,000/$3,000–$4,500**

# FURNITURE

An "S" chair, designed by Verner Panton
in 1960, and manufactured in 1968 by Vitra.
This is a later issue.
£100–£150/$150–$225

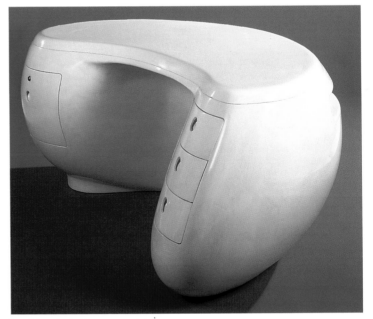

A white plastic "Boomerang" desk,
designed by Maurice Calka in 1969,
for Leleu-Deshay.
£10,000–£12,000/$15,000–$18,000

Some furniture designers exploited the possibilities of plastics, including vinyl, polypropylene, and fibreglass more than any other medium, and today their work is eagerly sought after by collectors, particularly those who specialize in collecting plastic furniture.

Plastics could finally realize the imaginative ideas of designers, and they were cheap to make, easy to keep clean (so ideal for children's and garden furniture, and in kitchens and offices), and could be moulded into hard or soft shapes for different purposes. New technological developments, such as injection moulding (where the raw material is conditioned by heat until it is fluid and then injected into a steel mould) gave designers virtually total freedom of shape for the first time.

Plastics also offered designers the chance to work with new, bright colours and they were also very strong. Further developments, such as vinyl, polypropylene, fibreglass, and polyurethane foam meant that not only could plastics look good but they could be comfortable (and comfy foam-padded chairs suited the 1960s laid back lifestyle!).

Verner Panton's "S" chair is perhaps the single most important chair of the 1960s. It was produced in 1968 by the German manufacturer Vitra on behalf of Herman Miller. The "S" chair was the first one-piece cantilevered plastic stacking chair to be mass produced. Panton originally designed it in 1960 but he had to wait for plastics technology to catch up with his idea before it could actually be made. He designed a similar chair in moulded plywood in 1956 and this broke new ground in plywood manufacture. The "S" chair was made from polyurethane and came in a variety of colours, including red and black. This chair continues to be produced today, and for a landmark example of 20th century design it is still affordable and a must for any collection. Early editions are now becoming particularly sought after and prices for these models are increasing.

The "Boomerang" desk was created by Maurice Calka (b.1921) in 1969 and made by Leleu-Deshay. It revolutionized the traditional perceptions of a pedestal desk and as such is an excellent example of Radical design. Its biomorphic shape seems to curl around the sitter. It has bulging, sack-like drawers at the sides, and a waterproof plastic surface instead of traditional leather. The "Boomerang" won the 1969 Grand Prix de Rome prize.

Gunter Beltzig (b.1941) designed the amazingly shaped "Floris" chair in 1967, and it was first exhibited at the Cologne Furniture Fair in 1968. This stacking

fibreglass chair was originally conceived as a child's chair for outdoor use but its surrealistic, sinewy form (created by moulds that were taken from Beltzig's body) made it just as appealing to adults. It was created in two pieces and suitable only for hand production so as few as between 35 and 50 original Floris chairs were ever produced in a limited run by Gebrüder Beltzig, and only five or six were finished in white, making this example extremely rare. It was reissued in red only in 1990 by Galerie Objecte in Munich in a limited edition of a thousand. These examples will have a number and the name "Gunter Beltzig" marked underneath the seat.

Peter Ghyczy designed the white fibreglass "Garden Egg" chair in 1968 for Reuter Produkts and it was produced into the 1970s. This organically styled chair could be folded down into a plastic pod for protection against the elements when used outdoors but was equally popular in the home. Examples were produced in a range of different coloured upholstery and the colour combination determines the chair's value. Bright Pop colours such as orange are more desirable than plain white versions. Condition is also important with this chair, as it is with other pieces made of fibreglass. Cracks, scratches, or dents in the body will affect the value.

*Above left*: A white plastic "Floris" chair, designed by Gunter Beltzig in 1967, and manufactured by Gebruder Beltzig.
Original: **£2,800–£3,500/$4,200–$5,250**
Later issue: **£600–£800/$900–$1,200**

*Above*: A "Garden Egg" chair, designed by Peter Ghyczy in 1968, for Reuter Produkts.
**£300–£500/$450–$750**

# Archizoom

Archizoom Associati began as an avant-garde architectural group in Florence in 1966 and led the way in Radical style. The initial members were Andrea Branzi, Paolo Degnello, Gilberto Corretti, and Massimo Morozzi. The name Archizoom is a fusion of the British architectural group Archigram and their journal *Zoom*. The group was one of the first counter-cultural syndicates in Europe to revolt against what they saw as excess and lack of meaning in modern consumer society and the pretensions of Modernist designers from earlier in the century. They produced kitsch artworks and designed objects that played with people's everyday perceptions of what constituted art and "good" design.

In both 1966 and 1967 the group organized two "Superarchitecture" exhibitions with Superstudio, another Florentine design collective. Archizoom expanded in 1968 with the addition of the industrial designers Dario and Lucia Bartolini, and began to produce furniture designs. In 1972 the group travelled to the USA, where their work was included in the landmark exhibition *Italy: The New Domestic Landscape* at the Museum of Modern Art, New York. The group were hailed as early

masters of the counterdesign movement that would come to fruition in the 1970s with Postmodernism.

The "Superronda" foam seating unit is the epitome of Pop design. It looks like a settee but can actually be rearranged to form a variety of different shapes including a flat bed or chaise longue, and as it is made of foam it is easy to move around. The "Superronda" is one of the most playful of Pop designs, with its wave-like, sculptural form and acid bright colour, intended to be more of a fun object than a serious piece of furniture. Designed by Archizoom in 1966, it came in a variety of colours including red, black, or white vinyl. This seating unit is still manufactured today, and it is difficult to tell original examples from newer ones other than by signs of general wear and tear.

The mischievously ironic "Mies" chair is arguably the first chair to be produced in the 20th century that directly mocks an early Modernist designer, in this case Ludwig

Mies van der Rohe and his extensive use of chrome-framed furniture. This makes it highly prized by collectors. It mocks the Modernist ideals of the use of exotic steel and leather in furniture as dictated by the Bauhaus designers, who wanted to design for the masses, but these materials were expensive and so Bauhaus furniture was actually only available to the rich. The seat was made from Pirelli rubber, which gave some comfort to the sitter, and the footstool was lit up by a series of small lights.

The "Safari" seating unit was made by Poltronova from 1968. Despite looking like a part of the *Barbarella* film set, this delightful object is making a serious point, although it is seen by some as the height of bad taste. It comprises two white rectangular and two square interlocking fibreglass forms, which have been cut away to create a seating and lounging area. The whole of the structure is upholstered in padded fake leopard skin, making an effect of a leopard skin rug within a piece of furniture, so challenging the viewer's existing notions of form and purpose in furniture. This seating unit was expensive to buy in the 1960s and so very few were made, hence their rarity and desirability today.

A "Safari" seating unit, designed in 1968, and manufactured by Poltronova.
**£8,000–£12,000/$12,000–$18,000**

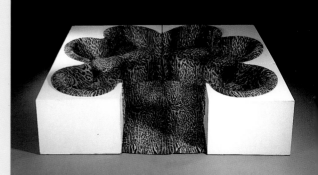

A "Mies" chair and matching footstool, designed in 1969 andmanufactured by Poltronova.
**£3,000–£4,000/$4,500–$6,000**

A "Superronda" foam seating unit, designed in 1966 and manufactured by Poltronova.
**£400–£800/$600–$1,200**

# Italy

The 1960s was without a doubt the golden age of Italian design, producing world-class designers, including the Castiglioni brothers, Joe Colombo, and Ettore Sottsass. It was a time of both experimentation and rebellion in design, which culminated in Radical style by the end of the decade.

Italy reached the peak of its economic boom in the mid 1960s, which meant there were more design-conscious customers with money to spend. Another reason for Italy's success was that the new designers were supported by manufacturers who specialized in plastics, including Kartell and Zanotta. These companies helped them to manufacture and market their work. Italian design became known throughout the world, thanks to extensive coverage in design and architecture magazines, including *Domus* and *Casa Vogue*. In 1961 the *Salon del Mobile Italia* was the first trade exhibition devoted entirely to Italian furniture, and this also made it popular worldwide.

Italian designers began to rework traditional furniture forms using new materials from the late 1950s onwards, with plastic in particular becoming very popular. The vinyl inflatable "Blow" armchair designed by De Pas, D'Urbino, and Lomazzi and manufactured by Zanotta has now become a highly collectable 20th century design icon. The widespread use of plastics went on for about a decade until the worldwide oil crisis in the 1970s, which led designers to return to more traditional materials. Italian designers were also interested in exploring the futuristic concept of total living units and Joe Colombo set the standard worldwide in this new experimental furniture form (*see pp.*140–1).

Paradoxically, as Italy was enjoying success with its more commercial modern designs in the mid to late 1960s, a new generation of designers were dissatisfied with what they saw as the empty rhetoric of Modernism and capitalism, and they rebelled against the establishment to form Radical design groups. A whole new style rejecting the key teachings of Modernism was started. Ettore Sottsass (*b*.1917) led Radical design, and its most famous groups included Studio 65 and Archizoom (*see pp.*136–7).

Giotto Stoppino's (*b*.1926) stacking tables were designed in 1968 for Kartell and are made from injection-moulded plastic. Kartell began to produce plastic household products in the mid 1950s and plastic furniture in 1967. While Stoppino's tables are not strictly modular furniture in the way that Verner Panton created whole living environments, they do stack together for ease of use, forming a neat cylindrical shape. They were light,

moveable, and affordable (the latter perhaps being most important to Stoppino, who believed that good design should be available to everyone). Their circular form reflects the geometric shapes that were popular throughout the 1960s and they were made in bright Pop colours, including orange, red, white, and black Cycolac, a type of ABS plastic that gave a shiny finish.

The "Tomato Soup" stools shown here were designed by Studio Simon in 1973 and, despite being manufactured in the early 1970s, absolutely typify the Pop style with their witty reinterpretation of Andy Warhol canvases. The designers have taken a familiar object, in this instance a stool, and completely reinterpreted it to make it look like a can of tomato soup. Campbell's cans were made famous by Warhol's paintings and silkscreens of 1962. Each stool is constructed from a metal canister (actually a recycled paint drum) with a lithographed design for the "label", and has a removable seat pad so they could also be used for storage. They were cheap to make and examples were probably discarded as Pop style went out of fashion in the 1970s, hence their value today. These stools should be labelled underneath, "Omaggio A, Warhol, Ultra mobile, Simon, Italy".

## Enzo Mari (b.1932)

Enzo Mari was born in 1932 and studied at the Accademia di Belle Arte di Brera in Milan between 1952 and 1956. He is best known for his unusual product designs that ranged from metal ashtrays to plastic vases.

In common with other Italian designers of the late 1950s and 1960s, he worked closely with and was supported by a commercial manufacturer, in this case Danese. He began working with the company in 1957 and a year later produced the unusual "Putrella" ashtray and container made of iron. Mari was a design theorist as well as a practitioner, and these objects illustrate his belief that decorative objects could be mass-produced without losing their beauty. Their plain, yet stylish shapes, consisting of a single piece of moulded iron, made them suitable for mass production.

Mari also experimented with plastics from the early 1960s and this led to several other important designs for Danese, including a PVC umbrella stand in 1962 and the very popular "Pago-Pago" vases of 1969, which were made from ABS plastic and came in a variety of colours. Mari has also worked with Olivetti, Zanotta, and Artemide, and his designs have become very collectable today.

A set of three plastic
stacking tables, designed by
Giotto Stoppino in 1968, for Kartell.
**£200–£400/$300–$600**

A set of three "Tomato Soup" stools,
designed in 1973 by Studio Simon,
for Simon International.
**£700–£900/$1,000–$1,350**

An iron section "Putrella" ashtray
(*far right*) and an iron section
"Putrella" container (*right*),
designed by Enzo Mari in 1958
and produced by Danese.
Ashtray: **£500–£600/$750–$900**
Container: **£650–£750/$970–$1,120**

# Joe Colombo

Joe Colombo
(1930–71).

Joe Colombo (1930–71) was one of the most influential and visionary designers of the 1960s, with an enormous output in his short life. He created radical designs in materials including plastic and wood. As well as lamps, clocks, tables, and chairs, he designed futuristic living units, with the aim of creating a utopian total living environment where all aspects of the design would work together to make a whole. In his own words, he wanted his designs to provide an "integral habitat".

Colombo was born in Milan, where he trained as a painter at the Brera Academy of Fine Arts before studying architecture at Milan Polytechnic. His father died in 1959, leaving Joe to run the family electrical business, and it was around this time that he began experimenting with new materials, including plastic and fibreglass, and new manufacturing methods. In 1962 he opened his own design office in Milan, and began to receive commissions for architectural and interior designs throughout Italy.

In 1964, Colombo received the IN-Arch prize for one of his hotel designs and produced his first chair design for the forward-thinking firm Kartell. This was followed by the "Elda armchair for Comfort" in 1963 and the "Universale" number 4860 chair, which was the first full-size chair to be made from injection-moulded plastic.

Colombo was interested in how the design of individual items worked together to make a whole. His pieces also had to be functional and adaptable to the needs of individuals. The "Minikitchen" is probably the most high-tech hostess trolley ever designed, enabling the food itself to be cooked in any room. Made in 1963 for Boffi, it features a hob, a pull-out work surface, a refrigerator, and storage trays, the whole unit set on castors for ease of movement. This design was extremely well received. It won a medal at the 1964 Milan Triennale and was included in the exhibition *Italy: The New Domestic Landscape* at the Museum of Modern Art in New York in 1972, along with his later "Tube" chair. In 1971 he designed a white laminated plastic "Living" centre unit for Rosenthal, featuring a pair of speaker grilles and a shuttered front, built into a wonderfully sculptural casing. By then, Colombo's living centres had metamorphosized into whole room interiors with plastic

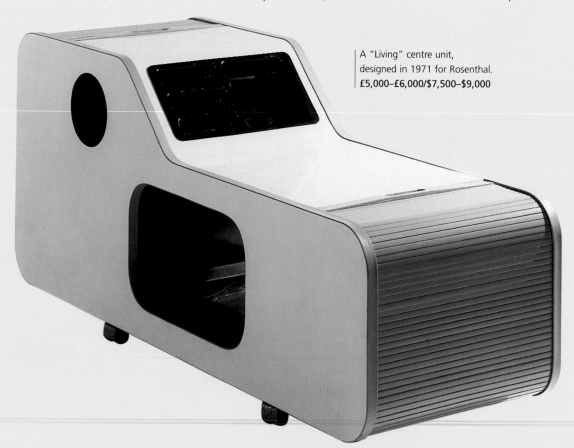

A "Living" centre unit, designed in 1971 for Rosenthal.
**£5,000–£6,000/$7,500–$9,000**

seating, lighting, and built-in television screens. The best known of these is the futuristic Central living block, shown at the *Visiona 1* exhibition in Cologne in 1969, complete with psychedelic soft furnishings and carpets.

Colombo was also hugely influential in advancing chair design, particularly the idea of multi-furniture, where a piece could work in a variety of different ways. The "Tube" chair is a superb example of this, demonstrating Colombo's love of circular forms – a trend reflected across all strands of design in the 1960s, from architecture to textiles. The chair's ingenious design meant that each of the four interlocking, plastic cylinders could be fitted together by steel and rubber joints to make various configurations, whether as upright chairs to sit in, horizontal settees to lie on, or even just a single circular stool. The chair was also extremely comfortable, as the plastic shells were covered in polyurethane foam upholstery and fabric which came in a variety of colours. It was also ingeniously packaged in a drawstring bag and could be stored away easily when not in use as the rings fitted inside each other.

A "Minikitchen", designed in 1963 for Boffi.
**£3,000–£4,000/$4,500–$6,000**

A "Tube" chair, designed in 1969 for Flexiform Prima.
**£6,000–£8,000/$9,000–$12,000**

# France

French design became known throughout the world after the landmark 1925 *Exposition* in Paris, but its commercial furniture output was severely disrupted by World War II. Some Mid-Century French designers were able to explore new furniture styles utilizing new materials, for example Jean Royère's "Bear" armchairs (*see pp.*76–77), but these were mainly very expensive commissions from private clients unaffected by the war.

In common with other European countries, France underwent a rapid period of development and economic expansion after the war and by the late 1950s the country had pretty much recovered from the devastation caused by the war. But by the mid 1960s the seeds of revolt were sown. Whereas in Italy rebellion against the establishment came through design groups such as the Radical style Archizoom, in France political unrest was displayed in a much more overt way.

In 1968 students revolted in Paris and there were mass demonstrations in the streets against the social order. Designers too had cause to rebel against a very traditional French decorative style, which in many ways was unchanged since the 19th century. French interiors were commonly filled with heavy, ornate antique furniture, which was often gilded, painted, and excessively decorated, and new fabrics and furniture for sale in shops were often reproductions of antique styles. The work of young French designers, such as Olivier Morgue and Pierre Paulin, was something completely different, and for a younger population intent on revolt their futuristic designs quickly became both popular and fashionable.

In France the key themes in design in the Pop era were space-age shapes; an inventive use of new materials; and a futuristic take on styling in the neo-organic style, which was a further development from the organic shapes popular in the Mid-Century style. Designers now had even more new materials to work with, which meant they could create increasingly dynamic, organic sculptural forms.

French furniture designers were influenced by other designers across Europe and the USA, particularly in the ways that they explored new possibilities of seating and how that seating fitted into a space. Morgue, in particular, was interested in how people sat and lived in rooms, and he wanted to explore furniture's relationship with its environment as well as to the individual.

Although France wasn't at the forefront of design in the Pop era it did produce several highly original designers, all of whom were working in the Pop style and interpreted it in their own completely unique ways. As a result, their work is increasing in value or, as is the case

with Morgue (whose furniture appeared in Stanley Kubrick's seminal 1968 film *2001: A Space Odyssey*), already has a very strong collectable value. The work of Paulin and Morgue is extremely similar and it is likely that they influenced each other.

Pierre Paulin (*b.*1927) studied sculpture at the Ecole Camondo in Paris and his classical training is reflected in the sculptural forms of his furniture from the 1960s. Paulin began his career designing somewhat conventional upholstered and metal-framed seating in the mid 1950s for the manufacturer Thonet, which was in complete contrast to his work in the Pop style in the 1960s. In 1958 he began working with the Dutch manufacturer Artifort, who went on to produce his later, more famous pieces. Paulin designed his first plastic chair, model number 157, in 1953 and this was way ahead of its time in terms of style and materials. Between 1958 and 1959, he travelled extensively and worked all around the world, including Japan, the USA, and Europe.

By the early 1960s Paulin had discovered the possibilities of new materials for his ideas and by 1965 his dynamic designs had come to fruition. He opened his own industrial design office in Paris in the same year. Like his co-designer, Olivier Morgue, Paulin's work found favour with the French authorities and he designed seating for the French government pavilion at *Expo 1970* in Osaka, and also produced visitor seating for the Louvre in Paris in 1965.

Paulin was fascinated by the forms of furniture and broke new ground with his inventive styling using foam, tubular steel, fibreglass, and polyester, typified by his lounge chair designed in 1966. By the end of the 1960s he had even created a revolutionary prototype of a long and snake-like "endless" sofa made of rigid foam, which was manufactured by the French firm Alpha in 1971.

Paulin designed lounge, dining, and commercial seating and he was always inspired by nature. This can be seen in his wonderfully organic, moulded plastic dining chair, which was made in 1968. It is perhaps the most overtly organic design produced by Paulin that does not relate to the human body (his "Tongue" chaise designed in 1967 really does resemble an outstretched tongue). The seat of this dining chair looks like a petal of an opening flower and the base appears as if it is growing out of the floor like a tree trunk, which gives the piece stability, both practically and metaphorically.

Paulin's number F598 armchair was designed for commercial use as it could be stacked and offered plenty of legroom for office workers or conference delegates underneath the seat. Constructed from a two-piece

A plastic dining chair, designed by Pierre Paulin in 1968 and manufactured by Boro.
**£400–£600/$600–$900**

A lounge chair, designed by Pierre Paulin in 1966 and manufactured by Artifort.
**£300–£500/$450–$750**

A DF 2000 chest of drawers, designed by Raymond Loewy's Compagnie de l'Esthétique Industrielle in 1965, and produced by Doubinski Frères for CEI.
**£800–£1,000/$1,200–$1,500**

tubular steel frame and covered in polyurethane foam and fabric, it is both an elegant and unusually shaped chair and very futuristic in its overall styling. It was produced in a variety of coloured fabrics, and the price of individual models today depends on the colour and condition of the fabric. His number 582 or "Ribbon" chair resembles a pair of bent human legs with their toes touching. The sinewy curvature of the chair's body comes down into a central point at the base, allowing the user to either sit normally in the chair or curl up in it. Paulin received many interior and commercial commissions based on the success of this chair. It won an Italian ADI (Associazione per in Disegno Industriale) award and was produced in variously coloured plain and psychedelic patterned upholstery by designer Jack Lenor Larsen and, as in the F598 armchair, the fabric can affect the value of an individual piece if it is worn, damaged, or in an unpopular shade or pattern.

The sculptural possibilities of new materials were also explored by Raymond Loewy's firm Compagnie de l'Esthétique Industrielle (CEI), and one of their most collectable pieces is the DF 2000 plastic chest of drawers. Loewy was born in France but based in America, and this piece shows how his design style matured and moved with the times throughout the mid 20th century. He replaced the sleek, streamlined forms that he popularized in 1950s America with pure Pop style. The plastic gives this item a fluid, sculptural, and effortlessly simple look, and its moulded plastic drawers and doors lend a uniform yet tactile feel to the whole piece.

Olivier Morgue (b.1939) became famous as a designer for both public and private commissions, including interiors for the French government pavilions at Montreal in 1967 and for Expo 1970 in Osaka. He is most famous for his expressive, neo-organic furniture based on the shapes of the human body. Like Paulin, he created fun, futuristic, comfortable, and portable chairs out of tubular steel, foam, and fabric.

Morgue trained at the Ecole Boulle and the Ecole Nationale Supérieure des Arts Décoratifs between 1954 and 1960. He spent time in Finland and Sweden in the late 1950s, so he would probably have seen the best examples of Scandinavian Mid-Century modern furniture. Morgue worked with the manufacturer Airborne from 1963 to 1966 and opened his own studio c.1965. He exhibited an entire bedroom at the 1965 Salon des Artistes Décorateurs in Paris and his work became popular in the USA, thanks to appearances in Domus and other architecture and design magazines. Like Paulin, Morgue won an Italian ADI award. After the success of his furniture designs in the 1960s he received interior commissions from across the world and went on to design interiors for major companies in the 1970s.

Morgue's most collectable and desirable furniture today is the wonderfully sculptural "Djinn" range, which included a sofa, chaise longue, and an armchair. It was designed in 1965 and consisted of a conventional tubular steel frame for the seat, legs, and back of each piece,

wrapped in urethane foam and upholstered in stretch nylon jersey. These chairs have a real personality, and both Morgue's design pedigree and their appearance in the film 2001: A Space Odyssey make them highly marketable to collectors today.

The name "Djinn" came from a shape-shifting spirit in Islamic mythology that was able to control men using its supernatural powers. This description really suits the furniture's anthropomorphic, organic shapes and the pieces do look like creatures that can spring into action and change their posture. Morgue saw a mystical and fantastic aspect in architecture and objects, and believed that this almost spiritual dimension was an integral part of their purpose, particularly in his own designs. He said, "Functionalism and rationalism cannot be the goal of design, an end in themselves; they are simply part of the honesty required for the construction of an object."

The low, squat forms of the "Djinn" range also reflect Morgue's interest in seating arrangements in relation to the body and living spaces in general. Looking back over his work in a 1983 Philadelphia Museum of Art exhibition he explained, "The good object is very moveable and displaceable; inventions and creations are light. It was in this spirit that I constructed my "Djinn" seats. In these models, simple in their construction . . . I was looking for several things: the use of new covering materials, but also lightness, so that one could carry it under one's arm. At the same time, I was concerned with something else: the floor seat or seating surfaces."

Interestingly, Morgue liked to call himself a constructor and a builder rather than a designer. So he wasn't content with just making a chair, and like Verner Panton and Joe Colombo, he was interested in entire living environments, not just furniture. By the end of the 1960s he had achieved his goal and designed a complete seating environment made out of carpeted squares on metal frames that could be moved around to make any configuration.

Plastic inflatable chairs became very popular in France at the end of the 1960s. Panton actually created the very first plastic piece of inflatable furniture in 1962 when he made a square plastic stool, but it was after the Italian designers Donato D'Urbino, Paolo Lomazzi, and Jonathan De Pas produced their revolutionary "Blow" armchair for Zanotta in 1967 that inflatable chairs became really well known. The "Blow" chair was the first mass-produced blow-up chair in Italy and thanks to extensive publicity photographs showing the designers seated comfortably on their new creations, it was widely copied and inspired other European designers to produce their own versions. In France, the principal creator of inflatable furniture was the company Quasar Khan, who sold this type of furniture through its futuristic interiors shop in Paris. Examples were also produced by other manufacturers, such as the one illustrated here. Plastic chairs were popular with both adults and children as they captured the fun and optimism of the 1960s in a way that perhaps no other piece of furniture has done since.

A late 1960s inflatable plastic armchair, designer unknown.
£200–£300/$300–$450

A "Djinn" sofa, designed by Olivier Morgue in 1965, and manufactured by Airbourne.
£2,000–£3,000/$3,000–$4,500

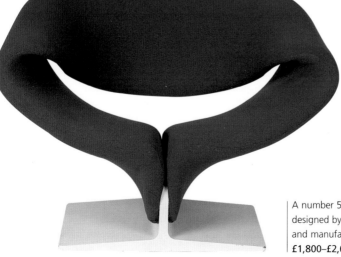

A number 582 or "Ribbon" chair, designed by Pierre Paulin in 1965 and manufactured by Artifort.
£1,800–£2,600/$2,700–$3,900

# Britain

In Britain, pop music and Pop art influenced all aspects of design from 1962 to 1972. It was also a decade of a return to mass ornament in Britain, ranging from spots and waves to psychedelic swirls. Pattern was everywhere, particularly circular and geometric patterns that came to symbolize the space age by the end of the decade. Britain embraced both plastic and throwaway furniture and some designers, including Ernest Race (see pp.72–3), continued to work with more traditional materials such as plywood, but in the Pop style.

Fashion reflected design and vice versa in Britain in the 1960s. The new styles in furniture and consumer design were popularized through extremely successful shops and boutiques, many of which became more than shops – they also became hip places to hang out. Britain led the world in shops and fashion, with Carnaby Street and the King's Road putting swinging London on the map in 1966. Biba and Habitat were launched in the late 1960s and Mary Quant's shop Bazaar opened on the King's Road, but perhaps most memorable of all was the shop Granny Takes a Trip, which changed its window display every few weeks and once featured an American car literally bursting out of the shop front. London was the place to be, and the outrageous shop exteriors and radical new pop interiors, themselves brimming with new plastic and inflatable furniture, were as colourful as the theatrically-clad shoppers themselves. Even The Beatles opened their own shop, the short-lived Apple boutique, in the late 1960s, and completed the crossover of pop music, art, and fashion.

There was practically full employment in Britain in the 1960s and economic prosperity meant a new generation of younger, more affluent consumers so many of these new shops targeted young people and teenagers. The consumer revolution and "throwaway" culture of the 1960s meant that young couples were no longer encouraged to buy good, traditional furniture that was intended to last a lifetime, but to fill their first homes with throwaway items. As Terence Conran explained in a contemporary interview from 1965, "Expendability is no longer a dirty word".

Throwaway materials touched all aspects of interior and industrial design, and even fashion. There were psychedelically-patterned paper dresses, cardboard furniture, and even inflatable plastic coat hangers, chairs, and cushions. These items were cheap to produce and cheap to buy, and were designed to be replaced like clothes, according to the latest fashion. Anything throwaway will have a value today, precisely because these pieces were meant to be expendable. Paper dresses and jewellery are particularly popular, and examples in their original unopened packaging are even rarer to find and as a result more desirable.

New, forward-thinking shops played an essential role in spreading Pop style throughout Britain. Much of the new Pop design created in Britain in the 1960s was sold through Habitat and other stores including Heal's, which actively encouraged young designers and sold the work of established designers, for example Lucienne Day's vibrantly patterned textiles (see pp.120–1).

Reasonably priced yet quality modern design became available in Britain when Habitat opened its doors in London in the late 1960s. Terence Conran, the store's founder, chose the name "Habitat" after looking up the word "house" in Roget's Thesaurus. Conran thought that everyone should have access to good design, and he wanted to make Scandinavian and Italian modern design furniture and household furnishings available at a reasonable cost to people in Britain. He believed in decent materials, such as natural timber, new plastics, and canvas and wanted the goods on sale in his store to be colourful and modern. Habitat was a great success, with a mail order catalogue launched in 1968 and more shops opening across the country in the 1970s and 1980s. The store is a familiar site on the high street today and in the late 1990s reissued a number of modern design classics, including pieces by Robin Day and Verner Panton.

Some British designers of the Pop era are remembered for just one or two designs. Peter Murdoch studied at the Royal College of Art and graduated in 1963. In 1968 he opened his own design office in London, specializing in graphics. In the same year, in conjunction with Lance Wyman, he designed the graphics for the Mexico City Olympics and he also acted as a design consultant to Hille International. He is most famous for the design of the archetypal British throwaway classic – the "Spotty" chair shown opposite. This chair was constructed from thick, Op Art patterned paperboard and was originally designed in 1963. He created the chair while still a student at the Royal College of Art. The "Spotty" chair was manufactured by the American firm International Paper between 1964 and 1965. It was aimed at children as the paperboard material made it light and the polythene coating was easy to clean and was meant to be thrown away when it became tatty. The chair had low production costs and so was also cheap to buy. It was sold in supermarkets and large stores, complete with instructions for assembly, which meant folding along lines and tucking

A "Spotty" chair, designed by Peter Murdoch in 1963.
£2,000–£3,000/
$3,000–$4,500

A chair designed by Wright and Schofield in the 1960s.
£300–£500/$450–$750

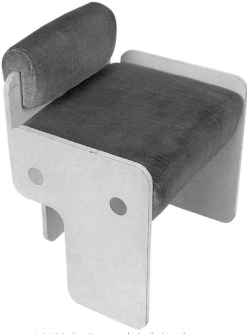

A "Maxima" range chair, designed by Max Clendining in the 1960s.
£300–£400/$450–$600

A "Penguin Donkey" bookcase, designed by Ernest Race in 1963.
£80–£120/$120–$180

flaps into slots. Only a small number of these chairs were originally made so they are very rare and highly collectable today. David Bartlett's "Tab" chair is extremely similar in style and construction to Murdoch's "Spotty" chair.

The "Spotty" Chair was relaunched and repackaged in 1967 in Britain by Perspective Designs utilizing plain paperboard. This chair was aimed more at young people and had the slogan "Fibreboard Furniture for the Young – Designed to Last" (the plastic laminate actually made them quite strong). This time, with a slightly modified design, the expanded range of chairs ("Chair Thing"), tables ("Table Thing"), and stools ("Stool Thing") were flat-packed and cleverly packaged, and were a commercial success. These chairs are also collectable today, even more so if they are still contained in their original packaging.

The British company Tomotom also produced cardboard furniture and their range was a great success in Britain and abroad, particularly in America where it was sold at Macy's department store in New York. The Tomotom design collection originated with the designer Bernard Holdaway's series of cardboard furniture made by the company Hull Traders in Britain. The Tomotom range came out in 1966 and was a complete break away from traditional furniture design. Individual pieces were essentially based on circles that could be joined together to make an overall design, or just used as stand-alone pieces. Large, strong, compressed cardboard tubes were used to make the frames of seats for furniture and tables, and then chipboard was used for the seats and table tops. The surfaces of the furniture were painted in vibrantly coloured enamels, which made them washable and strong. Optional cushions provided comfort and the strength of the materials actually made them last a long time, even though they weren't designed to have a lengthy life. One of the most sought-after designs is the six-sided "Cloverleaf" table, the shape of which is very reminiscent of Mary Quant's famous daisy logo.

The Tomotom range, like other paper-based furniture, was originally designed with children in mind but became popular with adults too. By 1969 there were over a hundred different designs in the range, including bins, lamps, and shelves, as well as tables and chairs. All of these are collectable today.

The original Biba shop was opened in Kensington, London in 1964 by the fashion illustrator Barbara Hulanicki and her husband. In 1966 the firm opened a larger shop on Kensington Church Street and began to attract a famous clientele including pop stars such as Cilla Black and Marianne Faithfull. Increasing coverage in the press and fashion magazines led to the launch of a Biba mail order catalogue in 1968. Biba products revived early 20th century ornamental styles, including Art Deco and Art Nouveau.

The distinctive Biba logo was created in 1966 by John McConnell, and featured a sinuous gold Art Nouveau flower with the Biba brand name below it. At the end of the 1960s Biba moved again, this time to an even larger store in Kensington High Street. It opened in September 1969 and an article in the *Sunday Times* hailed it as "the most beautiful store in the world". It was a real palace of opulence, with an abundance of peacock and ostrich feathers and velvet drapes. But in 1973 the company's fortunes changed when it moved into an old department store in Kensington. The new store became too big to control and it closed soon after.

The Biba collectors' market escalated in the late 1990s. Literally anything with the Biba logo is highly collectable today, whether clothes, make-up, original shop fittings, badges, playing cards, or furniture. Now is a good time to buy as items can still be bought cheaply and prices will inevitably grow as the store becomes even more recognized as an icon of its time. The table illustrated here is sure to increase in value as more and more collectors tune in to the Biba phenomenon.

## Mary Quant [b.1934]

Mary Quant's fashion designs revolutionized fashion in Britain and across the world in the 1960s. Quant brought the miniskirt and hotpants to swinging London and introduced bright, feel-good patterns based on Op Art and Psychedelia to the high street. Awarded the OBE in 1966, she has become one of Britain's best-loved designers, and her 1960s and 1970s clothes and accessories are now extremely collectable.

Quant was born in February 1934 and trained at Goldsmith's College of Art in London. She opened her first shop, Bazaar, on the King's Road in 1957, and it was immediately successful, becoming not only a cool place to buy clothes but also a hip place to hang out among the young.

Quant's designs were so popular because, like the transformation in Pop furniture and other areas of design, her look was totally new. Miniskirts were extremely daring compared to the staid fashions of the 1950s and hotpants even more so.

Original 1960s Quant fashions have become more and more collectable, and as such more expensive. Especially covetable are pieces that bear the name of her boutiques – Bazaar and, later, Ginger.

A "Tab" chair, designed
by David Bartlett c.1967.
£150–£250/$225–$375

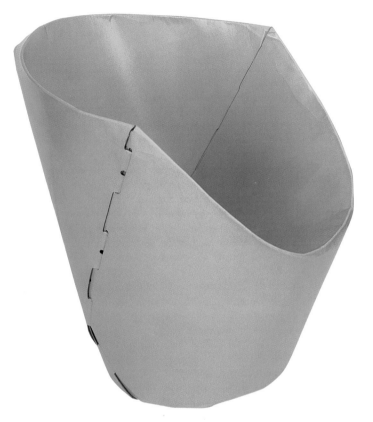

A "Holdaway" Tomotom chair,
manufactured in 1960.
£120–£180/$180–$270

A "Biba" table,
designed c.1969.
£300–£500/$450–$750

# Scandinavia

The popularity of Scandinavian modern design furniture continued throughout the 1960s – The Beatles even wrote a song called *Norwegian Wood* early in the decade. Modernist-inspired metal and new plastic furniture was popular with the young, swinging generation but many people continued to favour Scandinavian modern design for its quality and use of warm, natural materials.

Much of the furniture produced in the Scandinavian countries was unaffected by the onslaught of Pop and Radical style in the rest of Europe. Designers tended to use more durable, traditional materials such as wood, cane, and leather and continued to make furniture that was built to last. However, some designers, particularly Arne Jacobsen and Verner Panton, did experiment with new space-age shapes in furniture and lighting and explored the design possibilities of steel, aluminium, fibreglass, and moulded plastic, as seen in the rare Jacobsen side chair opposite. Designed c.1960, probably for Fritz Hansen, this chair is made from a single sheet of aluminium and came complete with a wool seat cover. It is highly collectable today because very few were made and the design might not have been developed past prototype stage. The material, too, makes it important in the history of Jacobsen's furniture design because many chairs of a similar shape were made in plywood.

Nanna Ditzel (*b.*1923) was also affected by the Pop movement in the 1960s. She explained in an interview in March 2001, "I take a great interest in avant-garde art at any time and that has an influence on my way of thinking and working."

The use of spherical shapes in furniture design, perhaps best illustrated by Eero Aarnio's "Globe" chair of 1963–5, was very popular. Hanging chairs also became fashionable and designers in Scandinavia adopted these new forms while keeping true to more natural materials, such as wood and rattan. Nanna Ditzel began experimenting with cane furniture in the 1950s when she designed a range of cane furniture with her husband Jørgen for the Italian manufacturer R. Wengler. This swinging chair was designed by the couple in 1959 and was popular from the beginning to the end of the 1960s, inspiring a host of imitations throughout the decade. Its wonderfully organic, egg-shaped form meant that people could either sit upright or curl up in the chair and it came complete with a fabric-covered upholstered seat. Nanna Ditzel described the chair as "an alternative to a rocking chair but with a freer movement." The swinging chair has been enormously successful and has been in production ever since it was designed. Jørgen

Ditzel died in 1961 but Nanna continued to design furniture for both private and public commissions. All Nanna Ditzel's work, ranging from her chairs to jewellery (*see pp.*122-3), is collectable today.

The "Hammock" chaise longue was created by the leading designer Poul Kjaerholm (1929–80) in 1965. Kjaerholm combined key Modernist styles and influences, in this case the understated elegance of chaise longues by Le Corbusier, Pierre Jeanneret, and Charlotte Perriand, and also examples by Marcel Breuer. His chair reflects Scandinavian styling through its combination of natural materials with tubular steel. The "Hammock" chaise longue is constructed from a light stainless steel frame with a woven cane seating section and came complete with an unobtrusive leather headrest to ensure maximum comfort for the sitter. Its design is similar to his cane "Easy" chair that was produced in 1955 and also had a cane seat. In the early to mid 1960s he produced a series of seating called the "PK" range and these chairs demonstrate Kjaerholm's instinctive understanding for the functionality of steel and how it could be combined with the tactile qualities of leather and woven cane.

Panton designed the space-age "Panthella" lamp (*see opposite*) for the Copenhagen lighting manufacturer Louis Poulsen in 1970. These single-form lamps consist of a hemispherical acrylic shade on a sinuous stem and cast a light that has no obvious source. Several sizes are available to collectors today.

It is still possible to buy inexpensive Scandinavian furniture from the 1960s by lesser-known designers at a reasonable price, but it is difficult to predict whether these pieces will increase in value in the same way as those by recognized designers. As more and more buyers become interested in modern design, prices will be affected but the collectability of a particular item of furniture will always ultimately depend upon the quality of its design, the condition of the piece, and its scarcity.

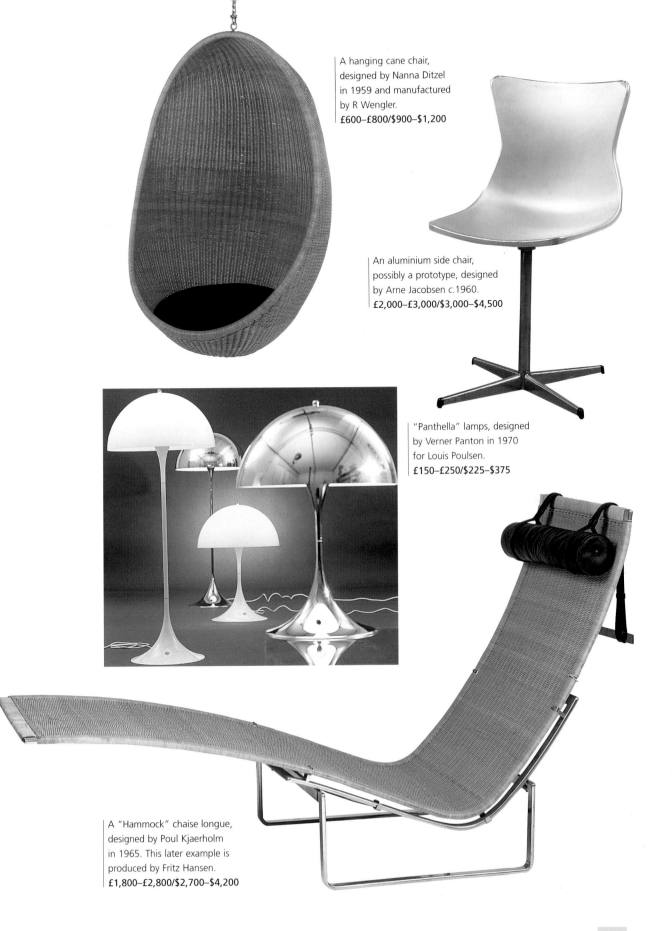

A hanging cane chair, designed by Nanna Ditzel in 1959 and manufactured by R Wengler.
£600–£800/$900–$1,200

An aluminium side chair, possibly a prototype, designed by Arne Jacobsen c.1960.
£2,000–£3,000/$3,000–$4,500

"Panthella" lamps, designed by Verner Panton in 1970 for Louis Poulsen.
£150–£250/$225–$375

A "Hammock" chaise longue, designed by Poul Kjaerholm in 1965. This later example is produced by Fritz Hansen.
£1,800–£2,800/$2,700–$4,200

# Verner Panton

Verner Panton
(1926–98).

Verner Panton (1926–98) was arguably one of the most inventive and original designers of the Pop era, and is one of the most collected and admired modern designers today. His work, whether lighting, furniture, textiles, architecture, or even inflatable furniture, was totally original when it first appeared in public, utilizing new materials and strong, bright colours for plastics, wire, and plywood. He recognized that working with these materials required radical new furniture shapes and he proceeded to create them. A contemporary magazine described him as "the enfant terrible of the Danish furniture world."

From the beginning of his career Panton brought imaginary forms into everyday households. His space-age interiors were set off with hanging, globular formed lights (see the double spiral on page 154), and co-ordinating textiles, including carpets and rugs. It is possible to recreate one of these space-age interiors today through collecting Panton design. Panton's work is much less Scandinavian than his contemporaries, although he believed in the importance of good-quality materials and construction despite embracing new, man-made materials and futuristic styling. Any original furniture by Panton will be collectable today and is of considerable value, as prices are rising all the time as more collectors begin to acquire Panton pieces and examples become harder to find.

Panton trained as an architect in Denmark between 1950 and 1952, and after graduating spent some time working with Arne Jacobsen on designs including the "Ant" chair. Panton opened his own office in 1955 and soon after this began experimenting with prototypes to create a single-form plywood chair. The "S" chair shown here was designed in 1965 for a competition and was the first single cantilevered chair to be made from plywood, although its fluid, organic design is very reminiscent of Gerrit Rietveld's famous "Zig-Zag" chair of c.1932–4. This example is extremely desirable to collectors today because it is such a rare prototype. Panton developed his design in 1965 and Thonet manufactured the "S" chair from 1966. Both white and red lacquered and natural finish examples

An "S" chair,
designed in 1965, and
manufactured by Thonet from 1966.
£1,500–£2,500/$2,250–$3,750

A "Moon" lamp,
designed in 1960 for
Louis Poulsen.
£200–£300/$300–$450

were available. The design for the "S" chair also reflects the plastic Panton chair designed in 1959–60 (*see p.*134). This was the first single-form injection-moulded plastic chair. Herman Miller acquired the production rights to the plastic chair in 1962 and the German furniture manufacturer Vitra mass-produced it in a variety of colours from the late 1960s to the present day.

Panton also began to embrace other new materials in the late 1950s and early 1960s, including fabric-covered foam and galvanized wire, which is beautifully illustrated in his "Peacock" lounge chair below and upholstered chaise longue (*see p.*155). The shape of the "Peacock" chair reflects the fan-like feathers of the bird's tail. Examples with their original fabric-covered upholstery are particularly desirable today.

Panton moved to Switzerland in the early 1960s and continued his interest in imaginative, experimental forms in furniture and lighting design. One of his earliest, most collectable lighting designs was the "Moon" lamp shown here, designed for Louis Poulsen in 1960. Consisting of a

A flower pot hanging fixture light, designed in 1968 for Louis Poulsen.
**£120–£180/$180–$270**

A "Peacock" lounge chair, designed in 1960 for Plus-linje.
**£1,800–£2,400/$2,700-$3,600**

set of circular bands arranged concentrically around a central pivot and attached to a hanging cord, the light was original because the bands could be moved around the support to create different lighting effects, ranging from a bright to a soft glow. This piece was space age in both its name and style and was used in commercial and private commissions to great effect. Its futuristic appearance and forward-thinking design in the context of Panton's early career make it particularly desirable to collectors today.

Panton's lighting designs found commercial appeal in the early 1970s when he produced a range of lighting for Louis Poulsen. Examples of these are becoming increasingly collectable today and because they were made in greater numbers than his furniture they are relatively easy to find. Among his more popular lights is the hanging fixture light (*see p.153*) and the "VP Globe".

The "Pantower" was made from a moulded steel frame covered in polyurethane foam, and was publicized worldwide by brilliant publicity photos showing Panton lounging and sitting in various positions and levels of the "Pantower". This piece of furniture was manufactured by Herman Miller between 1968 and 1969 and by Fritz Hansen between 1970 and 1975. It was expensive to produce, and had a limited market because such a large

A double spiral light, designed in 1970 for Louis Poulsen.
**£700–£900/$1,050–$1,350**

A "Pantower", designed in 1968, and manufactured by Herman Miller.
**£20,000–£30,000/$30,000–$45,000**

living space was needed to contain it. As a result few were made, which makes it rare and collectable today.

In the late 1960s and early 1970s Panton's work achieved worldwide recognition as a master of futuristic Pop design when he created interiors for trade fairs, the most famous of which is probably his undulating room installation for the *Visiona II* exhibition at the Cologne Furniture Fair in 1970. The event was organized by Bayer (a chemical company), and Panton's installations were part of a marketing and publicity exercise to show off Bayer's new synthetic home furnishings fabrics. The installation was put together in a way that meant it was possible to climb into it, sit in it, or lounge in it, and the lighting used in the exhibition gave the installation an dream-like psychedelic light of reds, purples, and blues.

A "VP Globe" light, designed in 1975 for Louis Poulsen.
**£1,200–£1,500/ $1,800–$2,250**

An upholstered 1-2-3 system chaise longue, designed in 1973 and manufactured by Fritz Hansen.
**£1,200–£1,500/$1,800–$2,250**

# STUDIO CERAMICS

"Shade", designed by
Ken Price in 1988.
£5,650–£6,200/$8,500–$9,350

A porcelain sculpture,
designed by Eileen Nisbet c.1983.
£900–£1,200/$1,350–$1,800

The international studio ceramics movement continued to develop throughout the 1960s and 1970s. Many traditionalists carried on in the Leach tradition but others were influenced by what was going on around them in other media, for example the new forms and colours of Pop design. Ceramic artists also began to work in new ways at this time – many used slab building instead of the wheel to create their works.

The market for studio ceramics from these decades is still specialized among what is a relatively small number of collectors, although more people are beginning to collect. Pieces are mainly sold through galleries and not the auction houses. Many contemporary ceramic artists are represented by galleries and the market is controlled by them. Also, a large number of these galleries are showing ceramic work alongside other media for the first time, so raising the game in terms of pricing. Some pieces are making it onto the auction market and the prices are high, which is largely due to the relatively small outputs of work and the original prices asked in the galleries.

Ken Price (b.1935) is one of the most important figures in American studio ceramics from the late 1950s and early 1960s to the present day, both in terms of driving the burgeoning American studio ceramics movement forward

and in developing his own unique style. Between 1957 and 1958 he was working with the father of American studio ceramics, Peter Voulkos (b.1924), at the Otis Art Institute in California. In the early 1960s, Price broke away from the traditional forms of pottery when his work began to reflect the wonderfully biomorphic and egg-shaped forms that were also occurring in Pop furniture. These pieces are very much surrealist ceramic sculptures and are rare and collectable today. Price lived in New Mexico between 1972 and 1980 and he continued to experiment with innovative forms and materials throughout the decade. By the 1980s, he was using new materials such as acrylic and metallic paint to create a range of lidded and other vessels that continued to extend the boundaries of traditional ceramic art. "Shade", shown above, is a desirable example of Price's work among collectors today.

The work of British ceramic artist Eileen Nisbet (1929–90) is held in major museum collections and her designs are becoming increasingly popular among collectors today. Her later work is characterized by minimal decorative techniques on elegant forms, as seen in the piece shown here. At this time, c.1980s, she was creating hand-built ceramic forms that demonstrate her

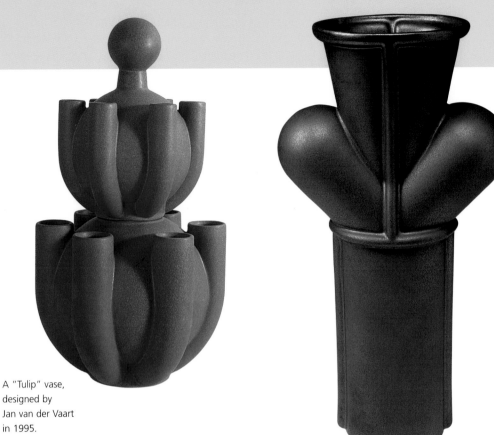

A "Tulip" vase,
designed by
Jan van der Vaart
in 1995.
£185–£200/$270–$300

A "Multiple" bronze vase,
designed by Jan van der Vaart
in 1997.
£80–£90/$120–$130

exact understanding of the materials and processes of the potter's art and how they work together to produce a unified whole.

Jan van der Vaart (1931–2000) was a leading Dutch ceramicist whose pieces are relatively affordable and widely collected, but they are highly sought after as most of them are already in museums and private collections. His work first became desirable among studio pottery collectors in the 1950s and his popularity increased in the 1960s when his work was bought by major museums collections across the world.

Vaart sculpted plain yet elegant pots using a restricted muted colour palette, including blue, white, black, and bronze. One of his most characteristic designs are his recurring, architectonic forms that make up his aptly named "Tulip" vases, which were produced from 1962 onwards. These vases really are a virtuoso display of the potter's art as they are a "modular" design. Each piece must be exactly designed and sized to fit the other pieces to make up the whole. "Tulip" vases are an interpretation of a traditional form and were made in stoneware and porcelain, and are easily recognizable. The shape of each element does vary, so some vases will have different looking parts or spouts. Each component works independently but can also be combined to create a spectacular construction.

Another key motif in Vaart's work is his love of mathematical forms, including geometric squares, cubes, rectangles, and hexagons. Many of his pieces are made up of the same cast elements in different combinations, giving a uniformity of style and making his work among the most distinctive of this period. He had a close affinity to the strict, functional style of De Stijl and the Bauhaus, and disliked ornamental or excessive decoration. He believed that his pieces spoke for themselves and as a result he did not name them. Vaart's designs have an almost mechanical quality and do not seek out the appearance of something that is handmade. His pieces are a good example of how ceramicists were beginning to work at this time. Vaart worked for major manufacturers such as the German firm Rosenthal, as well as producing one-off studio pieces, but due to their rarity his studio pieces will always be more desirable to ceramic collectors.

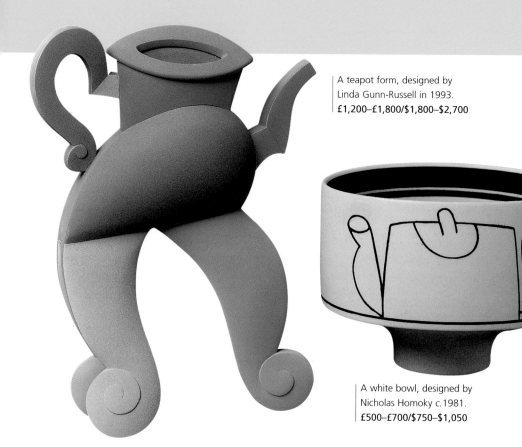

A teapot form, designed by
Linda Gunn-Russell in 1993.
£1,200–£1,800/$1,800–$2,700

A white bowl, designed by
Nicholas Homoky c.1981.
£500–£700/$750–$1,050

The work of the British ceramic artist Linda Gunn-Russell (b.1953) is also popular among collectors today. One excellent example of her work is the quirky teapot form illustrated here. Gunn-Russell is one of a generation of potters whose work shows the influence of Elizabeth Fritsh's unique language of drawn form (see p.220). Gunn-Russell's work takes this style into a more playful and decorative realm, as seen in this jaunty reinterpretation of the traditional teapot form.

The English potter Carol McNicholl was born in 1943 and trained at Leeds Polytechnic in north England from 1967 to 1970. She was a student of Hans Coper (1920–81) at the Royal Academy of Art, London, between 1970 and 1973, although her work does not reflect Coper's style (see p.111–13). McNicholl is one of a generation of studio potters who found fame in the 1970s (partly due to the influence of the Crafts Council in promoting her work).

McNicholl's work explores new colour harmonies and perspectives on the surface decoration and her ceramic objects from the early 1970s show sophisticated experiments with shade and form, some even recreating the effects of paper or cloth. McNicholl made bowls, vases, teapots, and other traditional ceramic forms in a

unique style. Some of the elements of her work are slip-cast and many pieces are almost a collage of these elements. There are two types of work: pieces which consist of many combined parts and those which are cast as a whole design. All her ceramics are hand-painted using visual motifs accentuating the shape and forms incorporated within the body of the piece, as can be seen in the coffee set illustrated opposite, with its vibrant surface decoration. McNicholl has produced hand-built studio pottery and more commercial wares from her studio. Both are collectable today although the studio pieces will always be more desirable because they are unique. Her ceramic objects will be signed underneath "Carol McNicholl".

Nicholas Homoky was born in 1950 in Hungary. His family moved to England in 1956 and settled in Manchester. He studied at Bristol College of Art and then the Royal College of Art in London, where he was taught by sculptor and artist Eduardo Paolozzi (b.1924) and, to a lesser extent, Coper. Like McNicholl, Homoky showed his work in Crafts Council exhibitions and this helped bring it to the attention of collectors and patrons.

His polished porcelain pieces are instantly recognizable as their inlaid designs look as if the decoration has been

A coffee set,
designed by Carol McNicholl
in 1991.
£500–£700/$750–$1,050

drawn on with a thin, black pen. The ornamentation is very simple, often just abstract black bands, which look particularly dynamic when applied to bowls and cylinders. The design is etched into the body of the vase before firing and black slip is applied.

Homoky's pieces represent a unique fusion of graphics with clay, combining two-dimensional caricatures of ceramic forms placed onto three-dimensional forms, so visual games are played out in clay. Homoky is fond of this theme, which started during his early studies at Bristol College of Art when he began experimenting with graphic and print design. He liked the effects he made and transposed them to ceramics.

Yasuo Hayashi (b.1928) lives in Kyoto, Japan. He trained as a painter at the Kyoto Arts and Crafts School from 1940 and in 1945 he entered the Kyoto Art Professional School. He became increasingly interested in ceramics (his father was a potter) and began to create his own distinctive ceramic sculptures from the late 1940s onwards. His pieces have included both small-scale ceramic sculptures and large-scale public commissions. Hayashi's pieces can be characterized by his graceful use of curved lines and surfaces, which are often offset by straight lines as seen in the piece here.

A stoneware sculptural form
"Focus 84-8", designed by Yasuo
Hayashi in 1984.
£1,400–£2,200/$2,100–$3,300

# STUDIO GLASS

"Bird", designed
by Alessandro Pianon
in 1962 for Vistosi.
**£800–£1,200/$1,200–$1,800**

"Pop Goblet",
designed by Gunnar Cyren
in 1967 for Orrefors.
**£200–£400/$300–$600**

Studio glass became an international phenomenon in the 1960s and pieces began to have fewer national characteristics. Young designers influenced by the Pop culture began to use glass to create fantastic art forms and to produce vibrantly coloured pieces with fluid shapes that had no real precedent in the history of glass.

Many artists worked with glass after training as fine artists or ceramicists, recognizing the new Studio Glass movement as an ideal way to express their individuality. As with ceramics, it is difficult to break studio glass up into movements in the way that is possible for furniture, instead it has been more of a continuous development since the 1970s with artists developing and continuing their own styles.

Throughout the 20th century outside influences altered the appearance of glass and the Pop era was no exception. Pop Art and its culture invaded all spheres of design including glass. In America and Italy this could be seen as early as the mid 1950s, but in Europe and Scandinavia it occurred in the mid to late 1960s. The background conditions in America were also more suited to the new wave of artist blown work in independent studios, whereas in Europe designers were largely attached to the major glasshouses. The European

designers were not necessarily stifled by these conditions since they were largely encouraged to develop and experiment with their work. These conditions did, however, mean that until the late 1960s European work developed along a different route to that in America.

The Italians, with their often brightly coloured and abstracted wares, imitated the spontaneity of art being produced during the post war era. Dino Martens (1894–1970) designed glass equivalents to Abstract Expressionism for Aureliano Toso in the 1950s, which was directly attributable to his background as an artist. Many of the pieces of Venini & Co. also exhibited a painterly approach, as did some items by Ermano Toso (1903–73) for Fratelli Toso, and the work of Ansolo Fuga for AVEM. Alessandro Pianon (1931–84) produced some quirky bird designs in 1962 for the leading Venetian glassworks Vistosi (*see above*), which seem to epitomize the exuberant attitudes of young people at the time. There are five different birds in this series.

A deeply engraved glass vase,
designed by Erik Höglund
1955–60 for Boda.
£600–£800/$900–$1,200

Seven bottle vases,
designed by Nanny Still
c.1958 for Riihimaki.
£700–£900/$1,050–$1,350

The Scandinavians, with their in-house workshops and designers, were also responding to prevailing artistic and cultural influences. Although experimentation was encouraged within these studio workshops the designs being produced did not display the freedom of expression that was coming out of America with the Studio Glass movement. It was the emergence of this movement in the early 1960s that was to revolutionize concepts and challenged the accepted Scandinavian design structure, particularly in Sweden, through the growth of independent workshop studios spear-headed by Asa Brandt (b.1940) on her return from England and a Royal College of Art course taken by Samuel Herman (b.1936).

Gunnar Cyren's (b.1933) notable work for Orrefors between 1959 and 1970, winning the Lunning Prize in 1966, included designs for engraved and acid-etched items. It was the unexpected "Pop" glassware of 1967 and his "Patriotic" series of enamelled wares that confirmed his versatility. The "Pop Goblet" shown here comes from the series started in 1967 and displays the multi-coloured stem that is the signature of this range.

Not so typical is the larger, angular chalice interpretation of the "Pop Goblet" (see p.162) designed by Kaj Franck (1911–89) in 1968. Unlike the Orrefors pieces, manufactured as a production run, Franck's goblet is an example of only a few made and differs in its dramatic scale. Other decorative goblets designed by him, such as the "Pokaaki" series of coloured cylinder-like bowled glasses, with built-up sectional coloured stems, and the "Sargasso" series of clear globular bowled pieces with hollow stems and foot internally decorated with random bubbling, were put into production around the same time.

It was the Finns who produced some of the less restrained Scandinavian pieces of this decade, notably the work of Oiva Toikka (b.1931), which captured the mood and style of the time with the way he combined experimental techniques with bright colours. Tapio Wirkkala (1915–85) and Timo Sarpaneva (b.1926) remained at the forefront of Finland's production. In 1964 Sarpaneva designed the "Finlandia" series of textured pieces, which were produced by blowing into a wooden mould with a charred surface, the heat of blowing leading to a variation in each piece.

A "Banjo" vase, designed
by Geoffrey Baxter in 1966 and
manufactured by Whitefriars in 1967–9.
**£450–£650/$675–$975**

"Pop" chalice (possibly unique),
designed by Kaj Franck c.1968
for Nuutajärvi Nötsjø.
**£800–£1,000/$1,200–$1,500**

Designing for Riihimaki another Finn, Nanny Still (b.1926) also captured the spirit of the decade in her work. The austere lines of the "Ambra" range of 1960 made way to the spiky "Pine Tree Top" series of 1963 that made use of subtle transparent pinks and blues. It was her handling of colour and modern forms that typified her work from the 1960s. The bottle vases (see p.161) were designed at the end of the 1950s and were so popular that they continued in production throughout the 1960s.

Erik Höglund (1932–98) of Boda Glass, Sweden introduced a range of wares that combined both bright colours (red and orange) with a style that echoed, in a restrained way, the freedom of American studio glass. Much of his work had a freer use of line than expressed in the vase (see p.161), and reflected the fact that he was a sculptor. His work ranged from functional vessels to highly sculptural pieces with pressed and textured surfaces.

Per Lutken of Kastrup and Holmegaard in Denmark is noted for his simple, transparent, sometimes asymmetrically formed pieces from the 1950s and early 1960s. In the latter part of the 1960s he designed a brightly coloured "Carnaby" range and at the very end of the decade his work began to exhibit the influence of the freedom within the modern Studio Glass movement. The

piece illustrated opposite reflects his desire to produce textured items, yet although it was designed in the 1960s, it was not actually produced until the early 1980s. He was successful, however, in making free-blown studio ranges in 1969 and 1970. The first range was mainly of cuboid forms with swirled brown and ochre decoration, followed by an opaque white range with random splashes of colour.

Although British glass manufacturers continued to employ their in-house designers, their approach was far less radical than manufacturing competitors in Scandinavia and Holland. Unlike those countries, there was generally a restraint in the working parameters governing design in the English factories. Although some of the cut and engraved glass continued to be highly stylish, the Stourbridge manufacturers in particular relied on their traditional markets of conservative cut glass, for which they were famed throughout the world.

Geoffrey Baxter (1926–95) also had constraints upon him, yet Whitefriars had long been associated with forward thinking, and it was this decade that produced some of the Baxter designs that are most highly prized among today's collectors. It is his textured pieces, designed in 1966, that are largely regarded as the high point of his work. The original designs were based on

Two "Forest-Art" pieces,
designed by Helena Tynell
in 1966 for Riihimaki.
**£800–£1,200/$1,200–$1,800**

pieces of bark that he collected and used to form a mould to make prototypes. Naturally this was too fragile to use for production, so three-part cast iron moulds were made to make the glass. Other patterns in the series used staggered blocks of wood to produce the form, some used nail heads to make textures, others had drilled holes, or were gauged with chisels. The "Banjo" vase illustrated opposite, as the largest and most imposing in the series, is generally regarded as the pinnacle of a Baxter collection. These pieces were usually coloured, often brightly, while Finnish textured glass was invariably clear.

There are parallels between Baxter's textured pieces and work produced by the Finns, particularly that of Sarpaneva, but also of Still and Helena Tynell. Sarpaneva's "Finlandia" series of 1964 is an obvious example, as well as Tynell's "Forest-Art" series from 1966 (*see above*). The architectural, sculptural "Forest-Art" pieces with their powdered-in colours also owe something to the Studio Glass movement with their free use of colour. It is thought that Baxter had seen and was influenced by the Finn's work. However, it may be that he did not see these textured wares until after the launch of his own range. Indeed, Wirkkala did not produce his textured tablewares until the late 1960s and early 1970s.

A "Lava" vase,
designed by Per Lutken c.1960 and
manufactured by Holmegaard in 1983.
**£400–£600/$600–$900**

Hot-blown vases,
designed and manufactured
by Samuel Herman in 1972.
£200–£400/$300–$600

During the 1950s there were a few individuals working away from the framework of industrial companies in America. They were Maurice Heaton, whose origins in glass-making came via Britain where his family worked in stained glass prior to moving to America; Michael and Frances Higgins, and Edris Eckhardt. Heaton used colour and lamination to great effect in his work.

Michael Higgins emigrated to America from England and was originally a graphic designer before moving into photographic reproduction. He eventually became the head of the Visual Design Department at the Institute of Design, Chicago. Michael and Frances went into partnership, particularly making fused, brightly-coloured enamelled glassware and glass jewellery, both individually and together. The ceramicist and sculptor Edris Eckhardt was also working in a similar way to Heaton and the Higgins, with the use of laminating in her initial work.

In many ways this "group" of artists were the forerunners of those who followed in the succeeding decades and traits of their work can be seen in the pieces of later designers. The big difference was the freedom displayed in the work of the later designers from the 1960s onwards. This freedom was inspired by seminal workshops held at the University of Wisconsin, America,

in 1962 under the guidance of Harvey Littleton (b.1922). The new availability of small furnaces, advances in refractory technology, and the easy access of standardized materials, combined with a formula for low-melting temperature glass – produced by Dominic Labino (1910–87) at these 1962 workshop seminars – produced a renaissance both in attitude and in the production of glass. This break through meant that an individual could design and make glass with relative ease and away from the industrial furnaces used by the major commercial producers. It led to a freedom akin to that experienced with other media such as the production of ceramics, textiles, and more obviously, fine art.

Samuel Herman moved to Britain in 1965 from America, where he had been studying at the University of Wisconsin. He went to Edinburgh College of Art, where Helen Munro Turner (1901–77) was Professor of Glass. Herman's revolutionary ideas, rooted in the new style of American free-blown glass, were totally alien to such an environment. In 1966 he was awarded a Research Fellowship at the Royal College of Art and in the following year he set up the first short course at that college. Michael Harris (1933–94) set up the first hot-glass blowing facilities at the college, after attending a lecture

by Dominic Labino (1910-87). Herman taught here until 1974 and had a huge influence on British glass students. His personal style was freely expressive and he produced strong forms that had a fluid style encapsulating swirling colours (see the pieces opposite).

Labino had been a major factor in the establishment of the Studio Glass movement in America. He set up his own glass workshop in 1965, retiring from a career in commercial glass technology and going on to develop his free-form method of expression. His work took two directions; one was the opening up of an asymmetric bubble form to produce an item and the other was the production of many layered pieces within a solid, sometimes giving a cascading effect. Many of these latter pieces are referred to as the "Emergence" series and were produced over many years. The piece shown above demonstrates stages in his colour experimentation.

While these pieces by Labino were entirely produced by hot-glass blowing techniques, other artists were beginning to develop in different directions, using techniques such as laminating or casting. Tom Patti (*b*.1943) has become one of America's foremost designers of glass. His work is painstaking and achieves a simplicity that belies its technical complexity. His glass sculpture

*Left*: A glass sculpture, designed and executed by Tom Patti in 1979.
**£2,500-£3,200/$4,000-$4,800**

*Above*: A glass sculpture from the "Emergence" series, designed and executed by Dominic Labino in 1984.
**£8,000–£10,000–$12,000–$15,000**

shown above is a transitional item, and depicts how glass was moving from the functional to the purely artistic.

The political structure and glass traditions in Czechoslovakia meant that its industry progressed in a different way to the rest of the world. There was a natural development process that produced art glass and sculptural work, in addition to providing functional glass for the home market and luxury glass to export. At the major world fairs it was the Czech's large-scale sculptural pieces that attracted most attention. René Roubíček (*b*.1922) was awarded the Grand Prix at *Expo 58* in Brussels for his glass collage. This piece had an important influence on the rest of the glass world, helping to change the course of working in the West in the 1960s.

# TEXTILES

The textiles of the Pop era are famous for their strong use of dynamic patterns and colour, often reflecting Op Art or Psychedelia. Pop textiles are easy to spot as their designs (frequently made up of bold geometric patterns or flowers) will be reduced to simple elements such as scrolls, circles, squares, and waves and their colours will be intense, including pinks, greens, oranges, and reds.

Textiles that are signed by a known designer or produced by a recognized manufacturer such as Heal's will always be attractive to collectors and will be worth much more than pieces by an unknown designer.

Collecting textiles is a great way to bring Pop style into your home, provided you are prepared to display them with care. Rugs and carpets need to be professionally cleaned (although gentle vacuuming is fine) and wall hangings and tapestries should never be attached directly to the wall but must be mounted onto backing board or ideally placed behind glass. Never expose a textile to direct sunlight or the colours will fade. Condition is paramount when buying textiles because as a general rule (the exception being if a piece is very rare) textiles that are threadbare or discoloured will not retain their value.

Wall hangings were extremely fashionable in the 1960s and heavy wool textiles and carpets also became

A wool carpet, designed by Pierre Cardin c.1968.
**£700–£1,000/$1,050–$1,500**

common, as large-scale murals were needed to fill wall space in open-plan and loft apartments. Styles spread from continent to continent through design magazines, and many of the leading furniture designers were also producing textiles.

Rugs, wall hangings, carpets, and lengths of fabric by Pierre Cardin (*see above*), Lucienne Day (*see pp.*120–1), and Verner Panton (*see opposite*) are particularly collectable today. Finnish textiles are also becoming desirable, and in the USA the textiles of Ray Eames are already fetching a premium. Also worth looking out for is fabric designed by Barbara Brown for Heal's; clothing by Mary Quant (particularly from the early 1960s) and Biba, and fabric produced by the Edinburgh Weavers Co. One of the fastest growing collectable areas in 1960s and 1970s textiles today is clothing produced by the British designer Ossie Clark. These pieces are especially sought after if the fabric was designed by his wife Celia Birtwell, who created superb prints utilizing floral and other motifs.

"Geometry 1" carpet, designed by Verner Panton c.1960.
**£1,500–£2000/ $2,250–$3,000**

The textiles by Verner Panton that are featured here have all the characteristics of Pop style with their dynamic, abstract designs based on circles, squares, and wave-like motifs. The geometric carpet is of particular note as it was designed in 1960 and featured in an exhibition installation in Zurich in 1961. Its pattern is heavily indebted to the Op Art paintings of Bridget Riley (*see p.*179).

## Pierre Cardin textiles

In the early 1950s Pierre Cardin (*b.*1922) worked for major fashion houses including Chanel and Christian Dior before starting his own fashion house, presenting his first Haute Couture collection in 1953. In the early 1960s Cardin was quick to recognize the new consumer power of young people and he utilized new materials in his work, including mouldable, fire-resistant, and washable fabrics.

By the mid 1960s the Cardin name had become a brand in its own right, and appeared on everything from sunglasses to wigs. Cardin clothing and textiles are much sought after at the time of writing, especially his space-age and futuristically styled costume and his rugs.

Cardin began to design rugs in the late 1960s and the example shown opposite is as much a fashion item as a home furnishing. He wanted to create a fusion between the clothes that people wore and their home furnishings. Rugs and carpets bearing Cardin's favourite motifs – circles, waves, and target patterns – are particularly collectable.

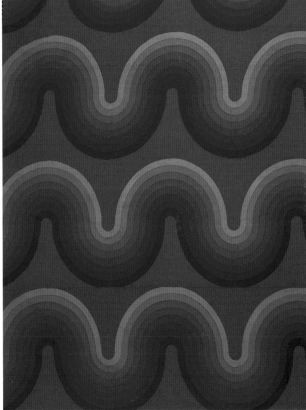

One from a set of four lengths of fabric, designed by Verner Panton in 1969 for Mira-x.
**£300–£500/$450–$750**

# JEWELLERY AND METALWARE

An "Alveston" stainless steel service,
designed by Robert Welch in 1958.
**£150–£200/$225–$300**

Robert Welch was born in 1929 and trained at the Birmingham School of Art and Design and at the Royal College of Art in London. By 1955 he had set up his own studio in Chipping Campden, southwest England, a place already famed for its metalwork because it had been the home of Charles Robert Ashbee's Guild of Handicrafts which led the English Arts and Craft movement in handcrafted metalware at the end of the 19th century.

Welch was one of the most successful metal designers of the 1960s because he was fully aware of the possibilities of mass production techniques and combined these with good design. In 1954 he travelled to Sweden on a scholarship where he studied industrial design and learnt how to adapt his silver designs into the more affordable stainless steel medium. He joined the English company Old Hall in 1958 and by 1959 had designed "Bistro", the first of his cutlery ranges, and by 1961 "Alveston" which would prove to be one of Old Hall's bestselling ranges. The "Alveston" and "Bistro" ranges have a fluidity and form that was inspired by the abstract expressionistic canvases of Jackson Pollock (Welch had seen his works on display in London in 1959).

By the mid 1960s there was a clear definition between Welch's silver and stainless steel wares, with the silver being much more exclusive, although in 1965 a range was developed and created by Heal's called the "Present Choice", which was vibrant and modern, and allowed Welch's silver to reach a larger market. Today, Welch's silver pieces are much rarer than his mass-produced stainless steel pieces, and the latter are still very reasonably priced although they are getting more expensive. Much of his silver is in private collections as these items were often made to order.

The Danish designer Arne Jacobsen (*see pp.* 100–103) produced cutlery for Michlesen (its futuristic design helped secure it a place in Stanley Kubrick's epic film *2001: A Space Odyssey*) and metal tableware for Stelton, all of which has become collectable in recent years. The beautifully fluid and organic designs that appear in his furniture translated easily into metal and the same effortless elegance of his most famous chairs can be seen in his flatware.

The mass-produced "Cylinda" line for Stelton was Jacobsen's most successful commercial design. It was

A silver candelabra,
designed by Stuart Devlin in 1965.
**£4,500–£5,000/$6,750–$7,500**

A silver tea service, designed
by Robert Welch in 1963.
**£3,500–£4,000/$5,250–$6,000**

extremely popular in modern homes in the 1960s and 1970s as an outstanding and fashionable example of good Danish design, and has now found a new cult status in smart retro-styled homes. It is still in production, although earlier pieces are more desirable to collectors. The "Cylinda" line included tea, coffee, and cocktail ranges (see p.170).

Stuart Devlin was born in Australia in 1931 and studied art at Melbourne College in 1957 where he took a degree in silversmithing and jewellery. As a talented student with a keen eye for good design, he was awarded scholarships, including one that took him to the Royal College of Art in London. In 1965 Devlin moved to London and opened a design studio and workshop, aiming to change the face of contemporary silver design and bring silversmithing up to date. Not only were Devlin's methods of production modern but he also mixed gold with silver to create modern, rough hewn bark effects. This technique become Devlin's signature style and makes these pieces instantly recognizable and collectable today.

In 1967 Devlin received a Royal Warrant as Crown Jeweller further elevating his position in Britain. Devlin now designs metalware ranging from trophies and medals to coins. He is mainly known in Australia for his coin and

A coffee service,
designed by Stuart Devlin in 1959.
**£7,500–£8,000/$11,250–$12,000**

A stainless steel "Cylinda" line coffee pot, designed by Arne Jacobsen in 1961.
**£150–£200/$225–$300**

medal designs (in 1964 he won a competition to design the new decimal coinage for Australia) and he has designed coins for over thirty-six countries, including the Sydney 2000 Olympic Coin. Today his silver is very expensive but pieces are only ever designed within his own workshops, which gives them an instant guarantee of authenticity and a strong provenance for the future. The coffee service (see p.169) on the previous page uses both silver and nylon in its construction, is incredibly rare and desirable.

Bjorn Weckstrom has been one of Finland's leading jewellery designers since the 1960s and his work is highly collectable today. He was born in 1935 and studied at the Goldsmiths School in Helsinki in 1956. Weckstrom ran his own workshop from 1956 to 1963 and worked for the jewellery firm Laponia from 1963 onwards. In 1981 he returned to independent design.

Weckstrom's design was a complete stylistic break from the traditions and ethics of contemporary Finnish design. His work is unrestrained with a beautifully naturalistic expression. Weckstrom never sketches preliminary drawings on paper but instead models them from clay, and this gives his work its immediate, organic quality. At an early stage in his career he went to the

Northern territory of Scandinavia to pan for gold and it was here that he became fascinated with the naturally occurring properties of this material.

The space race and the communications explosion in the 1960s fascinated Weckstrom and this can be seen in his work. He used a hands-on approach to designing through models. Very little drawing work was done and his main designs were created using a dentist's drill and scalpel on lumps of wax or plaster to achieve a solid form from which a mould was taken. Weckstrom believed that plastics would be an important material of the future. He also used silicon, resin, and silver, which were ideal for the sensuous shapes of his items. Weckstrom wanted to create small scale sculptures that represented people's emotions in the new Pop area, essentially playing on people's feelings of being lost in a strange new world. He did this by placing tiny figures in the resin parts of his silver objects. "Petrified Lake", one of Weckstrom's early pieces, was adopted by the artist Yoko Ono in the 1960s. This connection makes this piece one of Weckstrom's most famous and collectable designs today. "Icarus" was designed as a result of Weckstrom visiting an exhibition in New York about the effects of drugs on mankind. It was here that he began to understand a feeling of the human

A necklace and ring set,
designed by Torun-Bülow-Hübe in 1962.
**£1,000–£1,500/$1,500–$2,250**

race being lost in space and time.

Another collectable designer from the period is Torun-Bülow-Hübe. She was born in 1927 and studied at the National College of Art, Craft and Design in Stockholm. She designed from her own studio in the city from 1951 to 1956 and also worked in France between 1956 and 1968. While in France she developed her later, more sculptural jewellery including her famous neck torque with moss agate. These pieces of jewellery became works of art in their own right and fetch high prices at auction today.

Torun-Bülow-Hübe won a gold medal at the Milan Triennale in 1960 and has produced freelance work for Georg Jensen since 1967. Her designs are rooted in the Scandinavian modern design tradition but also show the influence of her travels. Her work is inspired by nature and she often combines natural materials such as pebbles, horn, and shells with silver. In her early work she simply strung these found objects onto silver torques and wires and these early pieces are very rare.

Her output as a jewellery designer has been immense and later jewellery designed for Georg Jensen is easier to find nowadays. You can buy pieces of her new jewellery from Jensen today and these will no doubt represent a good future investment.

*Top*: "Petrified Lake" ring,
designed by Bjorn Weckstrom in 1971.
**£800–£1,200/$1,200–$1,800**
*Above*: An "Icarus" ring,
designed by Bjorn Weckstrom in 1969.
**£800–£1,000/$1,200–$1,500**

# LIGHTING

A "Topo" ("Mouse") lamp,
designed by Joe Colombo c.1969.
**£150–£200/$225–$300**

"Mefistole" ceiling light,
designed by Ettore Sottsass
for Stilnovo in 1970.
**£500–£700/$750–$1,050**

The 1960s Pop style was perfect for lighting design, allowing new materials such as Perspex, plastic, and chrome to be modelled into futuristic, fun, and inventive shapes for both private and public spaces. Collecting lighting is an excellent way to accumulate representative styles of the period, as it is possible to track the development of avant-garde shapes from furniture and other products to mass-produced lighting available on the high street. Lighting by recognized designers such as Joe Colombo already attracts premium prices, but well-designed high street examples in the Pop style are a good and inexpensive way in which to begin a collection and their value is sure to increase in the future as examples become harder to find. As with many other collectable items, pieces in their original packaging or in unused condition can be particularly collectable. As a general rule watch out for broken or replacement light shades as this can affect the value. Some classic designs such as the "Arco" lamp are still made today.

In the 1960s and early 1970s designers began to explore the possibilities of lighting, not just in terms of form but also for effects. Pop and Radical interiors needed appropriate and co-ordinating lighting, and so designers worked to create lamps and fittings that would give soft atmospheric lighting or directional control according to the required purpose. Technical innovations such as fibre optics were new and offered plenty of opportunities for lighting designers to create original, futuristic effects. Lighting also became oversized, with pendant and floor lamps being particularly popular. Achille and Pier Giacomo Castiglioni's "Arco" lamp became a dominant part of room furnishings in many fashionable homes, and the enormous angle poise lamp shown opposite, designed by Gaetano Pesce, would have literally filled an entire room.

While some designers favoured a more creative approach, others continued to work with existing shapes and formats. The desk lamp had been a best seller since the early days of Modernism in the late 1920s, but by the Pop era it had become much more sophisticated. Colombo produced his "Topo" lamp in c.1969 and it retained the basic desk lamp design but brought it right up to date. The "Topo" is made from painted enamel and could be used either on its base or clamped onto a table.

A "Taraxacum" ceiling light, designed by Achille and Pier Giacomo Castiglioni in 1960 and manufactured by Flos.
£200–£250/$300–$375

A "Moloch" giant angle poise lamp, designed by Gaetano Pesce in 1970-1 and produced as a limited stamped production by Bracciodiferro.
£40,000–£53,500/
$60,000–$80,000

Radical style allowed designers to create lighting that was bold, brash, and challenged people's perceptions of how lighting should look in the home. Ettore Sottsass junior designed his "Mefistole" ceiling light for the manufacturer Stilnovo as a reaction to standard forms in lighting, and these lights would fill a room, hanging down from the ceiling. Each light is 1m (3ft) long and consists of a chrome shaft finished off with a red and black enamelled shade. They are readily identifiable by the "Stilnovo" trademark on the metal ceiling bracket of each piece.

Ettore Sottsass' lighting designs also reflected the new shapes and materials of his furniture. The bright blue "Asteroide" lamp (see p.174), made from ABS plastic, was also produced in pink. Both are extremely rare. Sottsass designed similar lamps in 1969 with rippled edging. These can still be found today and are called the "Ultrafragola" or "Super Strawberry" lamps. They have pink neon tubes inside them and when turned on become like a giant pink cloud. They are perfect pieces of Pop art.

An "Asteroide" lamp,
designed by Ettore Sottsass in 1968.
£4,000–£5,000/$6,000–$7,500

A "Snoopy" lamp, designed by
Achille and Pier Giacomo Castiglioni
in 1967 and manufactured by Flos.
£500–£700/$750–$1,050

The monumental "Moloch" angle poise lamp (see p.173) designed by Gaetano Pesce is the ultimate example of how radical styling was applied to everyday objects, in this case the desk lamp. The idea of a desk lamp has been taken completely out of its usual context and turned into a work of art, as this lamp is some four times bigger than an average size desk lamp. Measuring an incredible 2.3 x 3.12m (7½ x 10¼ft) this articulated light is constructed from gold and silver metal alloy parts and was based on an original design by the Swedish designer Naska Loris. Each example will have a Perspex plate attached bearing the maker's name "Bracciodiferro", a company set up by Pesce to promote his own designs, and an edition number. This lamp was made in limited quantities, and the highest serial number recorded on examples that have survived today is 27. Its rarity and unusual size make it highly desirable and important to collectors today.

Achille and Pier Giacomo Castiglioni were perhaps the most inventive lighting designers working in the Pop and Radical style and their names are two of the hottest in modern design collecting today. The "Taraxacum" ceiling light (see p.173) is one of their more organic styles and they produced several similarly modelled hanging lights in the early 1960s. These lights were partly inspired by George

Nelson's experiments with cocoon-like plastic lighting in the USA, and also by their quest to create original shapes and utilize new technology. The "Teraxacum" lights were made by spraying a film of plastic polymer over a metal frame, which gave a wonderfully light and cocoon-like shape to the finished lamp. Many of these would have perished over the years or been thrown away so they are becoming increasingly difficult to find today.

The architect and designer Achille Castiglioni (b.1918) has designed everything from lamps, telephones, and car seats to furniture. He studied architecture at Milan Polytechnic in the late 1930s and ran a design office with his older brothers Livio and Pier Giacomo in Milan in the 1940s. Due to World War II there were restrictions on materials and large-scale commissions, so the brothers initially specialized in smaller design products, including radios and a range of very successful cutlery. In 1939 they created the "Phonola" radio, which was the first Bakelite radio to be manufactured in Italy and won a gold medal at the Milan Triennale in 1940. Their experiments in lighting design were recognized as early as 1951 when they exhibited the "Tubino" light at the Milan Triennale, which was simply a piece of bent tubing with a lamp. It was radical, elegant, and practical, and one of their

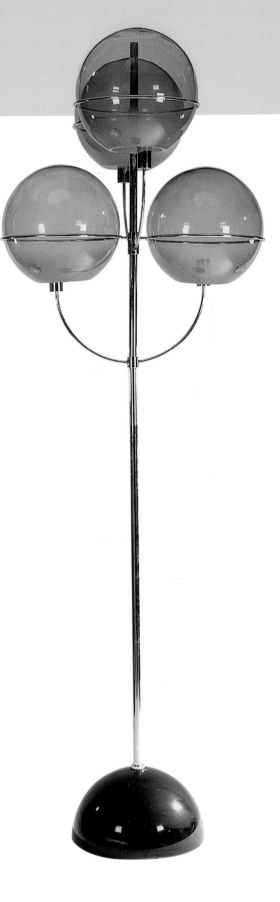

A "Colleoni" lamp,
designed by Vico Magistretti in
1971 and manufactured by Knoll.
£1,000–£1,500/$1,500–$2,250

earliest original lighting solutions. Pier Giacomo died in 1968 but Achille continued designing solo for companies, including Knoll, Kartell and Flos, and for Alessi in the 1980s.

Achille Castiglioni's designs work so well because they are imaginative and could actually be created. He re-examined existing objects and re-thought them in terms of form and manufacture, embracing new technology to create witty, unusual but inherently practical designs that also reflected popular culture. Castiglioni developed a long-term professional relationship with the manufacturer Flos, which was founded in 1960 by Dino Gavina and Cesare Cassina. The firm wanted to create lighting that complemented their modern furniture designs and that would appeal to a younger generation of shoppers. Castiglioni's self-assured style can be seen to great effect in his popular "Snoopy" lamp of 1967 (*see opposite*), which was named after the famous cartoon character. It has a highly expressionistic and quirky shade, which is very reminiscent of a dog's snout. Constructed from glass, metal, and marble, this lamp is a wonderful example of how Castiglioni mixed new and traditional materials, as the marble gives an elegant and stable base for the more modern glass and metal body of the lamp. Another highly creative design by Castiglioni was the "Boalum" lamp created for Artemide in 1969, which looks like a boa constrictor rearing up to strike.

Vico Magistretti (*b.*1920) was another influential and popular lighting designer from the Pop and Radical era. In the 1950s he concentrated on architectural commissions, but by the 1960s had discovered the sculptural possibilities of plastics, producing furniture for Cassina and plastic lighting for Artemide, both of which are collectable today. These lighting designs were very much in the Pop style, with their globular and circular shapes and coloured plastics, but Magistretti also produced more conservative lights. The "Colleoni" lamp was designed in 1971 and manufactured by Knoll and its design reflects traditional street lamps with its smoked glass shades. The example shown here is an early and rare example (the lamp was not manufactured in great numbers until 1977 when it was made by O-Luce production). Original "Colleoni" lamps will be stamped "K Collection Amp 1971 Venice", and examples are still being produced today.

# PRODUCT DESIGN

By the mid 1960s Pop style had filtered into domestic and office products, many of which were becoming electronic. This new technology needed designs that were fresh and forward looking and a host of goods from calculators, clocks, and televisions to radios and kitchen utensils were produced in multi-coloured plastics and decorated with Pop-inspired graphics. Many of these were mass-produced so are relatively easy to find today and are still inexpensive. Product design was practically dismissed as a collecting area until recently, but is now growing in popularity. Objects with their original packaging are even more desirable.

Ettore Sottsass (b.1917) designed for the Milan-based company Olivetti from the late 1950s, and by the mid 1960s had made European office design his own. He is perhaps best remembered for his later work with the Memphis Group, but his late 1960s and early 1970s typewriters for Olivetti are undoubtedly mass-produced masterpieces. Sottsass's ideas were driven by the design possibilities of an object, not the marketplace, and as such they were never great commercial successes and did not compete against inexpensive Japanese electrical goods.

The "Valentine" typewriter is possibly Sottsass's most vibrant typewriter design but despite winning the 1970

"Valentine" typewriter, designed by
Ettore Sottsass c.1970 for Olivetti.
**£100–£120/$150–$180**

Compasso d'Oro award it was only manufactured for a year and a half. His brief was to create a low-cost, portable typewriter that was easy to use, and he achieved this with ease. He said, "I wanted it to be a kind of 'biro' among portable typewriters." Sottsass removed the capitals and other service keys, designed the shell in a bright red plastic with a portable carrying case that was as much a fashion statement as a useful object, and gave the typewriter a light-hearted name. He wanted to bring colour and fun into offices, believing the "Valentine" would brighten up people's lives. This typewriter was much more streamlined than the large, bulky manual typewriters that were a common sight in offices across Europe at the time and as such was extremely radical.

By 1969, not only had Neil Armstrong walked on the moon but also over 18 million people in Britain alone owned a television set and were able to watch him take that first historical step. In the 1950s television was dismissed by some as an expensive novelty but by the end of the 1960s it had turned into an everyday piece of home

Grundig "Super-Colour" TV, c.1970.
**£1,000–£1,500/$1,500–$2,250**

Cardboard clock, designed by Paul Clark
c.1960 for Perspective Designs Ltd.
**£200–£250/$300–$375**

furnishing. Colour television, however, was still relatively new and big manufacturers such as Philips and Grundig wanted to promote their latest innovations to a younger, design-conscious audience. They did this by making sets in new materials such as plastic, and in space-age oval and spherical shapes. By the early 1970s, remote control models had also been invented and were on commercial sale. The Grundig "Super-Colour" TV (*see above*) is a wonderfully stylish early example. These sets are highly collectable today as only 2,250 of them were ever made, in colours including white, black, and brown. It is possible to buy vintage televisions that have been reconditioned to receive waves and transmit pictures today, but they still make great decorative objects in their own right, even if you can't actually use them.

Domestic design was also affected by the 1960s vogue for throwaway products, perhaps best illustrated by this cardboard clock (*see above right*) designed by Paul Clark for Perspective Designs Ltd. With its typical Pop throwaway case and funky, bold lettering it has become a collector's classic. Examples are already becoming rare as many of them would literally have been thrown away.

# GRAPHICS

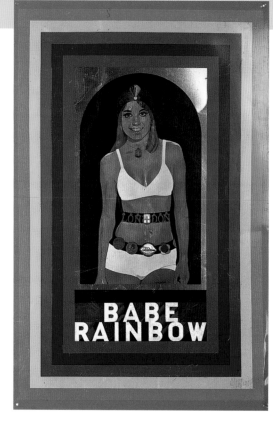

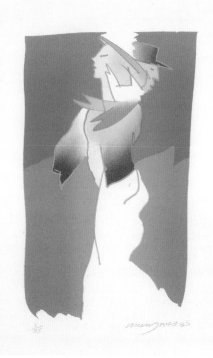

The 1960s was the decade when Pop Art came of age after its success in the 1950s through the works of Richard Hamilton, Roy Lichtenstein, and Robert Rauschenberg. There was a thriving avant-garde art scene in both Europe and the USA, and Pop Art paintings, graphics, and prints are now highly sought after by a new generation of collectors.

Developments such as silkscreens and screenprints (a printing technique that uses stencils and gives a flat image, making it ideal for reproduction) meant that modern art was much more available to art collectors and the public in the 1960s, and lifted it out of the realms of art galleries for the first time. During this decade the vibrant art scene spread into all aspects of design and everyday life, for example the Op Art paintings of Bridget Riley (*see opposite*) were extremely popular and their repeating psychedelic patterns appeared on dresses, furnishing fabrics, and in graphic design.

In Britain, key artists whose work is collectable today include Peter Blake, David Hockney, and Allen Jones. Peter Blake (*b*.1932) is best known for his love of images from popular culture such as comics, adverts, and packaging. His paintings rework these pictures into new iconic images that have already become a fascinating

*Above left*: A printed metal portrait of the female wrestler Babe Rainbow, by Peter Blake for Dodo Designs, 1968.
**£200–£300/$300–$450**

*Above*: A screenprint by Allen Jones, 1985.
**£400–£500/$600–$750**

legacy of the time. Ephemeral personalities such as Babe Rainbow, an imaginary female wrestler, are captured in fun and brightly coloured works that instantly immortalize them, as in this printed metal portrait (*see above*) that dates from 1968 and was created for Dodo Designs in London. Only a hundred of these tin screenprints were made, hence their collectability today.

Allen Jones (*b*.1937) is a painter, sculptor, printmaker, and designer. His prints have only recently become collectable as his best known works are pieces of furniture modelled as life-size women dressed in fetishistic clothes. His prints mainly depict women in exotic clothing and poses, as seen in the example here. The prints he produced in the 1960s now appear regularly in specialist auctions.

One from a set of nine Campbell's soup can screenprints, designed by Andy Warhol in 1968.(for the set)
**£10,000–£15,000/$15,000–$22,500**

"Study for Painting; Four Colours, Black and White, Green Bias", gouache on paper, by Bridget Riley, 1981.
**£500–£600/$750–$900**

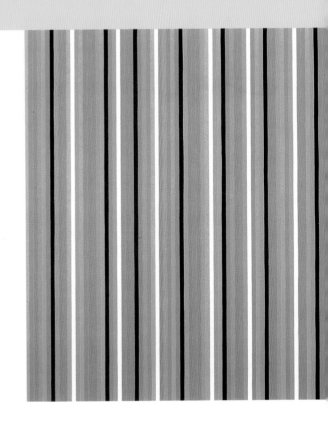

Andy Warhol (1928–87) was perhaps the most charismatic and flamboyant personality of the American Pop Art scene. He began experimenting with Pop Art during the early 1960s before unveiling a series of 32 paintings of Campbell's soup cans in 1962 (*see above*). These were exhibited in Los Angeles in the same year, and Warhol quickly found worldwide fame by introducing the playfulness of Pop Art to the public for the first time through lifting an everyday example of packaging design into the traditional realms of high art.

Warhol's other famous images include multiple portraits of Jackie Kennedy, Marilyn Monroe, and Elvis Presley, and pictures of Brillo soap pad boxes and Coca-Cola bottles, many of which were created at his appropriately named studio, The Factory. His celebrity images are extremely sought after and original examples can sell for tens of thousands of pounds. Silkscreen printing meant that Warhol's images could be produced over and over again, but the Campbell's soup can remains his most famous work. In 1965 Warhol officially resigned from art to devote his time to making films and managing the rock band The Velvet Underground, but he continued to produce portraits right up until his death.

## Bridget Riley

Bridget Riley was born in 1931 and studied in London at Goldsmiths College and the Royal College of Art. She was the leader of the 1960s Op Art movement, whose followers produced paintings that gave the effect of optical illusions.

Her first works in this style date from the early 1960s and were executed mainly in black and white. She found international acclaim when her paintings were shown in New York in 1965. By 1966 she was creating colourful paintings that gave an effect of movement on the canvas by using repeat forms such as straight lines, rippling waves, and stripes in an all-over pattern. The names of her paintings, including "Turn and Drift" illustrate this effect.

Riley won the International Painting Prize at the Milan Biennale in 1968 and she also produced designs for interiors and for the theatre. Her work has been issued as limited edition screen- and silkprints, and these are a very affordable way to own a piece of her work today.

*Left*: The Beatles, *Sergeant Pepper's Lonely Hearts Club Band*, designed by Peter Blake in 1967.
**£50–£80/$75–$120**

*Above*: *Magical Mystery Tour*, photograph taken by John Kelly with drawings by Bob Gibson, 1967.
**£40–£60/$60–$90**

The 1960s was the key time in music revolution. Pop music was born in this decade, whether it was the fabulous hits of The Beatles and The Rolling Stones in Britain or the folk-inspired songs of Bob Dylan, the up-beat sounds of the Beach Boys, or the rebellious psychedelic anthems of The Doors in the USA. By the middle of the 1960s young people across the world were taking the words of acid guru Dr Timothy Leary quite literally and tuning in, turning on, and dropping out. It was the decade of festivals such as Woodstock and the Isle of Wight, and apart from the music itself one of the most evocative legacies of this era are the often wild and wonderful music posters and album covers that were produced by Pop artists.

Posters and artwork created for the biggest stars of the 1960s attract the highest prices and are eagerly sought after by collectors, especially in the USA. Fillmore posters (named after the Fillmore Auditorium in San Francisco) are very popular at the time of writing, particularly those advertising concerts for rock legends such as Jimi Hendrix, Janis Joplin, Jefferson Airplane, and The Grateful Dead. The venue's promoter, Bill Graham, produced these posters and by the end of the decade thousands had been printed. They were not meant to survive, being ephemeral adverts for the current show, but many were taken down by fans and preserved. Concert handbills, designed to be given out as promotional goods can also attract a premium, as can record company promotional posters, counter-top displays from shops, and even ticket stubs. Do, however, look out for signs of display such as tape pull and stains, staple marks, moisture damage, and printing errors, which can all affect the value of printed graphic artwork.

Jimi Hendrix (1942–70) became the star of late 1960s psychedelic rock thanks to his technically brilliant guitar playing and fabulous fashion sense. When he died in September 1970 he immediately became a rock icon and anything relating to Hendrix is now extremely collectable. His career was short so he only released a handful of albums. The second of these was *Axis: Bold as Love* in 1967, and the cover depicts Hendrix surrounded by Indian music which reflects the vogue for this type of music that was entering the world of rock and pop at this time. The Bob Dylan poster advertises a documentary film about Dylan's 1965 UK tour when he was accompanied by Joan Baez and Alan Price, and it is suitably psychedelic in style.

The Beatles also worked with Pop imagery through the covers of *Sergeant Pepper* and *Magical Mystery Tour*. The

latter was made for a television film featuring The Beatles that included the hit songs *I am the Walrus* and *Your Mother Should Know*. The soundtrack from the film was released in December 1967 on the Parlophone label and was the first-ever double EP. The film and the soundtrack have now become cult classics among Beatles fans. They were released at the pinnacle of the band's later career when their music was fragmenting into new directions.

Peter Blake designed the cover artwork for *Sergeant Pepper's Lonely Hearts Club Band* which has become one of the most famous album covers of all time. It is a brilliant example of the links between art and music that were so strong in the late 1960s. The cover shows The Beatles in the guise of the Sergeant Pepper band with cut outs of their idols, ranging from Marilyn Monroe and Bob Dylan to Fred Astaire, Albert Einstein, and Marlon Brando. It shows Blake's love of circus imagery, badges, rock and roll stars, and costume to great effect. The Beatles went on to commission the Pop artist Richard Hamilton to design the minimal cover of their later *White Album*.

*Above left*: Bob Dylan documentary advertising poster for the star's 1965 UK tour.
£400–£500/$600–$750

*Above*: A copy of Jimi Hendrix's album *Axis: Bold as Love*, designed by David King and Roger Law in 1967.
£150–£200/$225–$300

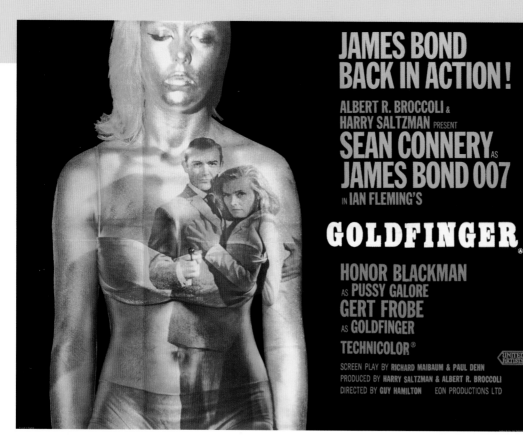

Film posters are much more than advertising tools. They capture the spirit of their time and immortalize the major Hollywood stars of the day. They have been collectable in America since the 1970s and their popularity has steadily grown in Britain, with specialist sales of posters becoming more and more common.

Posters are a particularly affordable collecting area, with prices beginning at around £100–£200/$150–$300. Rare images, including those for desirable films or those that feature a famous star will command very high prices. Posters from the golden age of Hollywood tend to be more expensive than those from later decades. The highest price ever paid for a film poster at auction was £300,000/$450,000 for the 1932 horror film *The Mummy*.

In America from the 1960s onwards, posters could be obtained directly from the National Screen Service. Greater quantities therefore became available for collectors. As a result of this, examples from this decade will be much easier to find than those from the early days of Hollywood.

The most common form of poster available to the collector today is the paper one-sheet, which was made in a standard size of approximately 104 x 70cm (41 x 27in) and is almost always found with two horizontal folds and one vertical fold. The British version of the one-sheet is

*Goldfinger*, 1964, United Artists, British quad poster, 76 x 100cm (30 x 40in).
**£600–£900/$900–$1,200**

the quad poster, measuring 76 x 100cm (30 x 40in). Even rarer are paper three-sheets, which measure 206 x 100cm (81 x 40in) and were printed in two or even three separate sheets. These posters were made to be pasted onto walls or billboards, and so very few survive. However, larger posters do not necessarily command higher prices as they can be difficult to display. Lobby cards were printed on heavy board and are much smaller and consist of a title art card that gives production credits and seven further cards showing photographic stills from the film, generally known as scene cards.

The condition of posters is important, except for very rare examples where only several copies exist. As British and American posters become harder to find, demand is growing for those printed for a film's release in Europe, and posters from Sweden, Poland, and Czechoslovakia are now beginning to appear on the market and at auction.

You can theme a collection around actors and actresses; directors; genres such as science fiction or horror; cult films (particularly from the 1960s); or enjoy posters purely for their artwork.

*Barbarella*, 1968, Paramount,
British quad poster, 76 x 100cm (30 x 40in).
**£300–£500/$450–$750**

*2001: A Space Odyssey*, 1968, MGM, American
one-sheet poster, 104 x 70cm (41 x 27in).
**£3,000–£4,000/$4,500–$6,000**

James Bond posters have seen a surge in prices since the late 1990s with a poster for *From Russia with Love* or *Goldfinger* selling for up to £1,000/$1,500 in the current market, whereas in the earlier years of the last decade they could be picked up for around £200/$300.

The film *2001: A Space Odyssey*, directed by Stanley Kubrick, includes key themes of the 1960s such as space travel and predictions of a space-age future. The poster for *2001* shown here is particularly unusual. It was made to be pasted as advertising around New York City and so few examples survive. It is also extremely representative of its time, with a filtered image of an eye appearing from a burst of typically psychedelic blue and orange colours and an acid-fuelled strap line "the ultimate trip".

Jane Fonda was one of the big stars of the 1960s, and her most famous film is undoubtedly the space fantasy *Barbarella*. It was released in 1968 and quickly gained a huge cult following that is still strong today. Robin Ray designed the artwork for this poster, which with its psychedelic colours is a piece of pure Pop Art.

# POSTMODERNISM
# TO THE PRESENT DAY

# POSTMODERNISM TO THE PRESENT DAY

Postmodernism grew from the 1970s into the 1980s as a style which opposed the Modernist idea that form followed function. Objects with a rich use of colour and strong elements of symbolism, as well as imagery for the mass media and everyday life were produced. Commonplace motifs were also used in design. "Postmodernism" is a very loose term and is used right across the arts from literature to furniture design to describe a state of mind in society in the 1970s and 1980s, as well as a design trend. While it is difficult to accurately describe what Postmodernism is, in general the term represents a complete rejection of Modernist principles and ideas.

Postmodern designers saw the sleek, cool, plain, and unadorned lines of Modernist architecture and furniture as cold and elitist and set out to turn the design theories from earlier on in the 20th century on their head. They also saw Modernism as having fallen short, and the utopian ideals of Le Corbusier's complete living systems and the Bauhaus designers' belief that good design would lead to a better society were cast aside as failures.

It was, however, only the theory of past design they rejected. In the 1970s and 1980s designers took signs and symbols from the past and added them onto new design as ironic comment, for example the precise forms of classical

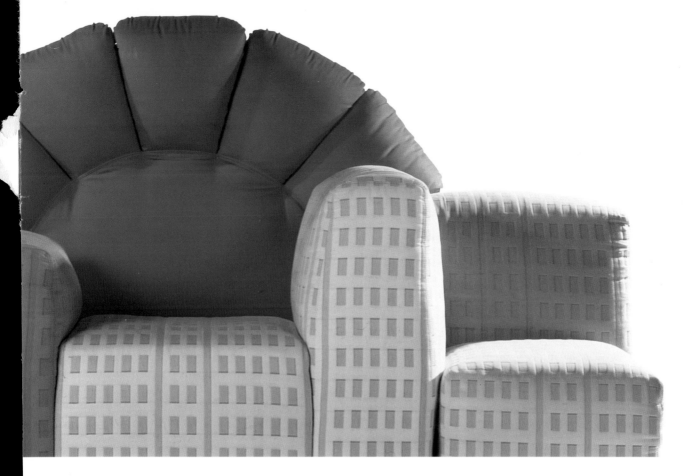

architecture appeared on a teapot. Styles including Art Deco, De Stijl, Pop Art, and Surrealism were reappropriated into the new Postmodern design. The Memphis designers reworked Art Deco styling with new and often unexpected materials, such as multi-coloured plastic laminates which looked more at home in a kitchen than on a piece of furniture, and so mocked everyday notions of good taste.

Postmodernism is extremely eclectic, designers were like magpies picking up styles from different periods and areas and merging them into new ideas. Postmodernism crossed over into all aspects of design, including furniture, glass, and fashion. By the early 1980s, designers were turning away from making items for mass markets and were concentrating more on producing one-off pieces for specialized and often very wealthy clients created by the economic boom of the decade. Materials that had never been used in design before were appropriated and reworked by those experimenting with salvaged materials. The star of this movement was Ron Arad (*see pp.*198–203).

Other design to come out of the mid 1980s to the present day includes the work of avant-garde designers from Europe and Japan who created their own looks that stand alone from Postmodernism. From Japan these have included Shiro Kuramata and Rei Kawakubo. In Britain, after a positive reaction to his Royal College of Art graduation, Jasper Morrison developed many designs for European manufacturers. The Australian Marc Newson has also found fame through his early aluminium experiments and designs from 1985 onwards, including the "Event Horizon" table in 1992 and more recently his creation of a concept car for the 21st century for the Ford Motor Company.

Today many firms are reissuing 20th century design classics, and modern design in one form or another is appearing in a growing number of homes. We now live in a society that is becoming increasingly design literate and the design classics of the last century are now incredibly fashionable.

Postmodernist designers experimented with colour, texture, and irony, wittily combining architectural elements into domestic designs for tea services or sofas, as can be seen in this New York "Sunrise" settee, which was designed by Gaetano Pesce in 1980 for Cassina. £4,000–£6,500/$6,000–$10,000

# FURNITURE

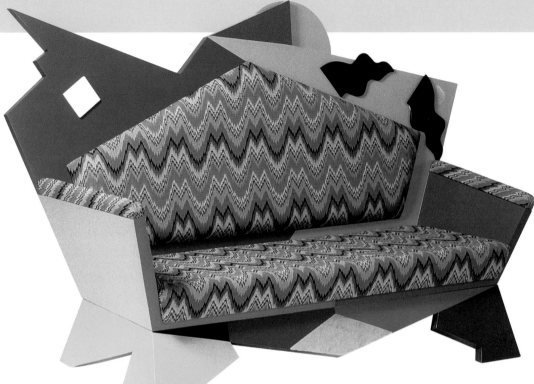

taly continued to be at the forefront of avant-garde design in the 1970s and 1980s. Following on from the original Radical design groups established in the late 1960s, more groups formed in the 1970s and they were part of the second wave of Italian radical design. The new groups, Studio Alchimia and Memphis being the most prominant, achieved worldwide recognition for their work and also sowed the seeds of a new design that became Postmodernism in the 1980s. The work of designers from these groups is already attracting large sums of money and prices will no doubt keep on rising as good examples become harder to find.

Many of the big name Radical designers of the 1960s, particularly Ettore Sottsass and Alessandro Mendini, continued to play a major part in Radical and later Postmodern design in the 1970s and 1980s. At the time design was very experimental and many pieces of furniture and lighting never made it beyond the concept drawing stage. The pieces that were finally made have become extremely collectable because of their rarity value.

The architect Alessandro Guerriero founded Studio Alchimia in Milan in 1976 with the philosophy of "materializing a non-existent object into being and doing

A "Kandissi" sofa, designed
by Alessandro Mendini in 1978
for Studio Alchimia.
**£8,000–£10,000/$1,200–$1,500**

things others consider impossible". Alchimia was a gallery space that displayed one-off experimental work that was either not suitable or not intended for mass production; so it can be argued that Alchimia was an art movement as well as a design group from the start. Sottsass, Andre Branzi, and the Florentine architect Michele de Lucchi joined Studio Alchimia in 1977.

The Alchimia name is derived from alchemy, a mythical process far removed from the scientific, rational, modern world, and it is significant that it was adopted by designers who wanted to set themselves apart from the mainstream with their fantastic, other-worldly designs. Annual exhibitions of the designers' work were held in the gallery.

The original line-up of Alchimia lasted only a few years with their first and second famous exhibitions – *bau.haus I* and *bau.haus II*. In 1980 Sottsass and Lucchi felt the group had become too intellectual so they left to develop their own project, which became the Memphis Group. But Studio Alchimia carried on producing designs and

A "Proust" armchair,
designed by Alessandro Mendini
in 1978 for Studio Alchimia.
**£6,000–£8,000/$9,000–$1,200**

A "Sinerpica" lamp,
designed by Michele de Lucchi
in 1979 for the bau.haus collection.
**£600–£1,000/$900–$1,500**

exhibiting them throughout the 1980s. Pieces were manufactured by a subsidiary called Atelier Alchimia and were only ever made in small quantities because of the limited market for expensive avant-garde furniture, hence their desirability to collectors today. Later designs by Mendini are often signed, as are pieces by Nuova Alchimia (a new series of manufactured furniture made by Zabro from 1984). These will be stamped "Zabro".

The Studio Alchimia designers rejected the Modernist principle that the form of an object should be more important than its decoration. Instead, they believed that applied decoration gave furniture its meaning and so meaning in design was now found in decoration alone. Also, due to the recession in Italy, many manufacturers were making traditional styled, plain furniture so Alchimia set out to bring a riot of colour back to design.

Alchimia pieces ranged from chairs, tables, and desks to lighting and mirrors. Apart from the bright colour, the furniture can also be recognized by its creative shape, as pieces are often angular, geometric, and have highly patterned and decorated surfaces. Materials, too, were highly experimental, with pastel-coloured laminated plastics, chrome, glass, and sharply-cut, angular plywood essential to the Alchimia style. Alchimia designs are easy

A unique chair from the "Infinite" series,
designed by Alessandro Mendini in 1981.
**£2,000–£3,000/$3,000–$4,500**

A unique "Scivolando" mirror chair
from the "Timeless Object" collection,
designed by Alessandro Mendini in 1983.
**£12,000–£18,000/$18,000–$27,000**

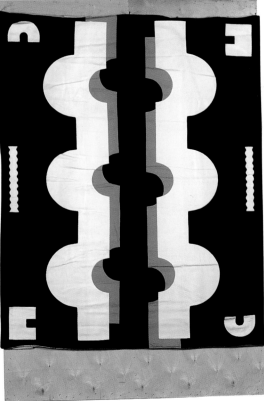

A cotton wall hanging, designed by
Alessandro Guerriero and Alessandro Mendini
in the 1980s for Museo Alchimia.
**£600–£800/$900–$1,200**

to spot because the members of the group reworked everyday and existing furniture designs with the addition of early 20th century motifs and themes ranging from the Art Deco style to the Bauhaus. This was because they believed that there could be no more truly original furniture designs, which was a key theory of early Postmodernism.

Alchimia designs were also intended as an ironic comment on society itself, with references to contemporary and past culture and even contemporary politics. Everyday and kitsch items were thereby elevated to the status of high-quality workmanship in a highly imaginative and intelligent way.

Mendini is arguably the central figure of Studio Alchimia and was its chief exponent in the 1980s when the group had split apart. He was born in Italy in 1931 and trained as an architect at the Polytechnic of Milan. He became a partner in Nizzoli Associati, an important firm made up of industrial designers, until 1970. Mendini was also involved in the radical architecture group Global Tools and was editor of the journal *Casabella* from 1970 until 1976. He founded his own periodical, *Modo*, in 1981 and became chief editor of the famous *Domus* journal between 1980 and 1985. He produced work for the Alessi

company at the same time.

Mendini believed in the concept of "banal" design because he thought that most mass-produced objects were literally banal and boring. To counteract this he applied bright surface decoration to his work, as can be seen in two of his best-known furniture designs – the redesigned "Wassily" chair and "Proust" armchair. He also experimented with mirrored surfaces, examples of which are the "Scivolando" chair (*see above*) and the fantastic "Kandissi" mirror (*see opposite*).

One of Studio Alchimia's most collectable designs today is based on what is possibly the most iconic chair of the early 20th century. Marcel Breuer's "Wassily" or "B3" chair (*see p.28*) designed in 1925–27, with its aluminium frame and archetypal Bauhaus styling, became Mendini's redesigned "Wassily" chair in 1978. Mendini took Breuer's chair and literally applied it with different coloured splodges of material. He also redesigned another

A "Kandissi" mirror, designed
by Alessandro Mendini in
1979 for Studio Alchimia.
**£1,000–£1,500/$1,500–$2,250**

20th century classic, Gio Ponti's "Superleggera" chair, by adding coloured motifs to it. Mendini's designs are fairly intellectual as they require the viewer to have an existing knowledge of 20th century design in order to identify that the original piece has been redesigned. His "Wassily" chairs became works of art as they were not mass-produced and were shown to the public through exhibitions. This gives them their collectable value today.

Another key collectable design is Mendini's "Proust" armchair (*see p*.189), which dates from 1978. He took a reproduction of a traditional, ornate armchair and literally covered it in tiny multi-coloured squares of paint in acidic colours including yellow, blue, and pink. The decoration became the primary element of the design, so challenging the Modernist teaching that form should follow function. The chair's name refers to the famous French writer Marcel Proust so it also makes a cultural reference.

The "Kandissi" sofa (*see p*.188) is perhaps Mendini's most extravagant design. It was created in 1978 and produced in 1980 as part of Studio Alchimia's ironically named bau.haus I collection. The sofa was loved by some and greeted with bewilderment by others. Mendini reworked a traditionally-styled Biedermeier sofa by adding garishly coloured wood cutouts in the style of a Kandinsky painting – hence the name. The walnut-veneered wood is just visible at the front of the sofa but it is the vibrantly coloured painted panels and beige and cream patterned fabric that make this piece so unusual and instantly recognizable. This sofa is a fantastic hybrid of art and design, and breaks new ground by fusing two separate disciplines, Biedermeier and Postmodern, in a unique way.

Michele de Lucchi produced designs for both Studio Alchimia and Memphis in the 1980s. His lighting designs are particularly innovative although many have remained at concept drawing stage. Born in 1951 in Italy, he went to Milan to work as a designer in 1978. It was here that he met Sottsass and became involved with the activities of Studio Alchimia and later the Memphis Group. In the early 1980s he became a consultant to Olivetti and was one of the founder members of Memphis. Lucchi's "Sinerpica" lamp (see p.189), designed for Studio Alchimia in 1979, is highly representative of his work and the Alchimia style.

# Memphis Group

The Memphis Group began with a designer's house party in 1980 and ended after it had successfully left its mark on everyday design and fashion throughout the world. The group was a truly international collective of extremely talented, visionary architects and designers who joined together to create a new design that reacted against Modernism and its belief in function over decoration. Ettore Sottsass, a founder member of the group, said, "A Memphis table is decoration. Structure and decoration are one thing."

Memphis formed in Milan in 1981 and grew out of Studio Alchimia's Radical style in the 1970s. Sottsass left Alchimia to pursue a new direction, and the idea for Memphis was born in December 1980 when young designers including Michele de Lucchi, Barbara Radice (Sottsass's wife), and Martine Bedin discussed their ideas for a new, revolutionary design for the next decade.

Memphis was named after the Bob Dylan song "Memphis Blues" that was supposedly playing at the party where the idea came about, but the name was also chosen for its other cultural and pop references, not least its being the homeplace of Elvis. The group executed hundreds of drawings and plans for their new designs before meeting again in February 1981 to discuss what they had produced. There was no set manifesto, they simply joined together with the common goal to revolutionize contemporary modern design. At this point the original group was joined by other designers, including Nathalie du Pasquier from France.

Memphis designers used new materials in their work, particularly patterned laminated plastics, to achieve fantastic, brightly coloured, and often kitsch effects. Memphis products went against accepted notions of good taste ("cheap" plastic laminates had been used for kitchen work tops, and in cafes and fast food shops, but never before for expensive pieces of domestic furniture) and the group dominated Italian avant-garde design throughout the 1980s.

The collectors' market for Memphis furniture is growing, and the value of pieces today depends both on the context of a particular design within the history of the group and its rarity. The Memphis designers wanted their items to be capable of mass production but the furniture in particular tended to be fairly labour-intensive to produce despite utilizing relatively inexpensive materials, so few examples were made.

The work of Memphis designers can be recognized by its characteristic patterns and shapes and most pieces will be marked "Memphis". Some also bear the designer's name, and the date and place of manufacture. As with other modern design furniture that utilizes plastic in its construction, condition is important. Plastic cannot be restored, and chipped, cracked, and damaged laminates can affect the value of a piece.

The Italian manufacturing company Artemide supported the Memphis initiative and its head, Ernesto Gismondi, became president of the collective. The company went on to manufacture many Memphis designs from 1982 onwards.

The first Memphis exhibition took place in September 1981 and a selection of over fifty original designs were shown at a gallery in Milan. This included a wide range of objects from furniture and ceramics to lighting and clocks, and the groundbreaking exhibition also featured the work of international designers including Shiro Kuramata and Masanori Umeda from Japan. The international design press quickly picked up on the iconoclastic new style and helped spread the name of Memphis design across the world. The group went on to produce textiles, lighting, silverware, and glass over the next seven years.

The Memphis designers produced a book called *Memphis – The New International Style* in 1981 and used this to promote their designs throughout the world. Pieces were displayed at the Artemide showrooms in Milan with new collections every year, just like in the fashion industry. Barbara Radice became art director of Memphis until 1988 when Sottsass disbanded the group.

Memphis style used decoration as the most important aspect of a design, as well as innovative new playful shapes. Their plastic laminates, many of which were produced to Memphis designers' own specifications, are a kaleidoscopic riot of animal skin prints, geometric lines, and bright colours. The new plastic appeared on tables, consoles, and chairs. Patterns reflected Pop Art and comic book graphics, and even organic shapes such as grains of rice, pasta, and coffee beans. Original drawings and Letraset figures were also used in pattern designs.

Laminates designed by Ettore Sottsass were made by the company Abet Laminati and his favourite colours for use on furniture were pastel blues, pinks, and yellows, and these colours went on to become the colours associated with the 1980s. The patterns created by Memphis quickly spread to mass-market designs and appeared on everything from wallpaper to clothes throughout the decade.

Memphis used other new materials, including neon lights, celluloid plastics, industrial paints, and coloured light bulbs – always removing them from their original

A "Super" floor lamp,
designed by Martine Bedin in 1981.
£500–£600/$750–$900

A "Kristall" table,
designed by Michele
de Lucchi in 1981.
£1,000–£1,500/$1,500–$2,250

A "Plaza" dressing table
and stool, designed by
Michael Graves in 1981.
£12,000–£16,000/$18,000–$24,000

context and putting them onto furniture in an unexpected and sometimes humorous way. Memphis designs also reflected past styles (following on from Studio Alchimia), in particular Art Deco, African (notably in the textiles of Pasquier), Futurist, De Stijl, and neoclassical motifs. They also placed inexpensive materials next to expensive ones, with plastic and marble being a characteristic combination in their furniture designs.

Martine Bedin's "Super" floor lamp was designed in 1981 for Memphis and consists of a blue plastic body with coloured lamp sockets on metal and rubber wheels. It has a real personality, with the shape of the body and the bulbs resembling a hedgehog, and will bear a metal label "Memphis Milano, Martine Bedin, 1981, Made in Italy". Bedin designed similarly styled floor lamps also for Memphis, utilizing primary coloured and pastel plastics and these are collectable today. She was born in France in 1957 and trained as an architect before winning a scholarship that prompted her to move to Italy. In 1978 she worked in Florence at the Superstudio before working with Sottsass and producing lighting and furniture for Memphis.

Michael Graves' glamorous "Plaza" dressing table and stool shown here is generally considered to be one of the most important pieces produced by the Memphis collective. With a thoroughly architectural feel, its Art Deco styling, use of coloured plastic laminates, embedded lights, and overall ostentatious look meant that it was an expensive piece to buy at the time and remains so in the collectors' market today. It was included in the first ever Memphis exhibition in Milan in 1981. They were made in extremely limited numbers and this heightens their rarity today. The design utilizes Perspex, laminated plastic, and more traditional maple wood veneer (one of Graves' favourite materials), and each example bears a metal label inscribed "Memphis Milano, Designer M. Graves 1981".

Michael Graves was born in Minneapolis in 1934. He studied architecture at the University of Cincinnati and later at Harvard. He has worked with some of the greatest designers and architects of the 20th century, including George Nelson, and opened his own architectural office in 1964. In the 1970s he began reworking Art Deco classical styles in his architecture and furniture and this came to fruition with his work for Memphis in the 1980s. He has also designed jewellery and ceramics and a range of highly successful household products for Alessi, including the neoclassically inspired "Piazza" tea and coffee set.

As well as furniture, Sottsass produced ceramics for Memphis, and it is possible to see the evolution of his ceramics style in the more restrained, organic pieces for Memphis after his large-scale Totem series of the late 1960s and 1970s (see p.133). Among his more collectable designs is the "Euphrates" vase (see opposite), which was designed in 1983 and consists of white, black, and yellow organic forms that resemble a surreal arrangement of cooking pots. The underside of these vases will be marked "Ettore Sottsass per Memphis". Pieces in their original box and packaging will attract a higher price today.

Sottsass's "Carlton" room divider is perhaps one of the most instantly recognizable Memphis pieces along with Michael Graves's "Plaza" dressing table and stool. Standing almost 2m (6½ft) high, it takes the familiar concept of a sideboard and reworks it into a work of art, making the piece the focal point of any room as well as offering a storage solution. The "Carlton" room divider was designed in 1981 and its open wooden structure is covered in a variety of brightly coloured plastic laminates. Originals will be marked with the manufacturer's label and each piece should be individually numbered.

## KEY MEMBERS OF MEMPHIS

Martine Bedin (b.1957)
Andrea Branzi (b.1938)
Michael Graves (b.1934)
Shiro Kuramata (1934–91)
Michele de Lucchi (b.1951)
Natalie du Pasquier (1895–1966)
Barbara Radice (b.1934)
Ettore Sottsass (b.1917)
George Sowden (b.1942)
Masanori Umeda (b.1941)
Marco Zanini (b.1954)

## Michele de Lucchi (b.1951)

The Italian designer Michele de Lucchi produced lighting and furniture designs for both Studio Alchimia and Memphis. His designs from the early 1980s are playful and show a strong use of imagery. He advocated the need for a softer, more child-like approach to design and used form, texture, and colour as parts of an expressive language. His designs reject the hard edges and sober colours of the new Functionalism.

The "First" chair was designed in 1983 and has a tubular steel painted frame with painted wood back and globular armrests. Its space-age design, the armrests and headrests resembling planets in orbit, looks back to the atomic styling of the 1950s and combines this with an ironic reference to the severe, cold lines of Bauhaus and early 20th century tubular metal furniture by the likes of Marcel Breuer and PEL.

Lucchi's "Kristall" side table (see p.193) was designed in 1981 and examples will have an original label to the side bearing the date, designer's name, and the Memphis name. It is made with a characteristic Memphis patterned laminated plastic top and sides and also utilizes MDF, a material that has become ubiquitous in household furnishings today.

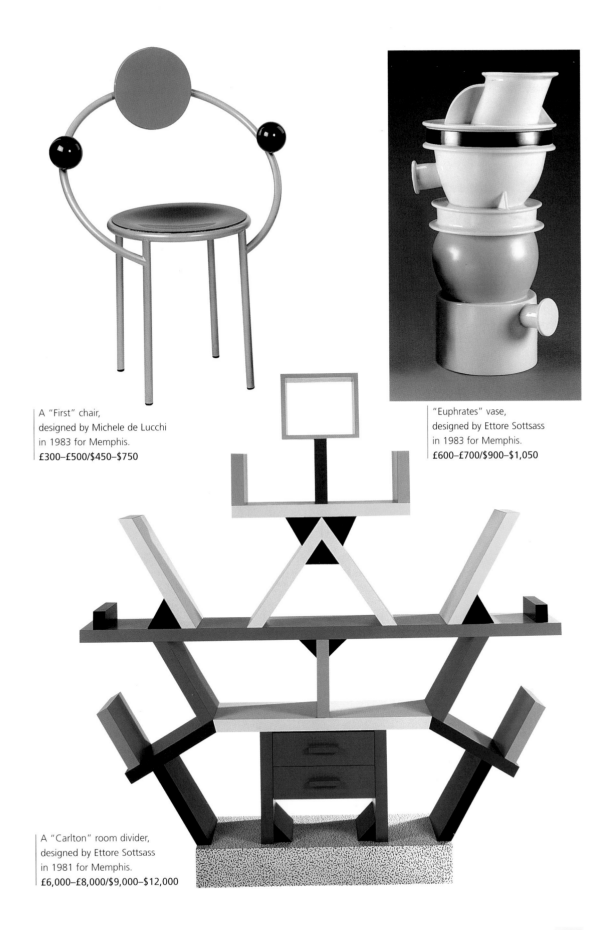

A "First" chair,
designed by Michele de Lucchi
in 1983 for Memphis.
£300–£500/$450–$750

"Euphrates" vase,
designed by Ettore Sottsass
in 1983 for Memphis.
£600–£700/$900–$1,050

A "Carlton" room divider,
designed by Ettore Sottsass
in 1981 for Memphis.
£6,000–£8,000/$9,000–$12,000

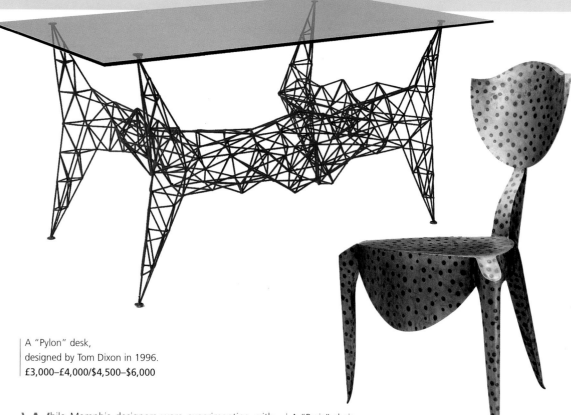

A "Pylon" desk,
designed by Tom Dixon in 1996.
£3,000–£4,000/$4,500–$6,000

A "Paris" chair,
designed by
André Dubreuil in 1988.
£2,000–£3,000/$3,000–$4,500

While Memphis designers were experimenting with outrageous pattern and decoration other designers were working with more traditional and found industrial materials, such as steel, concrete, and reinforced glass, and casting them into fantastic new furniture forms.

The work of Danny Lane, Ron Arad, André Dubreuil, and Tom Dixon has been dubbed Salvage Design and their pieces are now finding favour in today's collectors' market despite the fact that some of them are less than a decade old. Pieces of Salvage furniture were produced either as one-offs or in very limited numbers due to the painstaking work required by the designer to construct each item, so this heightens their desirability to collectors today.

The American designer Danny Lane (b.1955) has designed tables, screens, and wonderfully sculptural chairs in glass. He treats glass in a completely new and instantly recognizable way and also combines it with more traditional materials, including steel and wood. He smashes reinforced glass into irregular forms, leaving them with jagged, often harsh edges, then sandblasts and polishes the glass, and fits the different components together to make the finished piece.

The top of the low stacking table shown opposite is made from 2.5cm (¾in) -thick float glass and its irregularly

formed legs are attached to the top by stainless steel rods. Much of Lane's work is produced in limited numbers and exhibited in one-man shows in galleries in London and other European cities, although pieces are now appearing at top antique fairs. This makes his work exclusive from the outset. Most of Lane's glass furniture, particularly the more recent examples, should bear an etched Danny Lane name and the date of manufacture.

The French designer André Dubreuil (b.1951) has created dramatic and surreal items of furniture that resemble strange animals and insects with their scuttling legs and patterned surfaces. His pieces also have the drama of 18th-century Baroque furniture with their heavy reliance on extravagant shapes and rich decoration.

The "Paris" chair (see above) relies on surface decoration to achieve its effects, having a repeated pattern of spots applied to the steel body, which makes the chair resemble a surreal leopard with head, ears, neck, body, and tapering, pointed legs. Dubreuil also used wax on the

A low stacking table,
designed by Danny Lane in 1994.
**£1,800–£2,200/$2,700–$3,300**

surface of his pieces to give the steel a highly polished, smooth shine. His work has always been exclusive and made in limited numbers (often commissioned by private clients), with some designs being made in batches of less than fifty. This helps make his furniture collectable today.

The designer Tom Dixon, who is Tunisian by birth, was born in London in 1959. His work combines furniture with art as he admires the idea of "objets trouvé", or found objects, where ordinary objects are used as the basis of a piece of art. This idea was first popularized by the French artist Marcel Duchamp in 1917.

Dixon worked with scrap metal in the late 1980s and early 1990s, welding it together to produce his often bizarre and unexpected furniture based on his own observations of the world. The "Pylon" desk shown opposite is more an artistic statement than a desk, as the thin steel rods of its construction reflect the design of electricity pylons. Despite its fragile appearance the desk is very strong. Dixon produced a "Pylon" chair in 1991.

Dixon has also designed craft revival pieces that look unlike anything created by mass production and utilize natural materials. Another Dixon chair that is sought after by collectors today is the unconventional and sinuous "S" chair, which reflects Panton's plastic chair from the 1960s.

An early prototype
"S" chair, designed
byTom Dixon in 1986.
**£1,800–£2,200/$2,700–$3,300**

# Ron Arad

Ron Arad
(*b*.1951).

Ron Arad is perhaps the most exciting new designer to emerge in Britain in the last 20 years. His work challenges traditional notions of design and breaks new boundaries in form, technique, and materials. He has gone from a one-man designer producing expensive, limited edition chairs in the early 1980s to a designer whose name is recognized everywhere and who creates mass-produced chairs within the price range of most collectors.

His inventive and witty designs are original, and made out of the most unexpected materials including concrete and scaffolding. His chairs are as much contemporary pieces of sculpture as items of furniture and his output has included tables, interior schemes, lamps, architecture, and commercial interior spaces including the Opera House in Tel Aviv. He has also worked with some of the most exciting modern designers in other fields, for example Neville Brody (who was the most influential graphic designer of the 1980s) created Arad's typeface.

In common with other great designers of the 20th century, Arad has been supported by forward-thinking manufacturers throughout his career, particularly the Italian design company Vitra. He was also patronized in his early career by the fashion designer Jean Paul Gaultier. Today, most Arad pieces sell to museums, galleries, and dedicated collectors, but his mass-produced chair designs of the late 1990s, such as the "Tom Vac", are now putting his work within the reach of more and more collectors. These less expensive chairs are probably worth investing in now as their value is bound to increase in the future.

Ron Arad was born in Tel Aviv in 1951 but has spent his working life in England, moving to London in 1973. He studied at the Jerusalem Academy of Art from 1971 to 1973 and between 1974 and 1979 at the Architectural Association's School of Architecture in London. In 1981 he opened One Off Ltd. with Caroline Thorman in Covent Garden, London. This was his first design studio and showroom, and its welded steel interior perfectly matched the polished steel of his products. In 1989 he founded Ron Arad Associates (again with Caroline Thorman) in Chalk Farm, London and One Off was incorporated into Ron Arad Associates in 1993. Between 1994 and 1997 he was Professor of Product Design at the Hochschule in Vienna and in 1997–8 became Professor of Industrial and Furniture Design at the Royal College of Art in London.

A "Well Tempered" chair, designed in 1986 and manufactured by Vitra, produced between 1986 and 1993 for the Vitra Editions series.
£4,500–£6,700/$6,750–$10,000

Arad's early work at One Off is characterized by his use of found materials and ready-made items. Many of the pieces from this time were, as the name suggests, one-offs and he designed prototype chairs through simple sketches that would then be made into fantastic furniture by assistants in his workshop (Arad has no particular training in metalwork). He aimed to link industrial process with industrial design and one of his most memorable and witty early designs was the "Rover" chair, which consisted of a reclining leather seat, reclaimed from a Rover 2000 car, fitted onto a tubular steel frame. Look out for red leather examples of this chair as they are particularly rare.

The "Well Tempered" chair was designed in 1986, and produced by Vitra who wanted to manufacture Arad's fantastic furniture forms for a wider market. This commission was Arad's first from a major manufacturer and was part of the Vitra Edition series, which also included pieces by Ettore Sottsass and Shiro Kuramata.

The "Well Tempered" chair gave the armchair, in particular traditional club chairs, a whole new look through its oversized shape and polished sheet-steel material, while still retaining the overall appearance of an

A "Rolling Volume" chair, designed in 1989 and produced by One Off Ltd.
**£12,000–£18,000/$18,000–$27,000**

A "Single Rietveld" chair, designed in 1991 and produced by One Off Ltd.
**£14,000–£18,000/$21,000–$27,000**

armchair. The chairs were made from four separate sheets of steel, cut into shape from Arad's pattern sketches. It is a very simple design and literally looks like four pieces of fabric looped together and then tacked to keep it in place.

The steel sheets were made by flattening steel rods into sprung steel (a process which is called tempering), which makes the material try to spring back to its original flatness when pressure is removed. If the steel rivets were taken out of these chairs they would literally unravel out of shape. Bending was ideal for the design of this chair as it produced a graceful curve. Despite being made of steel, a material never before associated with upholstered armchairs, the chair is surprisingly comfortable.

"Well Tempered" chairs will be signed and numbered for easy identification. These chairs have been collectable from the time of production as they were only made in limited numbers. They were very expensive to buy, as were most of Arad's pieces in One Off, which were really produced as artworks in the 1980s. He encountered the same problem with the "Rover" chair. It was designed for

students and "bedsitland", but of course students would never have been able to afford it.

Some of Arad's designs from the 1980s to the early 1990s are even more abstract, including "Rolling Volume" (see p.199) from 1989 which looks more like a piece of Modernist sculpture than a chair, and the steel "Single Rietveld" chair (see p.199) of 1991 which reflects the geometric shape of Gerrit Rietveld's "Zig-Zag" chair of 1934 (see p.19). The "Single Rietveld" slides and adjusts on a single sheet of steel so that the sitter can change their sitting position as required. Arad's steel "Light" table (see over) was designed in 1988 and produced by One Off. It is the perfect complement to his monumental steel chairs, which he designed at around the same time, with their fluid curves and bulbous feet executed in such a non-traditional material for a table.

Arad has also produced some wonderfully inventive lighting. His "Tree" lights were designed in 1983 and produced by One Off and have wonderfully organic structures resembling the twisted branches of trees. The

A concrete stereo, designed in 1984 and produced in limited quantities by One Off Ltd.
**£10,000–£15,000/$15,000–$22,500**

original, handmade version of this light was made from a lump of concrete with a transformer embedded in it to make the base, and industrial conduit pipes, flexible tubes, and halogen lights at the top. The design was later standardized and is still manufactured by Zeus in Italy. Arad's other memorable light is the "Aerial" of 1981, ingeniously assembled from ready-made parts including a car aerial and a clutch motor. The fingerprints on the remote control of the "Aerial" light are Arad's own.

Stereo speakers, part of the set on the opposite page.

The unexpected juxtaposition of things and materials that began with the Surrealist artists earlier in the 20th century was carried on by Arad in the 1980s using contemporary found materials. His concrete stereo (see pp.200–1), designed in 1983, is a masterpiece of Postmodern design and a comment on contemporary society, reflecting the urban decay and recession of the 1980s. This piece completely contradicts the viewer's expectations of a stereo, traditionally made out of high-tech plastic or metal with visible switches. Arad's stereo consists of a turntable and electrical parts set into a block of rough-hewn concrete, a material more likely to be found on a building site or in the manufacture of paving slabs. It is this powerful contrast that makes the stereo such an important piece of concept design.

It was when Arad met an electronics expert that he realized that a hi-fi stereo did not have to be housed in a box or inside a chassis. The stereo was difficult to make as the electronics had to be protected with plastic and then lowered into liquid, quick-setting concrete while leaving the transistors and electrical parts visible underneath. Not surprisingly, the stereo did not produce a good sound through its concrete speakers (see p.201), and it is much more a work of art and piece of social commentary than it is a sound system. Only a handful of these stereos were made, making them instantly desirable to collectors today.

Arad did not just work in steel and concrete, he produced some upholstered designs for the Italian company Moroso in the mid 1990s. He also moved into mass-produced designs at this time, such as the moveable "Bookworm" shelf, designed in 1994 for Kartell, and the "FPE" ("Fantastic Plastic Elastic") chair, designed in 1997 also for Kartell.

The original prototype for the "FPE" chair was a handmade plywood and aluminium chair designed for use on Mercedes exhibition stands and produced only in limited numbers. Arad returned to the design a few years later and recognized its potential for mass production in less expensive materials. The "FPE" chair is made from two tubes of extruded plastic that are bent to form the shape of the frame. The seat and back are made from a plastic membrane which, when inserted into the bent frame, causes the extrusion to bite the plastic so locking the structure into place. The chair became the first in the history of design to hold itself together, so removing the need for rivets or glue.

A steel "Light" table, designed in 1988 and executed by One Off Ltd.
£8,000–£12,000/
$12,000–$18,000

The graceful "Tom Vac" chair was designed in 1997 and consists of a one-piece superplastic, aluminium, vacuum-formed shell mounted on a stainless steel frame. It was originally designed for a promotional commission for *Domus*, the Italian design magazine, to be used in Totem, a landmark made up of a hundred stacking chairs in the centre of Milan. The design was then adapted for mass production and Vitra released an injection-moulded version in plastic at the Cologne Furniture Fair in 1998. The chair is available today in a variety of colours including red and blue. It is similar in style and shape to Nanna Ditzel's "Butterfly" chair, designed in 1990.

A "Tom Vac" chair, designed in 1997 and produced by Vitra. £800–£1,000/ $1,200–$1,500

"FPE" ("Fantastic Plastic Elastic") chair, designed in 1997 and produced by Kartell. £80–£120/$120–$180

A "Domestic Animal" couch,
designed by Andrea Branzi
in 1985 and produced by Zabro.
**£5,000–£6,000/$7,500–$9,000**

In contrast to the industrial materials of Salvage Design was the work of Andrea Branzi and Frank Gehry. Branzi utilized completely natural materials for his furniture, and Gehry worked with cardboard to make a range of artistic pieces that developed the idea of disposable furniture even further than it had gone in the Pop and Radical era of the late 1960s.

Frank O. Gehry was born in Toronto in 1930 and is primarily known as an architect but he also designed some well-known furniture which, because of its quirky use of material, limited edition status, and fun shapes, has found favour with collectors today. Gehry designed the Vitra Design Museum in Weil am Rhein, Germany in 1989, but he is perhaps best known for the design of the space-age, controversial, titanium-covered Guggenheim Museum in Bilbao, Spain.

The remarkable looking "Little Beaver" chair and stool (*see opposite*) were originally designed by Gehry in 1980 and produced by the Swiss/German company Vitra in 1987. Both items are made from dark cardboard and get their name because it looks as though they have been gnawed by a beaver at the edges.

This was not Gehry's first venture into designing in cardboard. In 1972 he produced the popular "Easy Edges" series for the manufacturer Jack Brogan. The range was reissued by Vitra in 1982. It consisted of less than 20 different pieces of laminated, corrugated cardboard furniture, including low and side tables, and chairs. The "Easy Edges" items were designed to be available at low cost, and were an immediate commercial hit in American stores. They are collectable today because of their rarity value.

Gehry also made a range of cardboard furniture called "Experimental Edges". Fewer pieces were made than in the "Easy Edges" series and they were much more decorative and not as functional. In addition, he designed a range of lightweight, intricately woven plywood chairs in the early 1990s for Knoll and these have also become highly collectable.

The Florentine-born designer Andrea Branzi (*b*.1938) is perhaps best known for his pivotal role in Italian Radical

design in the 1960s and 1970s. Branzi was a co-founder of Archizoom in 1966 and also produced work for Studio Alchimia in Milan in 1979. He is one of Italy's best known designers and he won the Italian Compasso d'Oro in 1987 for his outstanding contribution to Italian design.

Branzi has always been interested in primitive furniture and animal-print decorations, but these references really came to fruition in his Postmodern work for the manufacturer Zabro in the mid 1980s.

The highly unusual and somewhat bizarre "Domestic Animal" ("Animali Domestici") series was launched in 1985 and in 1987 Branzi published a book under the same name to promote the new designs and the thinking behind them. The theory behind this range was that these pieces of furniture could have the same status as animals kept as pets in the modern home.

The "Domestic Animal" series was completely unlike anything seen before in domestic furniture design, utilizing man-made finished woods for the seats in combination with natural tree branches (usually silver birch) for the back and armrests. These give the chairs and couches a very primitive feel and it is hard to believe that these pieces were designed during the slick, highly polished, and glossy 1980s.

A "Little Beaver" chair and stool, designed by Frank Gehry in 1980.
**£5,000–£7,000/$7,500–$10,500**

A side chair and stool, designed by Frank Gehry in 1970 for the "Easy Edges" series.
Stool: £1,300–£2,000/$2,000–$3,000
Chair: £2,600–£4,000/$4,000–$6,000

A "Felt" chair,
designed by Gaetano Pesce in 1987
and manufactured by Cassina.
£5,300–£6,600/$8,000–$10,000

Gaetano Pesce is one of the most fascinating and consistently radical designers of the second half of the 20th century and was at the forefront of Italian avant-garde design in the 1980s along with Ettore Sottsass.

Pesce's "Felt" or "il Feltri" chair, shown above, was designed in 1987 and manufactured by Cassina, a company with whom he had enjoyed a very successful relationship since 1964. Cassina was founded in Milan in 1927 under the directorship of Cesare Cassina (1909–79). The aim was, and continues to be, to produce the work of innovative designers and sell high-quality products. The company began working with Mid-Century European designers from 1945 onwards and has manufactured furniture by some of the best designers of the 20th century, including Marco Bellini, Vico Magistretti, Gaetano Pesce, and Gio Ponti.

Pesce's "Felt" chair has an amazing, throne-like presence and imposing form, which made it an instant design classic. Its unusual shape combined with its innovative and experimental manufacturing method make it desirable to collectors today. The body of the chair is constructed from a thick wool felt that is impregnated with resin to reinforce the material and give the chair its rigid, yet soft shape. The felt is stitched with hemp

stringing. Versions of this chair were produced in a pink and blue colour combination, two typically Postmodern colours. Pesce's furniture designs from the 1980s place form over function, infusing them with symbolic as well as stylistic meaning.

Postmodern designers continued to experiment with the sculptural possibilities of metal and wire throughout the 1980s, most notably seen in the graceful work of the Japanese designer Shiro Kuramata (see pp.214–15). The American sculptor Forrest Myers also worked with wire and metal. Art furniture such as this is now becoming popular with collectors.

Myers was born in California in 1941 and is now based in Brooklyn, New York State. He produced Postmodern furniture as well as large-scale sculpture and installations in the 1980s. His favourite materials are stainless steel, aluminium, and steel wire and one of his most memorable furniture designs is the "La Farge" chair, which he designed in 1987–8. The chair's body consists of knitted and woven wire with an indentation in the centre for the sitter, making the piece resemble a high-tech nest. Its unusual form and limited edition status make it collectable today.

Ettore Sottsass continued to design in the Postmodern style throughout the 1980s after he had disbanded the

Memphis Group in 1988. He remains a leader of Italian design today, working with major companies such as Knoll and participating in international exhibitions.

By the mid 1980s Sottsass was producing ever more fantastic furniture ranging from chairs and coffee tables to bookcases, all demonstrating his inventive use of form and often classically-inspired motifs. He also designed beautifully and highly sought after jewellery, coloured art glass for Murano, the famous Italian glass factory (*see p*.118), and metalware for Alessi, as well as receiving architectural commissions. In the late 1980s he designed multi-levelled tables in materials including wood, metal, stone, and marble.

The "Park" table shown here is a fine example of Sottsass's eclectic Postmodernism. He has never been content to work within existing styles but continues to experiment and formulate his own personal style, constantly questioning design and breaking down boundaries with his work. As a result, his work is some of the most sought after of the late 20th century.

The 1980s saw new directions in Postmodern design, from the Salvage designers, who used found scrap materials in their work, to the Memphis Group, who decorated their pieces in a riot of colour. But some

*Top*: A "La Farge" wire chair,
designed by Forrest Myers in 1987–8.
**£4,000–£6,000/$6,000–$9,000**

*Above*: A "Park" table, designed
by Ettore Sottsass in 1983
for Memphis (very limited production)
**£5,000–£7,000/$7,500–$10,500**

designers who were rebelling against traditional Modernism turned away from functionalism and the real world to the extent of using magical and dream-like forms for their designs. Good examples are the work of Shiro Kuramata, whose beautifully-modelled "Feather" stool is illustrated opposite, and the work of Borek Sipek.

Sipek's work can only be described as extravagant. He has reintroduced decorative colour and form into furniture with often quite unexpected results, and created fantastically shaped glass for Murano. He has also produced ceramics and cutlery, all of which bear the characteristic stamp of his imagination.

Sipek was born in Prague in 1949 and studied furniture design at the School of Applied Arts until 1968. He went on to study architecture in Hamburg and philosophy in Stuttgart, and also travelled widely. Sipek's company Alterego, which he founded in association with the designer David Palterer, is based in Amsterdam.

Sipek's magical style utilizes traditional materials, including wood, leather, and fabric, and juxtaposes these with newer materials, such as polyurethane foam and steel. His style is easily recognizable as the legs of his furniture are often attenuated and the bodies may include surreal, unconventional backs.

A rocking chair from the "Angel Chairs" series, designed by Wendell Castle in 1990.
**£13,300–£20,000/$20,000–$30,000**

One of Sipek's most collectable designs is the "Bambi" chair, which was designed in 1983 and produced by Studio Sipek in a limited edition of sixty, making original examples sought after today. Originals can be identified from later editions because each should bear an individual number stamped underneath the seat. The chair consists of a lightweight, painted tubular-metal frame with a textile back and a brass and ebonized seat. The chair's attenuated, legs with their hoof-shaped feet reflect those of the character in the 1942 Walt Disney film *Bambi*, and the chair looks as frail as a young deer. The "Bambi" chair was later made by Neotu in Paris and these examples date from 1988 onwards.

Yet another direction in design came from the American designer and craftsman Wendell Castle, who wanted to reintroduce masterful woodworking and workshop techniques to design, an idea that was first developed a century before through the late 19th century Arts and Crafts movement.

A "Bambi" chair, designed by Borek Sipek in 1983 and produced by Studio Sipek. £3,000–£4,000/ $4,500–$6,000

A "Feather" stool, designed by Shiro Kuramata in 1990 for a limited edition of 40 produced by Ishimaru Co. Ltd. £14,600–£18,600/$22,000–$28,000

Castle was born in 1932 and led the craft revival in America in the late 1980s and 1990s. He has over 30 years experience of design and is recognized as the originator of art furniture in the USA through his skilful use of wood and sculptural techniques.

Castle trained as a sculptor at the University of Kansas and his furniture clearly reflects this background, as his pieces are often surreal, featuring unexpected juxtapositions of objects like a surrealist canvas. He experimented with the new styles and materials of Pop design in the 1960s, for example his famous plastic "Molar" sofa, which dates from 1969 and was based on the shape of human teeth. After this he turned towards wood carving, using increasingly sophisticated and illusionistic techniques.

The rocking chair illustrated opposite combines traditional materials with an understated, yet inescapable Postmodernist styling. Constructed from mahogany and curly maple it forms part of the "Angel Chairs" series, which was produced in 1990.

Another key figure in contemporary furniture and interior design is Australian-born designer Marc Newson. He has produced furniture for leading companies such as B & B Italia and Capellini, as well as glass, watches, interior

An "Event Horizon" table, designed
by Marc Newson in 1992.
**£36,600–£46,600/
$55,000–$70,000**

commissions, and installations for European, Asian, and American clients. He has even designed a bicycle, a concept car, and a private jet. His furniture, in particular, makes a very strong statement so it is ideal for contemporary living spaces.

Newson's often playful, biomorphically-styled furniture is highly original but also reflects aspects of Pop and Mid-Century styling. He combines these influences with his own late 20th and early 21st century vision. The beauty in acquiring a collection of contemporary design furniture is that it is available to buy new today. His earlier furniture is already attracting premium prices in major modern design auctions, and prices will no doubt keep on rising as his reputation as a cutting-edge designer continues to grow. However, it is impossible to predict exactly how much pieces will be worth in the future as the market for modern design furniture is still quite young.

Newson was born in Sydney in 1962. He studied sculpture and jewellery at Sydney College of Art in the 1980s and began to design furniture as well. His sculpture training can be clearly seen in his designs. Newson won a grant from the Australian Crafts Council in 1984 and this enabled him to set up his first exhibition in Sydney. He opened his own studio, POD design, soon after this.

An early Japanese patron, Teruo Kurasaki, offered to produce Newson's designs through his company Idée and this prompted the designer's move to Tokyo from 1987 to 1991. Here he developed the use of innovative materials and forms in his work, particularly exploring the sculptural possibilities of aluminium and fibreglass. Designs produced by Idée include the "Black Hole" table, which introduced the theme of space, science fiction, and physics into Newson's work. He is fascinated with set design, particularly that seen in Stanley Kubrick films such as *2001: A Space Odyssey*. This space-age theme appeared again with his "Event Horizon" table in 1992. These tables were produced in a limited edition and are particularly sought after by collectors today.

The colourful "Bucky" chairs are one of Newson's best-known designs and were commissioned by the Cartier Contemporary Art Foundation in 1995 for an interactive installation in Paris. These amoeba-shaped, delightfully biomorphic chairs reflect Pop classics such as Gaetano Pesce's "UP" chairs (*see pp.*128–9). In the original room installation a number of chairs were placed together to make a geodesic dome, creating a form made popular by one of Newson's heroes R. Buckminster Fuller. The "Bucky II" chair is similar in style to the original chair.

A "Bucky" chair, designed by
Marc Newson in 1995.
**£1,300–£2,000/$2,000–$3,000**

The "Orgone" lounge chair was originally made in 1993
and was cast in aluminium with a coloured interior. The
"Orgone" shape is recurrent in Newson's style. His work
seems to challenge existing perceptions of design and
objects, and this chair is a supreme example of his style.
Newson has also produced ranges of kitchen and
bathroom objects for Alessi. These pieces are bound to
increase in value in the future and are a fun and
affordable way to own his work today.

Postmodern design in the 1980s tended to be flashy
and ostentatious, matching the economic confidence and
spending power of the decade. The recession of the early
1990s brought with it a much more minimal approach.
Young furniture designers continued to explore and utilize

An "Orgone" stretch lounge chair,
designed by Marc Newson in 1993.
**£13,300–£20,000/
$20,000–$30,000**

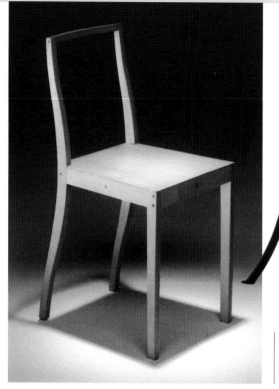

"Thinking Man's" chair,
designed by Jasper Morrison
in 1987 for Capellini.
**£2,000–£3,000/$3,000–$4,500**

A plywood chair,
designed by Jasper Morrison
in 1988 for Vitra.
**£300–£500/$450–$750**

new materials and develop imaginative solutions to design problems, in some cases fusing traditional handicrafts with the latest technologies. Other more established designers carried on developing themes begun in the 1980s including Ron Arad, whose "Box in Four Movements" (*see opposite*) dating from 1994 is a fantastic moveable creation in bronze.

Design in the Netherlands in the mid to late 1990s was dominated by Droog Design (which means Dry Design). The jewellery designer Gijs Bakker and design critic and editor Reny Ramakers formed Droog in 1993. The pair grouped together the work of young Dutch designers whose work was innovative, experimental, and minimal and exhibited it at the Milan Furniture Fair in that year. Almost immediately Droog was hailed by the international press as the future of Dutch design and the collective has retained its cutting-edge profile ever since.

Droog is not a design studio but a collective of designers whose work is experimental and shares a similar philosophy. Their pieces have become very popular but there is no actual group and no set manifesto, although many of the items that are included under the Droog umbrella are made by the designers themselves. Objects have included a washbasin made out of rubber designed

by Hella Jongerius and vases produced from baked sponges that have been soaked in kaolin by Marcel Wanders. Such unusual materials and shapes challenge everyday perceptions of design.

The "Knotted" chair (*see opposite*) was created by Wanders for Droog Designs. An ingenious construction, this incredibly light but strong rope chair is made from aramide braid with a carbon centre that is then knotted into the chair's shape. The shape is then impregnated with epoxy resin and left to harden while hung from a frame, with the force of gravity creating the form of the final piece. Wanders developed the technology for this chair in conjunction with the aviation and aerospace technology faculty at Delft Technical University. It won the Rotterdam Design Prize in 1996 and revitalizes the traditional skill of macramé (seen by some as dull and boring) by using it with the latest technology. Today the "Knotted" chair is produced and distributed by Capellini and is bound to become more collectable in the future.

In Britain, the minimalist work of Jasper Morrison (*b*.1959), who graduated from the Royal College of Art in London in a blaze of publicity in 1985, has brought the clean lines and traditional techniques of the past back into contemporary furniture design. Morrison also designs

A "Knotted" chair, designed by
Marcel Wanders in 1996.
**£4,000–£6,000/**
**$6,000–$9,000**

interiors and industrial products, and uses materials
including plywood and tubular steel.

Morrison began working with Capellini before
graduating from the Royal College of Art (having
previously trained at Kingston Polytechnic in Surrey).
After graduating he was commissioned by Vitra in
Germany, where he produced a traditionally-styled,
graceful plywood chair (*see opposite*) with an unusual
open back in 1988. This piece of furniture is now sought
after by collectors. Another one of Morrison's already
famous and collectable designs is the "Thinking Man's"
chair (*see opposite*), which was designed in 1987 and
manufactured by Capellini. This stylish chair follows the
traditional shape of lounge chairs with its fluid arms, and
comes with built-in hand rests. It is made from painted
tubular steel and flat-welded steel, and was designed for
indoor and outdoor use. Newson's commitment to
practicality, simplicity, and honesty in design, his eye for
elegance and his attention to manufacturing detail show
his appreciation for the values of Modernism, yet his work
remains very much part of 21st century culture.

"Box in Four Movements" (a bronze chair),
designed by Ron Arad in 1994 and
produced by One Off Ltd.
**£8,000–£12,000/$12,000–$18,000**

# Japanese design

Japan was a key player in Postmodern furniture design and also in industrial design, particularly in the field of electrical goods manufactured by corporations such as Sony and Sharp. Japan is still seen as being at the forefront of futuristic and inventive design in the West and the work of Japanese designers from the 1980s onwards is now highly sought after by collectors. Names to look out for at the moment include Kiro Kurakawa, Shiro Kuramata, and Masanori Umeda. Also becoming collectable is the work of a new generation of Japanese designers, for example the husband and wife team Shin and Tomoko Azumi, who are currently based in London.

Shiro Kuramata (1934–91) is one of the most admired Japanese designers in Western countries. Over a short but incredibly influential career he designed everything from vases to chests of drawers, as well as complete interior schemes for Japanese commercial buildings. Kuramata was an extremely prolific designer, supposedly able to produce a design per day. Thanks to commissions such as the Issey Miyake fashion boutiques in Japan and Paris, his work became known throughout the world in the 1980s and continues to influence designers and interior designers today.

By the end of the 1960s Kuramata was well established but it is his Postmodern work from the late 1980s that is particularly collectable today, and for which he is best known. Many of his designs were produced in limited numbers by Japanese manufacturers, which makes them instantly collectable. His work has been reissued by Western companies, including Vitra and Capellini.

Kuramata designed department store interiors in Tokyo and opened his own practice, the Kuramata Design Studio, in the city in 1965. He went on to design interiors for new Japanese restaurants and shops, fuelled by the economic boom of the 1980s. Kuramata won the Japanese Cultural Prize for Design in 1981 and opened a studio in Paris in 1988, which helped bring his work to a European audience. He was awarded the prestigious French "Ordre des Arts et des Lettres" in 1990.

Kuramata's highly individual style is a fusion of traditional minimal Japanese style and an industrial look. His design is very personal and he was not interested in the Modernist belief that design should be created for a specific function.

Kuramata's work can be characterized by its use of industrial materials such as glass, steel mesh, cast acrylic, and aluminium. From the West he adopted Memphis-style popular culture references including songs and films. This is reflected in the titles of some of his pieces, for example

the "Miss Blanche" chair, which was named after a character in Tennessee Williams' 1947 play A Streetcar Named Desire.

Kuramata's work appeals to collectors thanks to its beautiful, poetic quality. He gave his pieces names such as "How High the Moon" (a steel mesh armchair) and included references to the natural world in his work which gave it a wonderful humanity and sense of romance. Much of his furniture is sculptural, seeming to be like a work of art rather than a piece of furniture. All his designs are highly imaginative and some have a dream-like quality. Kuramata felt that the modern world, despite its technological successes, had lost a sense of romance, beauty, and love and he tried to reintroduce these through his designs.

Kuramata broke new ground in design by creating optical illusions and exploring the spatial dimensions of objects, for example the use of steel mesh allowed him to make furniture that was transparent. He created unexpected juxtapositions such as embedding silk red roses in a transparent acrylic chair and designing a chest of drawers that was shaped like a sinuous curve in the "Furniture in Irregular Forms" series .

Kuramata worked extensively with both transparent and coloured acrylic, and one of his most beautiful pieces created from this new material is his "Flower Vase" series, which dates from 1989. The vases were designed for a solo exhibition of his work at a Paris gallery. He said, "I prefer artificial materials such as plastic or laminates which don't show the maker's intentions."

The "Flower Vase" number 2, which is simply a rectangular acrylic block with a glass tube at an angle to hold the flower stem, was designed by Kuramata in 1989 for the Spiral Collection, and manufactured by the Ishimaru Co. Ltd. Its design is wonderfully minimal with the only colour coming from the pink central block and the flower. "Flower Vase" number 1 and 3 were produced at the same time and vary slightly from this example, number 2. These are also collectable today.

Kuramata's beautifully romantic "Miss Blanche" chair is also highly collectable. It consists of silk flowers cast in transparent acrylic with tubular aluminium legs. Kuramata was commenting on time and motion as the flowers seemingly float in the space within the chair, a fantastic effect achieved after much painstaking research at model and prototype stage. This chair was designed in 1988 and produced by Ishimaru Co. Ltd. in a limited number of 56 (Kuramata's age when he died, the edition finishing after his death under the direction of his wife,

An "Anthurium" table,
designed by Masanori Umeda
in 1990 and produced by Edra.
**£500–£800/$750–$1,200**

A "Rose" chair,
designed by Masanori
Umeda in 1990 and
produced by Edra.
**£2,000–£2,200/
$3,000–$3,300**

A "Miss Blanche" chair, designed
by Shiro Kuramata in 1988 and
produced by Ishimaru Co. Ltd.
**£33,300–£46,600/$50,000–$70,000**

"Flower Vase" number 2,
designed by Shiro Kuramata in 1989
and manufactured by Ishimaru Co. Ltd.
**£700–£900/$1,120–$1,440**

Mieko). Again it makes use of transparent acrylic, one of Kuramata's favourite materials. He said in an interview with *Domus* magazine in 1984, "I feel attracted to transparent materials because transparency doesn't belong to any one place in particular, and yet it exists."

Some Postmodern Japanese designers felt that the downside of their country's cultural, economic, and technological success story in the 1980s was a loss of beauty and tradition. They attempted to comment on this through their Postmodern designs. This is particularly seen in the work of Masanori Umeda.

Umeda (*b*.1941) trained at the Kuwasawa Design School, graduating in 1962. He went to Italy in 1966 and began working in the Castiglioni design studio in Milan, remaining there for two years. He then became a design consultant to Olivetti up until 1979 and here he met and befriended Ettore Sottsass. Umeda went on to design for Memphis, including the famous full size "Tawaraya" boxing ring, furniture, and ceramics. He opened his own design studio, called U-Meta Design, in Tokyo in 1986 and has worked on interior spaces throughout Japan.

The beautiful and symbolic "Rose" chair (*see p*.215) was designed by Umeda in 1990 and produced by the Italian firm Edra. It is simply a chair upholstered in red velvet with each cushion shaped like an individual rose petal. The chair is still in production today and is available to order in a variety of different coloured velvet upholstery.

The floral symbolism of the "Rose" chair represents Umeda's attempts to reintroduce elements of the natural world into modern-day Japan and his efforts to rediscover the roots and traditions of his country. He believed that modern industrialism in the Western world had destroyed the beauty of the natural world. As a result, his designs are full of animal, plant, and floral references to remind people of the beauty of nature through his work.

The "Getsuen" armchair has a similar sentiment. It too symbolizes the natural world and is made from foam-covered velvet on a steel frame. The flower that inspired the chair is the kikyo flower (Chinese bellflower), one of Umeda's favourite blooms. The chair is portable as it has a roller skate wheel at the back, perhaps representing the fusion of the natural world with the industrial world.

Umeda produced the "Anthurium" side table for Edra and it is also a comment on the loss of beauty in the modern world. It has an organic form with a stamen-shaped central section and a red lacquered tabletop.

A new wave of Japanese designers found fame in the 1990s and their work is now becoming collectable. The "Table=Chest" was designed by Tomoko Azumi in 1995. It is in complete contrast to Umeda's work in its practicality and functionality. It is actually two pieces of furniture in one, converting from a table into a small chest with two drawers. The beautifully economic design is constructed from beech and veneered plywood, and is already included in the collections at the Victoria and Albert Museum in London as an example of important contemporary design, despite being only six years old.

The "Table=Chest" is sold under the name Azumi. This award-winning company was set up in London in 1995 by Azumi and his wife Shin, an industrial designer, after the pair graduated from London's Royal College of Art. The company experiments with materials as well as form, and looks for new ways in which furniture and other objects can be used. Azumi works with British, European, and Japanese manufacturers and has created products including lamps, stereo speakers, and stools. It is, of course, difficult to predict how the collectability and value of items that are so new will grow in the future, but it is likely that good quality contemporary modern design will continue to be desirable in the years ahead.

## OTHER COLLECTABLE JAPANESE DESIGNERS

The following furniture designers are principally known in Japan but their work is now becoming increasingly popular among collectors in the West, and will more than likely increase in value in the future.

Atsushi Kitagawara (*b*.1940)
Setsuo Kitaoka (*b*.1946)
Natsuki Kurimoto (*b*.1961)
Hiroshi Morishima (*b*.1944)
Masaki Morita (*b*.1950)
Sinya Okayama (*b*.1941)
Toshimitsu Sasaki (*b*.1949)
Shigeru Uchida (*b*.1943)

## Toshiyuki Kita (b.1942)

Born in 1942, Toshiyuki Kita is one of the most prolific Japanese designers today, having offices in both Italy and Japan. He trained in interior design and opened his first office in Osaka in 1967. His work is international in scope but he continues to assert his cultural roots and identity through the use of materials such as paper and lacquer.

One of Kita's most famous and collectable designs is the "Wink" chair, which was designed in 1980 and manufactured by Cassina. It is a legless lounge chair which has remained in continuous production since it was designed. The joints inside the chair allow it to be used in either an upright or a vertical position and the wings that form the headrest can be moved from side to side. Kita explained, "One sits sideways, straddles or sits cross-legged. I have often imagined a chair which would gently receive our changing moods at all times."

Other designs for Cassina include the "Kick" table (1983) and the "Luck" sofa. He has also designed for Alessi, Luci, Cesa, and Pendo Mokko. In 1980 he was presented with the Kunii Industrial Art Award. Kita designed the Japanese pavilion for the Seville Expo in 1992.

A beech veneered "Table=
Chest" by Tomoko Azumi,
designed in 1995 and
produced by Azumi.
£1,000–£1,500/$1,500–$2,250

A "Getsuen" armchair,
designed by Masanori Umeda
in 1990 and produced by Edra.
£2,000–£2,200/$3,000–$3,300

A "Wink" chair, designed by Toshiyuki Kita
in 1980 and manufactured by Cassina.
£1,500–£2,500/$2,250–$3,750

# CERAMICS

An untitled plate,
designed by Peter Voulkos
in 1999.
**£14,000–£15,500/$21,000–$23,000**

An "Amaya Stack",
designed by Peter Voulkos
in 1999.
**£60,000–£65,000/$90,000–$100,000**

The 1970s, 1980s, and 1990s brought a new wave of young ceramicists to public attention, including a number who had trained at the Royal College of Art in London. This school is very much part of the British tradition, and the best of the ceramicists who train here gain an international reputation. The young artists used new materials, glazes, and firing techniques to create some fantastic ceramics that are becoming more and more collectable today. Since the early 1980s in particular, studio pottery became very experimental and developed a more sculptural approach. It continues to be experimental today. The ceramics did display elements of Postmodernism, but, as in the Mid-Century and Pop eras, studio wares continued to be an expression of the individual potter's style rather than following a particular movement.

Mid-Century ceramic artists, including Dame Lucie Rie (1902–95) and Hans Coper (1920–81), continued to work in their own style. The way they worked was influential to their pupils but probably the most important aspect they achieved was to elevate ceramics from "craft" to "art" or "ceramic art" – breaking down the stigma that surrounded "craft" and paving the way for the younger generation to be viewed in that context. Many of their pupils became established as studio potters in their own

right and went on to break down the barriers between sculpture and ceramic art even further than their teachers. The mid 1970s also saw a huge interest in traditional crafts and handicrafts. This was brought to public attention and given formal recognition with the formation of the Crafts Council, which supported and showcased the work of talented new designers throughout Britain.

One of the main technical shifts in ceramics that occurred in the late 20th century was the trend towards hand-building, rather than throwing ceramics. This was particularly popular throughout Europe and the USA. Hand-building allowed potters a much greater freedom to construct their pieces (essentially breaking free of the ceramic tradition that had built up over the years) and more expressive and unusual styles became possible.

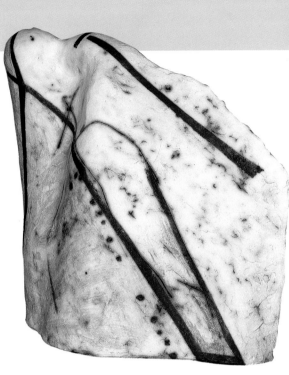

"Enigma" series,
designed by Gordon Baldwin
c. 1986.
£1,300–£1,400/$2,000–$2,200

Developed earthenware bottle,
designed by Gordon Baldwin
c. 1986.
£2,800–£3,000/$4,200–$4,500

Before the advent of hand throwing, ceramic pots that were made on a wheel were symmetrical in one plane and then sometimes squeezed or altered to form pouring lips, which added a human touch. With hand-building, ceramicists could create uneven, textured pots. The "Amaya Stack" (*see opposite*) by Peter Voulkos (*b.*1924) is an excellent example, with its irregular, asymmetric form. It is a combination of thrown elements and pieces added to the central form – once this is constructed cuts and slices are taken out of the piece, adding expressive elements. Voulkos hand-sculpts his pieces, and then adds pieces of clay to the surface, cuts holes in the body, and presses engobes (small ceramic beads) into the structure to create a textured surface. Hand-building also meant that ceramic shapes had changed forever, making vessels singular pieces of artistic expression rather than functional objects. However, many ceramic artists who hand-built pots retained the idea, albeit a much more theoretical one, of vessel form and functionality above objects as "pure" sculpture.

The greatest American ceramicist from the period is Peter Voulkos, whose expressionistic, sculptural work from this era is both highly respected and collectable today. Very few of his pieces exist outside America and

American work is not collected globally, unlike British and Japanese ceramics, in which interest is much more widespread. Voulkos set up his own highly influential ceramics department at the Otis Art Institute in Los Angeles in 1954 and began to create pieces that had no real precedent in the history of American ceramics. He also helped to establish studio pottery in America.

Voulkos' work falls into three recognizable categories. The early work is often finely potted and covered in light green and buff glazes and is almost devoid of any surface texturing and applied design. The middle or "transitional" period begins to be more roughly finished and often has painted motifs and designs painted in the glaze. The late period work becomes increasingly expressive and although based on several themes (the dish, the stack or vase, and the ice bucket) often ceases to be functional as an object despite retaining the concept of the vessel form. The stoneware plate illustrated opposite is an excellent example of this; its rough textured, dry surface is blistered with irregularly formed lumps of clay to create an unconventional, rugged, and challenging one-off piece. Voulkos' ceramics can be identified by their style and his name will be etched into the clay. The majority, but not all, of his pieces are dated.

Large stoneware sack form,
designed by Ewen Henderson
in 1990.
£3,000–£4,000/$4,500–$6,000

A "Floating Particles" vase,
designed by Elizabeth Fritsch
c.1985.
£5,000–£7,000/$7,500–$10,500

Gordon Baldwin (b.1932) is another artist whose style has developed an increasingly abstract, sculptural approach while still retaining the concept of the vessel. Like Voulkos, his work has a sculptural feel which is partly due to his admiration of the sculptor Eduardo Paolozzi (b.1924). Baldwin's work from the 1980s is predominantly white glazed earthenware (see p.219) in jagged, although actually strangely smooth and organic, expressionistic shapes. Baldwin often created monumentally sized pieces. His early work is very inexpensive and plentiful but the later works became more complicated and were made in smaller quantities. In the 1980s his work became internationally popular and he was beginning to get represented by galleries who helped to control the prices and lifted them higher. His monogram is "GB" and this will appear on all his work. Pieces usually have a date too, for example "86" for 1986.

The British designer Elizabeth Fritsch (b.1940) is a visionary and highly influential potter who broke new ground through achieving spatial effects in her stoneware high-fired pottery. She is famed for her stoneware vases, bottles, and bowls. Fritsch's training was initially in music, but she later studied at the Royal College of Art in London from 1967 to 1970.

Fritsch hand-paints coloured slip glazes that show optical illusions of space and perspective, referred to by her as "two and a half dimensions". Her work is improvized (she never makes sketches before starting a piece) and reflects themes of time, physics, the art of ancient civilizations, and, perhaps most importantly, music. The result is beautifully patterned vases such as the "Floating Particles" vase illustrated here, which shows the influence of science and music through the harmonious coloured blocks in the design. Thanks to Fritsch's masterful use of illusion the blocks literally seem to shoot out of the vase. The pieces also work well when seen in small groups; Fritsch designed many of her ceramics along themes, each individual piece seeming to gain something from the next while developing their own character.

Martin Smith (b.1950) studied at the Royal College of Art in London, where he is head of the ceramics department at the time of writing. Smith's use of clay is

A hand-built red earthenware vessel,
designed by Martin Smith
in 1990.
£2,000–£3,000/$3,000–$4,500

very different to that of most ceramic artists. His early
work is black and white Raku (*see p*.50) with geometric
designs playing visual games with the form they are
decorating. He then produced "redware" work. This
often used pre-made elements, such as building bricks cut
and glued together to make angular forms. Sometimes
these forms are laminated with slate or have a covering of
gold, platinum, or copper leaf. He used machinery such as
diamond edge saws to work on pieces of pre-fired clay.
Smith's work challenges our idea of what clay actually is
and how it is worked (after all, it is essentially the same
material used to make basins and roof tiles).

Smith's work attracted the attention of collectors from
the late 1970s onwards. He is particularly famed for his
hand-built, architectonic ceramics in red moulded
earthenware that date from the 1980s onwards. Pieces
such as the example shown above are often geometrically
shaped and angular with a highly controlled quality.

The work of Ewen Henderson (1934–2000) has
already found favour with collectors despite its fragility
and sometimes unstable forms. Henderson believed that
all pieces were a work in progress. By the 1980s he was
sculpting often large scale, hand-built, fantastic ceramic
forms that have no clear function or symmetry and are

A wall plate,
designed by Claudi Casanovas
in 1989.
£2,000–£3,000/$3,000–$4,500

simply highly individual expressions of his art. They look like naturally occurring boulders or pieces of rock and their decorative effect is achieved through the jagged quality of the finished work (see p.220). Henderson's work develops along evolving themes. It is sometimes sculptural, and sometimes loosely retains the concept of a vessel, although not always remaining functional. One theme of Henderson's work that occurs throughout his working life are his "teabowls". These are relatively affordable and have many of the elements of his larger, conceptual work.

Other collectable designers include Pierre Bayle (b.1945) from France and Claudi Casanovas (b.1956) from Spain. Bayle produces ceramics that have spectacularly gentled coloured effects and controlled glazes with organic shapes. Casanovas constructs large-scale pieces on a mould, which are then supported and fired to high temperatures with the mould still in place to create his wonderful forms, that are like the volcanic surroundings of his native Catalunya in northern Spain.

Collectable studio ceramics from Japan are dominated in the West by a handful of key designers. In Japan a vast range of artists are able to sell their work at very respectable prices but relatively few of them are known in

"Shun II" ("Flash of Light II"),
designed by Fukami Sueharu
in 1998.
**£16,700–£18,500/$25,000–$27,500**

the West. Fukami Sueharu was born in 1947 and is based in Kyoto. He is one of the leading figures in contemporary ceramics in Japan. Within Japan, even at the beginning of the 21st century, very few artists produce purely sculptural work – most still use the "tea ceremony" as a source of inspiration, producing teabowls, water jars, flower vases, and dinnerwares. Sueharu has revolutionized the way porcelain, a traditional material for ceramic artists, is used.

Sueharu is inspired by natural forms and weather conditions. He works in porcelain, essentially trying to capture the essence of a natural occurrence in his pieces. Porcelain allows him to create works that leave no trace of the potter's hand and the results are sleek pieces that are beautifully formed, with an impeccable sense of line. In the example shown above, the effect is that of the curved edge of a samurai sword. His pieces are made through slip-casting, carving, and then glazing, and are often made to order, which heightens their collectability today.

Magdalene Odundo (b.1950) was born in Kenya,

*Above*: A ceramic form,
designed by Pierre Bayle
*c.*1985.
£1,200–£1,800/$1,800–$2,700

*Above right*: A vase,
designed by Magdelene Odundo
*c.*1983.
£3,000–£4,000/$4,500–$6,000

*Right*: A bone china vase,
designed by Jacqui Poncelet
*c.*1972.
£1,200–£1,800/$1,800–$2,700

moving to England in 1971. Her pieces are hand-built and show the influence of traditional African pottery forms, as well as elements of the European ceramics tradition. No two pieces are ever the same but many of them combine similar elements such as a round base. The shapes of her pieces (as seen in the vase shown here) often reflect the curves of the female body.

Another successful, collectable contemporary ceramicist is Jacqui Poncelet (*b.*1947). Her early pieces in cast bone china are plain white, extremely fine, and almost translucent. Her work developed into stoneware from the mid 1970s onwards and used coloured decorative motifs.

# GLASS

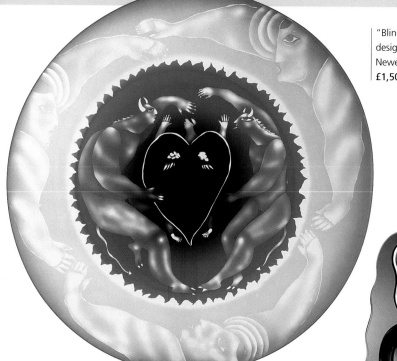

"Blind Heart in Hell", a glass charger designed and executed by Stephen Newell in 1990.
**£1,500-£2,500/$2,250-$3,750**

"Cosmic Tides",
designed by Ray Flavell in 1990.
**£2,500–£3,500/$3,750–$5,250**

The 1970s and 1980s saw a consolidation of the Studio Glass movement and the realization that there was only a finite number of things that one could do to the "bubble" before the challenge faded. The new wave of artist-designers saw infinitely more possibilities for glass, edging it further and further away from functionalism and towards a pure art form.

The combination of other materials with glass, such as metal, the introduction of different treatments of glass, for instance laminating, and the re-introduction of pâte de verre, and the use of the lost-wax casting methods all helped to give rise to a new, more sophisticated treatment of glass. Cutting, polishing, etching, and sandblasting were employed to great effect.

Towards the end of the 20th century the major Scandinavian factories not only consolidated their position with the amalgamation of rivals, but they also allowed their designers a freer rein. In both America and Europe by the 1990s, it became clear that because of the diversity of styles within the countries involved, and the cross-over of ideas generally, a new international glass movement had been established. It has its own vocabulary which transcends the factories, styles, and commercial parameters as well as national boundaries.

In Britain Ray Flavell (b.1944) reacted against Samuel Herman's (b.1936) form of free-expression with hot-glass blowing, feeling that there was not enough attention to technique. Flavell decided to remedy this by going to Sweden to attend the Orrefors Glass School. It was here that he developed a more disciplined and controlled approach to his design than that of Herman's, a trend which was to become apparent in other artists' work. Flavell works with clear glass, often combining transparent coloured sections with his pieces. He also employs cutting, polishing, and sandblasting, making his work very sculptural. The piece shown above is typical of his work and his sculptural style.

Although Stephen Newell (b.1948) is American, he has pursued a career in Britain. He was an early member of The Glasshouse, which became one of the longest running glass cooperatives in Britain. Most of his work is of fantasy subjects etched or sandblasted to the surface of bowls or large plates. Many of his pieces utilize his own personal repertoire of symbolism. Particular symbols are

Cast glass bowl, designed
and executed by Tessa Clegg in 1990.
**£450–£750/$670–$1,120**

"Blue Figure", designed and
executed by Clifford Rainey in 1989.
**£2,800–£3,500/$4,200–$5,250**

used time and again and can be traced throughout his
work. As with the charger illustrated opposite, his
individual work is all titled.

A few British artists use casting techniques, a high
proportion of whom were taught by Keith Cummings
(*b*.1940) at the University of Wolverhampton in central
England. One of his students was Tessa Clegg (*b*.1946).
Over the years she has developed her own unique style.
Many of her pieces have a pleated effect, or use deep V-
shaped grooves to produce the looks she desires. In the
early 1990s she was influenced by Norman and
Romanesque patterns in the production of monumental
bowls that were both architectural in stature and
conception. The bowl illustrated above demonstrates her
use of deep-grooved decoration.

Clifford Rainey's (*b*.1948) work encompasses the
monumental, sculptural, and architectural, and has an
international following. He was probably the first British
glass artist to combine the material with other media and
has been influential, not only through his works, but also
through his teaching. His cast figures, like the one shown
here, give rise to a number of emotions and call on several
influences and references. One obvious reference here is
to St Sebastian – the sheets of glass set at angles

Internally coloured vase with
etched surface, designed and
executed by Pauline Solven in 1990.
**£400–£500/$600–$750**

"Cerulean Blue Persian Set with Red
Lip Wraps", designed and executed by
Dale Chihuly and a blowing team in 1990.
**£10,000–£14,000/$15,000–$20,000**

becoming the arrows. Rainey's work is truly an art form and is far removed from most of the early pieces of the hot-glass (or studio glass) artists whose work now seems more like a craft.

Pauline Solven (b.1948) was an early pupil on the course held by Herman in 1967 at the Royal College of Art in London, and she was strongly influenced by him. Her work at that time was similar to Herman's, but utilized a more muted palette. After having worked at and run The Glasshouse in Covent Garden, London, in 1975 she set up her own workshop in Newent, Gloucestershire, southwest England. She formed the Cowdy Glass Workshop Ltd. in 1978, with her husband Harry Cowdy (b.1944), which produced functional work mainly by her, but also by other invited artists. Although her work was initially somewhat faltering, she developed a style that showed her skills as a colourist, often taking inspiration from nature, both in the round and in detail. The piece shown above illustrates her confident use of colour, a feel for gentle forms, and her continued use of hot-glass blowing.

In America, the movement towards glass as a pure art form had also taken place. However, as in Britain, some artists continued to work in hot-glass while others embraced new techniques.

Dale Chihuly (b.1941) was one of the early pioneers of the modern hot-glass movement in America. Chihuly is an accomplished communicator, both through his work and in the promotion of it. The publicity he has received and created has made the public more aware of glass as an art form. He continues to work in the modern tradition of hot-glass blowing, but has formed a team of recognized artists that make the pieces he creates under his direction. The composite items produced depend on an inter-relationship of the individual pieces that form the whole. They also rely on the skill of the workers, combined with spontaneity during the course of the work to help produce the overall flamboyant effect. The work is organic in nature, and ostentatious with its vivid use of different colours. The pieces can be individual, shell-like forms or be used in multiples to create a composite design as shown above. Nowadays Chihuly's works can be huge sculptural conceptions.

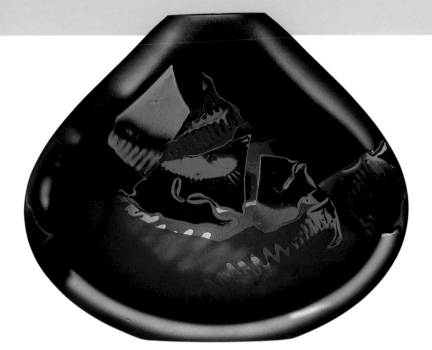

"Continuous Fragment" vessel,
part of a series, designed
by Joel Philip Myers in 1982.
£2,500–£3,000/$3,700–$4,500

Another of the early students of studio glass was
Joel Philip Myers (b.1934) who trained as a ceramicist. He
took a position with Blenko Glass in 1964, succeeding
Wayne Husted as design directior, and stayed until 1972.
During his time with Blenko he learnt how to blow glass.
He was interested in the studio movement so some of his
more commercial designs reflected this, but he also blew
his own individual items. Since those early days his work
has developed, as has his technical mastery. His
"Continuous Fragment" series illustrates this amply, as
can be seen from the example shown above. Many of the
pieces from this series are opaque, often black, decorated
with coloured pieces of glass in a marquetry technique, a
method that he has perfected.

Cast-glass forms are a speciality of Howard Ben Tré
(b.1949) who also uses sandblasting, copper inlays, and
patinas to create the effects he requires on the industrial-
looking pieces he produces. At first sight, many appear to
be sections of steel girder made in glass, yet on second
inspection they are far more subtle and involved than

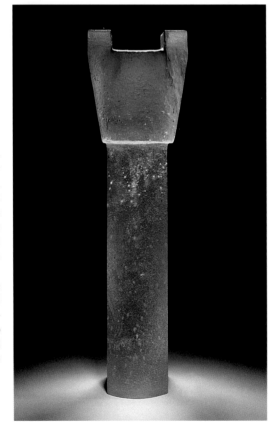

Cast glass sculpture designed
by Howard Ben Tré in 1986.
£6,000–£7,500/$9,000–£11,000

"3 Curiosities Against a Wall",
designed by Philippe Starck for
Christallerie Daum in 1988.
**£1,500–£2,000/$2,250–$3,000**

that. A section through his forms details how varied, yet balanced, his pieces really are. One can read all sorts of meaning into his stylized sculptures, from highly stylized human features to industrial icons or futuristic totems. There is a strange, almost primitive presence about his work, as can be seen in the piece shown on page 227.

Kreg Kallenberger (b.1950) studied, and later taught, at the University of Tulsa between 1979 and 1984. Since 1985 he has been an independent artist. He is fascinated by the anonymous industrial aesthetic pervading our lives, whether consciously or not. He believes that glass is a metaphor of our time, encompassing as it does coldness, impersonality, resilience, and fragility. He translates these thoughts into his work. Once he has blown or cast the basis of a piece he then embellishes it by cutting and polishing with optical precision, enhancing the original form with the complex effects produced. The piece from the "Interlock" series shown opposite exemplifies these themes through being a sort of industrialized sculpture. Kallenberger's work exploits the inherent beauty of glass with his sophisticated cut techniques.

The versatility of Dan Dailey (b.1947) is demonstrated by his ability to combine different materials with glass and to use glass alone, but decorated by sandblasting or acid etching. Both approaches are invariably accompanied by his own comic treatment. He studies people's habits and idiosyncracies then uses this to inspire his work and as a means to evoke reaction to that work. When building mixed-media sculptures, he enlists the help of his wife Linda MacNeil (an accomplished glass artist in her own right) to construct the metalwork. Dailey produced work for the likes of Steuben, Venini, and Daum during the 1980s. The example of work illustrated here is made from pâte de verre which is a paste made from finely crushed glass mixed with metal oxides. The paste is first placed in a mould, then fused and vitrified in a kiln.

In the same way that Steuben in America had invited outside artists to design work, Michel Daum (b.1910)

"Le Vent", designed by Dan Dailey
for Christallerie Daum in 1986.
**£3,500–£4,000/$5,200–$6,000**

introduced the idea at the French factory of Christallerie Daum. Designers for the limited editions ranged from Salvador Dali (1904–89) through to Philippe Starck (b.1949). Many of these works included pâte de verre in order to give colour to the item. This had been reintroduced to the factory in 1965 after an idea by Jacques Daum (b.1909) to enrich a particular collection of heavy crystal being made by the company.

As can be seen from the table-like piece shown opposite, Starck combined the use of pâte de verre with clear plate glass in his designs. Some of the items from this series by Starck, introduced to celebrate the twentieth anniversary of the limited edition project, are less traditional in feel. The horns can be made of various colours and in various forms. By simply turning the sheet of plate glass on its edge the horns became vertical, making the item very sculptural. Others in the series use a single horn as support, sometimes with the horn pointing directly onto the sheet of glass. Starck uses this horn-shaped motif in other disciplines of design within his work as a designer and architect.

The work chosen for this section was picked as being representative of the period and giving a cross-section of techniques employed by today's artist-designers. It may be too early to say which designer one might collect, although some names have become established through both their

"Interlock System No. 214",
designed and executed in 1984
by Kreg Kallenberger.
**£1,800-£2,000/$2,700-$3,000**

work and their longevity in the field. The main difference between buying contemporary work and earlier pieces is that one is purchasing first hand, not second hand with the benefit of hindsight. Occasionally however, as with the pieces illustrated, items do appear at auction. When they do, prices do not always reflect those asked in the studio or gallery. This is a challenging form of collecting where one has to rely on recognizing the integrity of an artist and using one's personal judgement.

A mint condition watch,
designed by Dieter Rams in 1978.
**With box: £1,000–£1,200/$1,500–$1,800;**
**Without box: £700–£800/$1,000–$1,200**

An later plastic example of the steel carafe,
designed by Eric Magnussen in 1976.
**£80–£100/$120–$150;**
(steel carafe) **£200–£250/$300–$375**

By the early 1970s Bjorn Weckstrom had won some prestigious competitions, including the Rio Grand Prix in 1965 and the Lunning Prize in 1968, putting him at the forefront of Finnish modern design jewellery. The "Space Apple" necklace (see opposite) represents one of the first successful commercial applications of mixed material methodology from Weckstrom. During the 1970s the Miss World contest came from Finland and the winner was given a set of Weckstrom jewellery, which brought him further fame. This tradition continues today.

In 1977 Weckstrom's work reached a worldwide audience when it was worn by Carrie Fisher in the role of Princess Leia in George Lucas's film Star Wars. This suite of jewellery, called "Planetoid Valleys" (see p.232), is a wonderful example of Weckstrom's love of space-age styling combined with a hint of romanticism. This jewellery found a perfect home in Lucas's science fiction fantasy film and this connection helps make the "Planetoid Valleys" suite desirable to collectors today.

Erik Magnussen was born in 1940 and educated at the School of Arts, Crafts and Design in Copenhagen. He specializes in designing ceramics and tableware. In the 1970s he was particularly interested in creating functional and well-designed tea ware for the commercial market.

Magnussen wanted to solve the problem of handling hot objects when pouring drinks and so worked with thermoware. By 1976 his work in this field had been noticed by the firm Stelton, and Magnussen designed the famous Stelton coffee carafe in the same year. This has now become a contemporary design classic. Original examples were made in steel, and these are particularly rare and collectable today. Slightly later versions were produced in multicoloured plastics including red, white and orange. These have also found favour with collectors both as stylish objects, and to use in the home.

One of the greatest industrial designers to come out of Germany in the late 20th century was Dieter Rams (b.1932). He is best known for his pioneering industrial and product design for Braun. Rams joined the firm as a designer in 1955, becoming head of product design in 1968 and general manager of the company in 1988.

Rams was trained within the Bauhaus tradition and wanted to produce functional, minimal, yet decorative

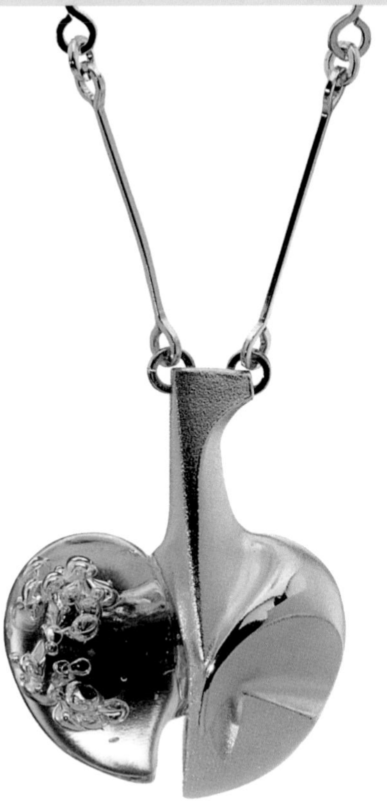

A "Space Apple" necklace,
designed by Bjorn Weckstrom in 1969.
**£1,500–£1,800/$2,250–$2,700**

objects. He finally achieved the Bauhaus aim of creating good design for mass production. His works are masterpieces of minimal decoration and sleek styling, and are also idealistic, as he wanted his designs to simplify the hectic modern world that he saw as driven by consumption and consumerism. He liked to call his products "silent butlers", and wanted them to become indispensable and reliable objects that everyone could afford.

During his early years at Braun, Rams created many stylish objects, including audio equipment such as radios and stereos. He also produced kitchenware, including coffee percolators and food mixers, and cameras, clocks, and electric razors. Ram's watches are particularly collectable today, and the current trend for 1970s styling has put his work right back into fashion again as a new generation of collectors discover it.

Rams continues to design today and his retro watches such as the example shown here are relatively easy to find, notably in specialist jewellery and modern design sales at

Very rare yellow gold and enamel
"Tower" rings on a frosted acrylic stand,
designed by Wendy Ramshaw in 1975.
**£9,000–£10,000/$13,500–$15,000**

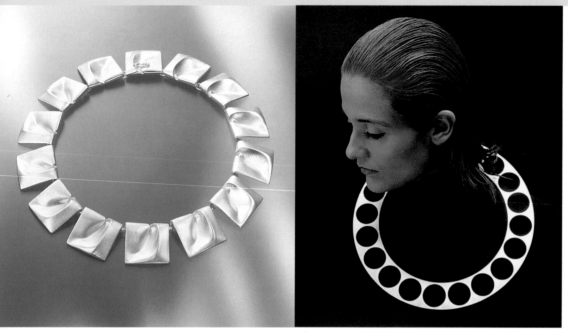

A "Planetoid Valleys" necklace,
designed by Bjorn Weckstrom in 1973.
£1,000–£1,500/$1,500–$2,250

A "Torus" gilded brass necklace,
designed by David Watkins
in 1989.
£6,000–£7,000/$9,000–$10,500

major auction houses. His work is still reasonably priced, apart from early key examples of stereos and watches which are already fetching four-figure sums.

Wendy Ramshaw's jewellery from the 1970s is becoming extremely sought after today, particularly her highly collectable "Tower" rings (see p.231) and beautifully modelled necklaces. She was born in 1939 and studied at the College of Art and Industrial Design, Newcastle. She designed commercial Perspex Op Art jewellery in the 1960s with her husband, David Watkins (b.1940). She has designed jewellery in one form or another since the age of 16. Early pieces were made from inexpensive materials such as copper, brass, and nickel silver. In the later stages of her education she was producing copper plate etchings and became interested in the look that could be created by rubbing ink into the recesses of the plates. She set out to replicate this effect in her jewellery. Ramshaw is mainly influenced by industrial art as well as by nature, and the natural appeal of all materials including gold, silver, and precious stones. She also admires simple, early medieval jewellery and the more ostentatious jewellery designs of the 1920s.

Ramshaw developed the concept of her "Tower" rings because she liked the idea of jewellery that could be manipulated by the wearer and worn as a single part, or as a whole group. At first the towers were created to display her rings, and as time went on they became an intrinsic part of the piece of jewellery, creating a sculptural tower. These rings are becoming harder to find today because the production levels of Ramshaw's jewellery are decreasing each year as she turns more towards large-scale commissions, such as gates and sculptures. Her work continues to develop, reflecting and anticipating more contemporary styles.

In the London of the "swinging sixties" Watkins and Ramshaw designed an innovative collection of flat-pack paper jewellery which was sold in boutiques throughout Britain and exported worldwide. In the 1970s and 1980s Watkins explored the possibilities of new materials and techniques in jewellery, combining plastics with precious metals and harnessing computer technology to design mechanistically-styled, yet extremely wearable Postmodern jewellery. In 1974 the Science Museum of London acquired examples of his acrylic work because of his incorporation of a wide range of innovative techniques in modern plastics. Watkins' work was remarkable at this time for the inclusion of bonding, surface dying, heat forming, and machining in one piece.

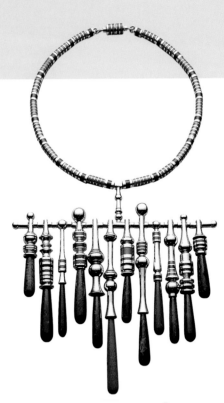

A gold necklace,
designed by Lara Bohinc in 2000.
**£750/$1,120**

A very rare silver, enamel,
and lapis lazuli necklace,
designed by Wendy Ramshaw in 1971.
**£9,000–£10,000/$13,500–$15,000**

Examples of David Watkins' jewellery are to be found in most important international collections of applied art. His approach to jewellery design has been very influential, and his teaching at the Royal College of Art has encouraged and nurtured a generation of young jewellers. The "Torus" necklace shown opposite was produced using the most up-to-date machine processes, combined with precious metals and traditional handbrushed techniques. From the outset he shared Ramshaw's belief that pieces of jewellery could be deconstructed and seen as dynamic sculptural works of art in their own right. Both husband and wife are recognized as key figures in modern jewellery and this makes their work collectable today.

Lara Bohinc is the *enfant terrible* of the next generation of British jewellery designers who are breaking new ground with their innovative jewellery forms and use of unexpected materials. She was born in Slovenia and came to London to study jewellery at the Royal College of Art, graduating in 1994 and receiving instant critical acclaim. Her work is already attracting the interest of a growing number of collectors and is regularly seen on fashion catwalks including shows for Julien MacDonald, Exté, Maria Chan, and many more.

Bohinc's jewellery can be recognized through its modern use of materials such as leather and rubber combined with silver. She also uses Perspex, which she dyes and folds into fantastic shapes. Bohinc believes that her work should be clean and dynamic, an ethos that can be traced back to the beautifully refined silver jewellery of the Scandinavian designer Nanna Ditzel (*see p.123*).

Bohinc's strongest inspirations come from the work of the Danish designer Verner Panton, Russian Constructivism, and Japanese graphics. She is also influenced by the natural world and the whole experience of living in 21st century London with its strong sense of individual fashion and style.

At the time of writing Bohinc's pieces are affordable and sure to become highly desirable items of the future. The beauty of collecting contemporary jewellery such as Bohinc's is that it is possible to obtain examples from each new range as it is released, so your collection will develop along with the designer's career.

# Directory

## DEALERS AND MARKETS

These dealers and markets sell modern design classics and reissues of modern designs.

- **Aero** 347–349 King's Road, London, UK tel: 020 7351 0511
- **Alfie's Antique Market** 13–25 Church Street, Marylebone, London, UK tel: 020 7723 6066
- **Atomic Interiors** Plumptre Square, Nottingham, UK tel: 0115 9415577
- **Domane** 5 Bridge Street, Leeds, UK tel: 0113 245 0701
- **Eat my handbag bitch** 6 Dray Walk, The Olde Truman Building, 91–95 Brick Lane, London, UK tel: 020 7375 3100
- **Elastique** 19 Grüngrasse, 8004 Zürich, SWI tel: 00 41 79235 2761
- **Full House** 1 North Street, Brooklyn, New York, USA tel: + 718 599 2410
- **Inside** 69 Venn Street, London, UK tel: 020 7622 5266
- **Places and Spaces** 30 Old Town, Clapham, London, UK tel: 020 7498 0998
- **Ron Arad Studio** 62 Chalk Farm Road, London, UK tel: 020 7284 4963
- **SCP** 135–139 Curtain Road, London, UK tel: 020 7739 1869
- **Skandium** 72 Wigmore Street, London, UK tel: 020 7935 2077
- **Themes & Variations** 231 Westbourne Grove, London, UK tel: 020 7727 5531
- **20th Century Marks** 12 Market Square, Westerham, UK tel: 01959 562221
- **Twentytwentyone** 274 Upper Street, Islington, London, UK tel: 020 7288 1996
- **Zoom** 312 Lillie Road, Fulham, London, UK tel: 020 7386 9522

## WORLDWIDE ONLINE SUPPLIERS

These are a selection of some of the best online sites where you can buy both original and reissued modern design pieces.

www.mancha.demon.co.uk – selling Charles and Ray Eames, Scandinavian glass, ceramics, and furniture
www.classiconline.com – 20th century classic furniture designs by Le Corbusier, Ludwig Mies van der Rohe, Eileen Gray, and Gerrit Rietveld
www.internetauctionlist.com – portal site to worldwide internet auctions
www.ebay.com – probably the best auction site on the net
www.scandinaviandesign.com – for new furniture, information, and news
www.danish-design.com – specializing in Danish furniture
www.retrogallery.co.uk – post-war decorative glass, specializing in Murano and Scandinavian design
www.fearsandkahn.co.uk – particularly good for 20th century plastics
www.icon20.com – articles available to buy plus a reference directory of 20th century designers
www.banaldesign.com – specializing in Postmodern design items

## AUCTIONEERS

These auctioneers currently hold regular sales featuring modern design. This list is by no means exhaustive. As modern design is growing in popularity more regional auctioneers will offer selections. The major London auction houses have branches worldwide and their contact details can be obtained from the London offices.

- **Bonhams & Brooks** Montpelier Street, Knightsbridge, London, UK tel: 020 7393 3900 www.bonhams.com
- **Christie's** 85 Old Brompton Road, London, UK tel: 020 7581 7611 www.christies.com
- **Hagelstam Fine Art Auctioneers** Bulevardi 9 A, 00120, Helsinki, FIN tel: + 358 9 602 785 www.hagelstam.com
- **Phillips** 10 Salem Road, Bayswater, London, UK tel: 020 7313 2700 *and* 101 New Bond Street, London, tel: 020 7629 6602 www.phillips-auctions.com
- **Rago Arts** 333 North Main Street, Lambertville, NJ, USA www.ragoarts.com
- **Rosebery's** 74/76 Knight's Hill, London, UK tel: 020 8761 2522 www.roseberys.co.uk
- **Sotheby's** 34–35 New Bond Street, London, UK tel: 020 7493 8080 www.sothebys.com
- **Treadway/Toomey** 2029 Madison Road, Cincinatti, OH, USA www.treadwaygallery.com

## DESIGNER'S WEB SITES

Some of the great 20th century and contemporary designers have their own web sites with information, biographies, and items for sale. Among the best are:

www.eamesoffice.com
www.eero-aarnio.com
www.ronarad.com
www.fornasetti.com
www.marc-newson.com
www.vernerpanton.com
www.nanna-ditzel-design.dk

## MUSEUMS AND COLLECTIONS

The following institutions have particularly strong collections of modern design including furniture, ceramics, glass, textiles, graphics, and metalware:

- Alvar Aalto Museum, Jyvaskyla, FIN
- Bauhaus Archiv, Berlin, GER
- Design Museum, London, UK
- Geffrye Museum, London, UK
- London Transport Museum, London, UK
- Manchester City Art Galleries, Manchester, UK
- Metropolitan Museum of Art, New York, USA
- Museum of Applied Arts, Helsinki, FIN
- Museum of Decorative Arts, Copenhagen, NTH
- National Glass Centre, Sunderland, UK
- Vitra Design Museum, Berlin, GER
- Vitra Design Museum, Weil am Rhein, GER
- Victoria and Albert Museum, London, UK
- Whitworth Art Gallery, Manchester, UK

# Bibliography

Aav, Marianne and Stritzler-Levine, Nina (eds.) *Finnish Modern Design – Utopian Ideals and Everyday Realities 1930–97* (Yale University Press, 1998)

Baker, Fiona and Keith *20th Century Furniture* (Carlton Books, 2000)

Bangere, Albrecht and Armer, Karl Michael *80s Style – Designs of the Decade*, foreword by Ettore Sottsass, (Thames & Hudson, 1990)

Benton, Tim and Campbell-Cole, Barbie (eds.) *Tubular Steel Furniture*, conference paper, (Art Book Co., 1979)

Boudet, François *Eileen Gray* (Thames & Hudson, 1998)

Collins, Michael *Post-Modern Design* (ed.) Andreas Papadakis (Academy Editions, 1989)

Conway, Hazel *Ernest Race* (The Design Council, 1982)

Crow, Thomas *The Rise of the Sixties* (Everyman Art Library, 1996)

Dormer, Peter *Design since 1945* (Thames & Hudson, 1993) *The New Ceramics: Trends and Traditions* (Thames & Hudson, 1997)

Favata, Ignazia *Joe Colombo and Italian Design of the 60s* (Thames & Hudson, 1988)

Fiell, Charlotte and Peter *Modern Furniture Classics since 1945* (Thames & Hudson, 1991) *1000 Chairs* (Taschen, 1997) *Design of the 20th Century* (Taschen, 1999) (eds.) *60s Decorative Art Sourcebook* (Taschen, 2000)

Fitoussi, Brigitte *Memphis* (Thames & Hudson, 1998)

Friedeman, Mildred (ed.) *De Stijl 1917–1931: Visions of Utopia* (ex cat) (Minneapolis and Oxford, 1981)

Garner, Philippe *Sixties Design* (Taschen, 1996) (ed.) *The Encyclopaedia of Decorative Arts 1890–1940* (Grange Books ,1997)

Gilbert, Anne *60s and 70s Designs and Memorabilia* (Avon Books, 1994)

Gowing, Christopher and Rice, Paul *British Studio Ceramics in the 20th Century* (Barrie & Jenkins, 1989)

Green, Oliver *Underground Art* (StudioVista, 1990)

Greenberg, Cara *Mid-Century Modern Furniture of the 1950s* (Thames & Hudson, 1995)

Harnsen, Eileene Beer *Scandinavian Design – Objects of a Life Style* (American-Scandinavian Foundation, 1975)

Hayes, Jennifer *Lucienne Day: A Career in Design* (Whitworth Art Gallery, 1993)

Jackson, Lesley *The New Look – Design in the Fifties* (Thames & Hudson, 1991) *The Sixties* (London, Phaidon, 1998)

Julien, Guy *The Dictionary of 20th Century Design and Designers* (Thames & Hudson, 1993)

Kirkham, Pat *Charles and Ray Eames, Designers of the 20th Century* (MIT Press, 1998)

Klein, Dan and Ward Lloyd *The History of Glass* (Little, Brown & Co., 1993)

Marcus, George *Functionalist Design* (Prestel, 1995)

Marsh, Graham and Normand, Tony (eds.) *Film Posters of the 1960s* (Avrum Press, 1997)

McDowell's *Directory of 20th Century Fashion* (Muller Blond & White, 1984)

Mellor, David *The Sixties Art Scene in London* (Phaidon 1993)

Oda, Noritsugu *Danish Chairs* (Chronicle Books, 1999)

Overy, Paul *De Stijl* (Thames & Hudson, 1991)

Radice, Barbara *Ettore Sottsass* (Thames & Hudson, 1993) Memphis (Thames & Hudson, 1994)

Sparke, Penny *Ettore Sottsass Jnr* (Design Council, 1982) *A Century of Design* (Mitchell Beazley, 1998)

Sudjic, Deyan *Ron Arad* (Laurence King Publishing, 1999)

Waal, Edmund de *Bernard Leach* (Tate Gallery Publishing, 1998)

Watson, Oliver *Studio Pottery* (Phaidon, 1993)

Weltge, Sigrid Wortmann *Bauhaus Textiles – Women Artists and the Weaving Workshop* (Thames & Hudson, 1993)

Whitford, Frank *The Bauhaus* (Thames & Hudson, 1984)

Woodham, Jonathan *Twentieth Century Design* (Oxford University Press, 1997)

### CATALOGUES

*Forces of Nature: Axel Salto Ceramics and Drawings*, catalogue (Antik, New York, 1999)

*Achille Castiglioni Design!*, exhibition catalogue (Museum of Modern Art, New York, 1998)

*A Lifetime Sale of Dame Lucie Rie*, auction catalogue (Bonhams, 17 April 1997)

Mauriès, Patrick *Fornasetti – Designer of Dreams* (Thames & Hudson, 1991)

*Design Since 1945*, exhibition catalogue (Philadelphia Museum of Art, 1983)

Also various modern design specialist-sale catalogues from Christie's, Phillips, and Sotheby's auctioneers, from 1997 to the present day.

# Index

# Acknowledgments

Key for acknowledgments

**FC** Front Cover, **BC** Back Cover, **SPI** Spine, **t** top, **b** bottom, **l** left, **r** right, **c** centre

**20thC:** 20th Century Design; **A:** Alfie's, London; **AJP:** A. J. Photographics; **AKG:** AKG, London; **ANT:** Antik/Axel Salto; **B:** Bonhams Auctioneers; **BAL:** Bridgeman Art Library; **BAUHAUS:** Bauhaus-Archiv, Berlin/VG Bild-Kunst, Bonn, Germany; **BC:** The British Council; **CASS:** "Cassina I Maestri" Collection; **CB:** photo Clarissa Bruce; **CF:** Christoher Farr; **CI:** Christie's Images; **CP:** Charlotte Perriand; **CSK:** Christie's South Kensington; **DAY:** Robin and Lucienne Day Archive; **DES:** Design Council/DHRC, University of Brighton; **DW:** David Watkins; **FBS:** photograph supplied by the Festival of Britain Society; **FDE:** Flying Duck Enterprises; **FLG:** Frank Lloyd Gallery; **GC:** Galerie Carla Koch; **HM:** Hermann Miller, Inc.; **IB:** photo Ian Booth; **JBM:** Joan B Mirviss Ltd., Japanese Fine Art, New York, / Fukami Sueharu; **JM:** Jasper Morrison; **KIM:** Kunst Industri Museet, Denmark; **LAMA:** Los Angeles Modern Arts, USA; **LB:** Lara Bohinic; **LD:** Lucienne Day; **LJ:** Lapponia Jewelry OY; **LTM:** London Transport Museum; **MKG:** Collection Museum für Kunst und Gerwerbe, Hamburg, **ML:** Memory Lane; **MN:** Marc Newson; **MW:** Marcel Wanders; **NB:** at Neil Bingham; **ND:** Nanna Ditzel Design A/S; **OPG:** Octopus Publishing Group; **PB:** Planet Bazar; **PC:** Private Collection; **PHIL:** Phillips, London; **RA:** Ron Arad Associates; **SJC:** Studio Joe Columbo, Milan; **SL:** Sotheby's, London; **SPL:** Sotheby's Picture Library; **SS:** Schopplein Studio; **ST:** photo Steve Tanner; **TA:** Tomoko Azumi; **TG:** Target Gallery; **TM:** photo Tony Mann; **TR:** photo Tim Ridley; **TT:** Treadway.Toomey Gallery, Cincinnati, Ohio, USA; **TTO:** Twentytwentyone; **V&A:** Victoria and Albert Museum, London; **VITRA:** Vitra Design Museum; **VP:** Verner Panton Design; **WAG:** The Whitworth Art Gallery, University of Manchester; **WCG:** Courtesy of The Worshipful Company of Goldsmiths; **WM:** photo Wilhelm Moser; **WR:** Wendy Ramshaw; **YORK:** York City Art Gallery; **Z:** Zambesi; **ZA:** photo Zakowski

Acknowledgments in page order

**FC: tl** SPL, **tr** TTO, **bl** WAG, **br** BAL/PC; **BC: bl** OPG/TR/TTO, **bc** OPG/TR/TG, **br** OPG/TR/TTO, **SPI** CI, **5** PHIL, **6** SPL/©DACS 2001, **7l** BAL/PC, **7r** CI, **8cl** B, **8bl** OPG/TR/TTO, **9l** OPG/IB/CSK, **9r** CI, **14–15** CI/© DACS 2001, **19t** CI/© DACS 2001, **19bl** CI/©DACS 2001, **19br** Cassina S.P.A./Mario Carrieri/© DACS 2001, **21tl** PHIL/© DACS 2001, **21tr** PHIL/© DACS 2001, **21bl** PHIL/© DACS 2001, **21br** PHIL/© DACS 2001, **23tl** CI, **23tr** V&A/© DACS 2001, **23bl** BAUHAUS/photo Gunter Lepkowski/© ARS, NY and DACS, London 2001, **23br** BAUHAUS/photo Atelier Schneider/© DACS 2001, **25tl** PHIL, **25tr** CI, **25bl** CI, **25br** PHIL, **27t** PHIL, **27cl** PHIL, **27b** CI, **28tr** CI, **29t** PHIL, **29b** PHIL, **31tl** AKG, **31tr** CI, **31cl** TT, **31br** PHIL/© DACS 2001, **32tr** AKG/Gert Schutz, **32bl** CI, **32bc** CI, **32br** CI, **33** SPL, **34** CI, **35t** CI, **35b** SPL, **37t** CI, **37c** CI, **37br** CI, **39r** TT, **39tl** BAL, **39b** CI/© ADAGP, Paris and DACS, London 2001, **40t** CP/photo Pierre Jeanneret, **40c** CASS/photo Leo Torri/© FLC/ADAGP, Paris and DACS, London 2001, **40b** B/© FLC/ADAGP, Paris and DACS, London 2001, **41tr** CASS/photo Oliviero Venturi/© FLC/ADAGP, Paris and DACS, London 2001, **41b** CASS/photo Bella & Ruggeri/© FLC/ADAGP, Paris and DACS, London 2001, **42** SPL/© FLC/ADAGP, Paris and DACS, London 2001, **43tr** CI/© FLC/ADAGP, Paris and DACS, London 2001, **43cl** CI/© FLC/ADAGP, Paris and DACS, London 2001, **43b** CI/© ADAGP, Paris and DACS, London 2001, **45tl** V&A , **45tr** PHIL, **45b** CI, **47tl** PHIL, **47tr** PHIL, **47bl** PHIL, **47br** PHIL, **48** PHIL, **49tl** BAL/V&A, **49tr** PHIL, **49br** YORK, **50l** V&A, **50r** PHIL, **51l** PHIL, **51tr** YORK, **52l** PHIL, **52r** PHIL, **53** PHIL, **54** CF, **54t** CI, **54b** SPL/© DACS 2001, **55r** CF, **55t** CI, **55tl** CI, **55br** CI, **56tl** CI, **56tr** CI, **57** PHIL, **58** PHIL, **59tl** CI, **59tr** PHIL, **60tl** CI, **60tr** PHIL, **61tl** SPL, **61tr** CI, **62l** LTM, **62r** LTM, **63l** LTM, **63r** LTM, **66–7t** CI, **68t** FBS, **68bl** FBS, **68br** OPG/TR, **69l** CI, **69r** OPG/IB/B, **70tl** OPG/IB/CSK, **70tr** CI, **71** OPG/TR/NB, **72tr** DAY, **72b** OPG/TR/NB, **73tr** OPG/ST, **73cl** OPG/IB/CSK, **73cr** OPG/TM, **73br** OPG/ST, **75tl** CI, **75tr** OPG/TR/TTO, **75c** CI, **75b** PHIL/©ADAGP, Paris and DACS, London 2001, **77t** PHIL, **77cl** CI, **77cr** CI, **77b** PHIL, **79tl** CI/© ARS, NY and DACS, London 2001, **79tc** OPG/TR/20thC, **79b** OPG/TR/20thC, **80t** HM, **80b** CI, **81t** OPG/TR/FDE, **81bl** CI, **81br** OPG/IB/CSK, **83tr** OPG/IB/B, **83cl** OPG/TR/TTO, **83cr** OPG/TR/TTO, **83b** OPG/TR/TTO, **84t** © 2000 Lucia Eames/Eames Office (www.eamesoffice.com), **84b** CI, **85t** CI, **85b** B, **86** B, **87tr** CI, **87bl** LAMA, **87br** CI, **88** B, **89l** OPG, **89tr** CI, **89br** CI, **90** OPG/TR/20thC, **91bl** B, **91br** OPG/IB, **93tl** OPG/IB/B, **93tr** OPG/IB/CSK, **93bl** CI, **93br** OPG/IB/CSK, **95t** CI, **95cb** PHIL, **95c** CI, **95b** PHIL, **96t** PC, **96bl** CI, **96br** CI, **97tr** CI, **97cl** TT, **97b** CI, **99tl** PHIL, **99tc** OPG/TR/TTO, **99tr** OPG/IB/B, **99b** OPG/IB/CSK, **100t** Fritz Hansen, **100bl** CI, **100br** CI, **101bl** OPG/IB/B, **101br** OPG/IB/SL, **102** CI, **103tr** PHIL, **103bl** PHIL, **103br** CI, **105tl** OPG/IB/CSK, **105tr** SPL, **105cl** SPL, **105br** CI, **106t** Fritz Hansen, **106b** OPG/IB/B, **107t** CI, **107bl** TT, **107br** OPG/TR/TTO, **108l** ANT, **108r** ANT, **109** PHIL, **110r** PHIL, **110tl** PHIL, **111l** PHIL, **111r** PHIL, **112l** PHIL, **112r** PHIL, **113l** PHIL, **113r** PHIL, **114l** CI, **114r** OPG/IB/CSK, **115l** OPG/IB/A, **115r** OPG/IB/CSK, **116l** OPG/IB/CSK, **116r** OPG/IB/CSK, **117** CI, **118l** CI, **118r** OPG/IB, **119l** OPG/IB/A, **119r** CI, **120** DAY, **121tl** OPG/ST/LD, **121cl** OPG/ST/LD, **121cr** OPG/ST/LD, **122** SPL, **123tl** ND, **123tr** ND, **123b** SPL, **126–7** PHIL, **128l** B, **128r** TT, **129t** PHIL, **129b** TTO, **130** B, **131tl** B, **131cr** CI, **132tr** DES, **132bl** CI, **132br** CI, **133r** CI, **133bl** CI, **134tl** OPG/TR/PB, **134tr** CI, **135tl** CI, **135tr** OPG/TR/PB, **136b** CI, **137tr** CI, **137cr** CI, **139tr** OPG/TR/Z, **139c** CI, **139b** PHIL, **140tr** SJC, **140b** CI, **141t** CI, **141b** CI, **143tl** OPG/TR/TTO, **143tr** OPG/TR/TTO, **143b** OPG/TR/TTO, **145t** OPG/TR/PB, **145c** PHIL, **145b** OPG/TR/TTO, **147tl** V&A, **147tr** OPG/TR/TG, **147bl** OPG/TR/TG, **147br** B, **149tl** OPG/TR/TG/© 2001 All Rights Reserved, DACS, **149tr** OPG/TR/TTO, **149b** OPG/TR/TG, **151tl** CI, **151tr** CI, **151cl** VP, **151bl** CI, **152t** VP, **152bl** OPG/IB/SL, **152br** OPG/TR/TTO, **153t** TT, **153b** PHIL, **154l** PHIL, **154r** PHIL, **155t** CI, **155b** OPG/TR/TTO, **156l** PHIL, **156r** CI, **157l** GC, **157r** GC, **158l** PHIL, **158r** PHIL, **159t** BC/Carol McNicoll, **159b** PHIL, **160tl** OPG/AJP, **160tr** PHIL/© DACS 2001, **161l** CI, **161r** CI, **162l** CI, **162r** CI, **163t** CI, **163b** CI, **164tl** CI, **165l** CI, **165r** CI, **166** PHIL, **167r** CI, **167t** CI, **168** OPG/TR/TG, **169tl** WCG/CB, **169tr** WCG/CB, **169br** WCG/CB, **170** OPG/TR/TTO, **171tl** CI, **171tr** LJ/ZA, **171br** LJ/ZA, **172l** OPG/TR/TTO, **172r** CI, **173lB**, **173r** CI, **174l** CI, **174r** PHIL, **175r** CI, **176** OPG/AJP/B, **177l** OPG/TR/Boom!, **177r** OPG/TR/TG, **178l** OPG/TR/A, **178r** CI, **179l** CI/© The Andy Warhol Foundation for the Visual Arts, Inc./ARS, NY and DACS, London 2001, **179r** SPL, **180** OPG/TR/ML, **181l** OPG/TR/ML, **181r** OPG/TR/ML, **182tl** CI, **183t** CI, **183b** CI, **186–7** CI, **188** VITRA, **189tl** CI, **189tr** SPL, **189br** SPL, **190l** SPL, **190r** CI, **191** CI, **193t** CI, **193bl** PHIL, **193br** CI, **195tl** PHIL, **195tr** SPL, **195b** CI, **196tl** PHIL, **196tr** CI, **197t** PHIL, **197br** CI, **202t** RA, **202b** PHIL, **203t** CI, **203b** PHIL, **204** PHIL, **204cl** CI, **204br** CI, **205** CI, **205t** CI, **205b** LAMA, **206** PHIL, **206** CI, **207r** PHIL, **207t** CI, **207tl** RA/WM, **207c** RA, **207b** CI, **208** CI, **209t** PHIL, **209b** CI, **210** CI, **211t** PHIL, **211c** MN, **212l** JM, **212r** JM, **213t** MW/photo Hans Van der Mars, **213b** CI, **215tl** PHIL, **215tr** PHIL, **215bl** PHIL, **215br** CI, **217t** TA, **217tr** TA, **217c** PHIL, **217bl** Cassina S.P.A./photo Andrea Zani, **218l** FLG/SS, **218r** FLG/SS, **219t** CI, **220l** CI, **220r** PHIL, **221t** CI, **221b** PHIL, **222** JBM, **223tl** PHIL, **223tr** PHIL, **223b** PHIL, **224l** CI, **224tr** CI, **225t** CI, **225b** CI, **226l** CI, **226r** CI, **227t** CI, **227b** CI, **228** PHIL, **229t** CI, **229b** CI, **230l** CI, **230r** KIM, **231l** LJ/ZA, **231r** WR/photo Mike Hallson/WCG, **232l** LJ, **232r** DW/photo DW/MKG, **233l** WR/photo Bob Cramp/WCG, **233r** LB